the
best
creative
NONFICTION

Volume Volume Volume Volume

2

ALSO EDITED BY LEE GUTKIND

*Keep It Real: Everything You Need to Know About
Researching and Writing Creative Nonfiction*

The Best Creative Nonfiction Volume 1

In Fact: The Best of Creative Nonfiction

Silence Kills: Speaking Out and Saving Lives

*Hurricanes and Carnivals: Essays by Chicanos, Pochos, Pachucos,
Mexicanos and Expatriates*

*Our Roots are Deep with Passion: Creative Nonfiction Collects
New Essays by Italian-American Writers*

Rage and Reconciliation: Inspiring a Healthcare Revolution

On Nature: Great Writers on the Great Outdoors

Healing: A Creative Nonfiction Reader

Lessons in Persuasion

*Connecting: Twenty Prominent Authors Write About Events
That Shaped Their Lives*

The Essayist at Work: Profiles of Creative Nonfiction Writers

*Surviving Crisis: Twenty Prominent Authors Write About Events That
Shaped Their Lives*

Our Roots Grow Deeper than We Know

the
best
creative
NONFICTION

Volume Volume Volume Volume Volume Volume

2

EDITED BY LEE GUTKIND

W. W. NORTON & COMPANY

New York London

For information about special discounts for bulk purchases, please contact
W. W. Norton Special Sales at specialsales@wwnorton.com or 800-233-4830

Manufacturing by Courier Westford
Book design by Chris Welch
Production manager: Devon Zahn

ISBN 978-0-393-33024-3 (pbk.)

W. W. Norton & Company, Inc.
500 Fifth Avenue, New York, N.Y. 10110
www.wwnorton.com

W. W. Norton & Company Ltd.
Castle House, 75/76 Wells Street, London W1T 3QT

2 3 4 5 6 7 8 9 0

coordinating editors

HATTIE FLETCHER

JESSICA MESMAN GRIFFITH

DINTY W. MOORE

blog editor

KATHLEEN TARR

contents

The "L" Word—
And All the Rest of Us "Outsiders"

LEE GUTKIND

In my memoir, *Forever Fat,* I tell the story of my bar mitzvah, during which I am being tortured by the brown wool suit my mother forced me to wear. The wool is itching like crazy and I am sweating so profusely that perspiration from my forehead is dripping onto the sacred parchment of the Torah as I read from it. The rabbi is appalled, as was my mother, who, when she read this excerpt, looked up at me and said, politely but clearly annoyed, "Lee, you have a very vivid imagination." Both parents insisted that they never bought me that suit, and so the scene I described with the rabbi could never have happened. They were adamant, which made me feel uncomfortable and guilty—until I ran into Alan Levy some months later. He had just read my book.

"I know exactly how you felt," he said, "because I was forced to wear that same hothouse of a suit for my bar mitzvah." Levy's family had shared a walk-up apartment with my grandparents, a tailor and a seamstress. His parents were too poor to buy him a new suit for his bar mitzvah, so my grandmother refitted my old brown suit for Alan to wear, he said.

Of course, I immediately recounted the details of my chance meeting with Alan Levy to my mother, who waved her hand as if she were brushing away an annoying fly. "Alan Levy," she said, "is crazy."

"But he *says he* wore the suit! "I protested.

"No," she replied, "he didn't."

Did he wear the suit or didn't he? Did the suit even exist? Either way, the experience confirmed what I have long believed—that the factual details of memoir are considerably less important than the writers' intentions in revealing, describing, and re-creating stories. It is unreasonable to expect memoirists to document every detail of their stories. Even if Alan Levy had not confirmed my recollection, the story I had written was mine, as true as I could make it to my memory, whether real or partially imagined.

I was reminded of this by a recent essay published in *Harper's Magazine* about truth and labeling in memoir, "A Lie That Tells the Truth." In it Joel Agee recounts his struggles to avoid having his books, which he describes as "amphibious," labeled as memoir and thus consigned to "the purgatory gloom of 'nonfiction,'" banished from the realm of "that fabled unnameable beast—Literature."

This need for categorization that Agee finds so uncomfortable seems unnecessary in some respects. While categorization may guide us in our selection of reading material, most readers are simply seeking enjoyment and enlightenment from books—no matter how they are categorized. (The publisher of the James Frey book, *A Million Little Pieces*, set aside $2.35 million, anticipating disgruntled readers would demand refunds following the discovery of Frey's trickery, but only 1,729 people did.) Publishers and newspaper reporters care the most about categorization, I think—not so much readers.

And, as Agee's agent tells him, even "in publishing circles nowadays the L-word is the kiss of death"—a statement Christina Nehring would probably agree with. In a recent essay online at truthdig.com, Nehring uses *The Best American Essays 2007* as a jumping-off point to describe what she sees as the lamentable state of the form. She quotes essayist Joseph Epstein and agrees with his overall assessment of the tone of the modern American essay: "middle-aged." By this, he means (in a good way) quiet. She means "Slow-moving. Soft-hitting. Nostalgic. Self-satisfied." And even "eye-crossingly dull."

Nehring also laments the homogeneity of the writers whose work ends up anthologized, and creates a composite portrait she calls the Preferred American Essayist: "Educated at Harvard, he or she has spent significant time at the Bread Loaf Writer's Conference, written proposals for New York Public Library Fellowships (often lovingly paraphrased in the essays) and received medical attention at Sloan Kettering Hospital. Chances are good she's a doting dog owner who has done such things as lace her pet's dinner with [antidepressants] or write gourmet cookbooks for his discerning palate."

Nehring is making fun, but she's got a point—the "literary establishment" in America, with some exceptions, has turned into a rather uninspired and predictable group. More and more, the popular American essayists are writing for each other and for other insiders, the type of people Nehring lampoons in her composite sketch.

But these are not the writers you'll find in *The Best Creative Nonfiction*. True, this volume does include some writers who were educated at Ivy League schools; some live in New York, and some have attained a measure of insider status and fame—writers like Stefan Fatsis, Heidi Julavits, and Ander Monson. But for the most part the writers published here are outsiders—folks with other jobs, making time to write between family responsibilities and other passions. They come from all over the country (and a few live overseas), and their perspectives are as varied as the places they call home. K. G. Schneider, a librarian from Tallahassee, Florida, writes mostly technical pieces for librarians, but also essays and travelogues. Hauquan Chau, a Canadian who teaches English in Japan, describes himself as a "modern nomad." Patricia Brieschke has worked in a fertilizer factory and a five-and-dime store, among other places. Gwendolyn Knapp is a cheese monger in New Orleans. Laura Sewell Matter is a high school teacher in Albuquerque, New Mexico.

It is also interesting to note how many of these writers are at the beginning of their careers. Sewell Matter's story "Pursuing the Great Bad Novelist" was her first national publication. "Spite," the first piece in this collection, was Anne Trumbore's first attempt at writing creative nonfiction. Many of the other writers are currently in MFA programs, honing their craft.

What is different and special about *The Best Creative Nonfiction* is that we are introducing new voices, at the tipping point of discovery, that are not part of the homogenous, composite world Nehring is so critical of and bored by. The places we found their work are similarly diverse. (All of the pieces in *The Best Creative Nonfiction* have been previously published except for two, Emily Bernard's "Figurines" and Pagan Kennedy's "The Dangerous Joy of Dr. Sex.") There are pieces here from some cornerstones of the literary establishment, magazines and journals with rich histories—like *Harper's* and *The Georgia Review*—as well as from younger publications, like *The Believer*, that have begun to make their mark. Chances are good, however, that you're unfamiliar with many of the print and online publications from which we've pulled stories, among them *Eclectica*, *The Big Ugly Review*, *Etude*, *Willow Springs*, and *Obit*. You probably don't subscribe to *PMS poemmemoirstory*, *Hayden's Ferry Review*, *Swink*, or even *Creative Nonfiction*, but if you did—and perhaps you should—you would see that there's an expansive and ever-increasing body of literature out in there in the hinterlands, far beyond the pages of *The New Yorker* and *The Atlantic Monthly*, where writers are capturing the tone and spirit of our country and many parts of the world, in poetry, fiction, and nonfiction, and in forms which defy categorization. The creative nonfiction pieces in this collection represent the power and vitality of the rising tide of these voices and the scope of its achievement and impact. They demonstrate the versatility and strength of this genre we call creative nonfiction.

The week after Nehring's critique appeared online, the *Chronicle of Higher Education* published "Creating Nonfiction," an essay by Rachel Toor, a creative writing teacher from Spokane, Washington. In it, Toor rehashed the overworked debate about why creative nonfiction is called "creative nonfiction" and not "narrative nonfiction" or "literary nonfiction." This is a subject that has been beaten to death over the past couple of decades—yet never seems to die. Toor summarized the usual answers: "Narrative" and "literary" are problematic because (1) some brilliant, beautiful nonfiction is simply not narrative, and (2) no one has the power to determine what is literary and what is not (the "L" word, again).

But Toor pursues the subject with dogged repetition. She also squeezes in a sarcastic reference to "James Frey and his ilk," a group that includes, according to Toor, Annie Dillard, who referenced a cat that did not exist in her Pulitzer Prize–winning book *Pilgrim at Tinker Creek*; Bruce Chatwin, who may have never met in Patagonia some of the people he described; and David Sedaris, recently outed by *The New Republic* as "a maker-up of things." Toor also goes after the difficulties with the word "nonfiction," pointing out that the word causes us to be "defined by what we are not."

Ultimately, Toor's complaint boils down to this: "I don't like the ghettoization of nonfiction from literature"—which echoes Agee's concerns about the narrowness of labels. Both writers are well meaning, earnestly telling readers what they think, and attempting to motivate readers to think more deeply and analytically about their ideas and vision as it relates to a subject for which they have a great deal of interest and passion. Which is exactly the reason creative nonfiction has become so popular, so quickly—it allows writers to declare themselves in the most passionate and revealing way possible. When you read the work of creative nonfiction writers (whether or not they have been stamped with an "L" of approval), you not only learn about the subject being discussed (walking across Andorra, egg donation, the burial of the "N" word), but you also meet another human being, a real person, a writer searching for meaning, identity, insight, and courageous enough to share his or her angst and passion with the world.

Speaking of angst and passion and sharing with the world, as in volume one, we've included voices from the blogosphere, selecting blogs that, while generally rough around the edges, are thrilling in their immediacy and intimacy. Our blog editor, Kathleen Tarr, went on a crazy, endless search she calls "bloginfinitus." "I got so deep into linking and clicking that I completely lost track of where I was and how I got down certain cyberpaths," she told me. "And this is part of the blog experience, isn't it? You follow one narrative and then another and another and before long, you've just connected with an eclectic group of humanity across the globe."

Many of the blogs published here were discovered by Hattie Fletcher, managing editor of *Creative Nonfiction* and Jessica Fischoff, a graduate student intern. And coordinating editors Hattie Fletcher, Dinty W. Moore (who edits his own online journal, *Brevity*), and Jessica Mesman Griffith (Hattie's predecessor at *Creative Nonfiction*), screened all of the approximately five hundred pieces nominated this year for *The Best Creative Nonfiction*. We worked together quite diligently—for months!—in order to winnow the mass of nominations and blog entries down to the pieces you find in this collection.

And then we added one more special feature: statements from the editors of the publications from which our selections have been taken. We are pleased to identify them here—and praise them. It is easy to forget that editors, often anonymous, are the vital link, the connective tissue, between writers and readers. Editors help writers focus their messages and hone their identities. Writers don't say much about editors one way or the other, and critics don't say anything at all, unless they feel that the editing is uneven or shoddy. There are few awards, special fellowships, teaching positions, or studios in art colonies for editors. But in the end, it is an editor's touch and insight that shapes and defines what the "L" word is really all about.

acknowledgments

Thanks to the following for their help and encouragement:

- The staff at *Creative Nonfiction*—Nancy Raynovich, Jessica Fischoff, and Larkin Page-Jacobs;
- Amy Cherry, our editor at W. W. Norton;
- The hundreds of editors who nominated work from the pages of their journals, magazines, newspapers, and book lists;
- Friends and past contributors who made nominations for this volume: Eula Biss, Jeff Gordinier, Donna Hogarty, Paul Morris, John O'Conner, Sunshine O'Donnell, and Alexis Wiggins.

Finally, *Creative Nonfiction* would like to thank the Juliet Lea Hillman Simonds Foundation and the Pennsylvania Council on the Arts, whose ongoing generosity is essential to its success.

the best creative

NONFICTION

Volume Volume 2 Volume Volume

Spite

ANNE TRUMBORE

"After almost two decades of writing in a variety of genres," Anne
Trumbore *says, "I've discovered that, ultimately, writers are never
so invested in anything as we are in telling our own story, and that
the first word we write in our own voice is as remarkable and
memorable as the first word we speak." This story, which appeared
online in* The Big Ugly Review, *was the author's first attempt at
writing creative nonfiction.*

The facts are indisputable. On a Friday evening in the late spring
of 1977, in a small house in the suburbs of Philadelphia, a thirty-
five-year-old woman with multiple sclerosis fell while taking a
shower. She screamed for her husband. He did not hear her.

She clutched at the shower handle on her way down and turned it
all the way to HOT.

Three ribs, weakened by twelve years of steroids, snapped on
impact. The scalding water draped her back like a blanket. She could

not get up. She screamed and screamed and screamed until her husband heard her.

They did not go to the hospital until the next morning. She came home with second-degree burns on her torso and two more prescriptions.

They returned angry, my father's mouth in an iron line, my mother in the wheelchair she refused to use, head down, weeping softly. He cornered me once the new pills sent her to sleep. "Did you hear what happened last night?" he asked, brows pulled down, eyes predatory. "Did you know what was happening?"

No, Dad. I didn't hear anything.

"Really?" His voice went an octave higher in disbelief.

Yes.

My legs at eleven were long and straight and suntanned, twinkly in the sun with fine golden hairs. My body was long and lean: a brown wiggly line. The neighborhood mothers called me "a stick." My mother said I had a fat ass.

Since she said I had a "fat ass" with a cigarette clenched between her teeth (she had to smoke like a longshoreman because her hands shook so much from the MS that she was always setting fire to the couch), you might think she had close-cropped steel wool hair, thick shoulders, broad hips, and a balloon waist. You might think she had dropped out of high school and worked at a canning plant at some time in her life. You might think she wore a hair net to sleep and scrubbed the kitchen floor on her hands and knees.

You would be wrong. She had dual degrees in history and French, porcelain-pale skin, blue eyes, and soft black hair. Her cheekbones were softly sculpted and I never saw her without her lipstick, one red and one coral, which she kept in an enamel bowl right next to her crystal ashtray. She dieted in high school, in college, throughout both pregnancies, during her diagnosis, confinement to a wheelchair, and her last stop in a hospital bed in the dining room. She allowed herself half a cup (we measured) of Coke from a glass bottle each day. Every month, my father would drive to a beverage distributor and pick up a wooden flat of it. She never ate chicken with skin, bread with dinner, or dessert, except on birthdays. In later years, when she pretty much just sat on the couch all day and my father was doing well at work, she allowed herself a single Godiva chocolate at 4 P.M., right after her Prednisone.

And I did have, at least in comparison to the rest of me, a fat ass. Also my father's nose, which looked broken, small eyes, and a strong jaw. I hated brushing my hair, which she used to have shaved by the barber on the corner when I was small. "I can't take care of it," she would cry with me while he buzzed my scalp. "You have an enormous head," she would say afterwards. She was right. The only hat I have ever tried on that fit belonged to her father, a former small-time Irish boxer. "What a sweet boy you have," women in skirts would say when I helped her out of her black VW bug with the red leather interior. "She's not a boy," my mother would sniff. "It's a pixie cut."

This fact is also without question: I listened to the whole thing. My bedroom shared a wall with the bathroom, and the painted wicker headboard of my bed was flush against this wall.

"Jack!" she screamed. "Jack! Jack! Oh God help, Jack!"

My fifth-grade math teacher gave the class brain teasers on Friday afternoons, and this was the last one of the year. Although most of school was very easy for me, I was stumped. An old man said to a young man, "I have a daughter. She has as many brothers as she has sisters. Each one of her brothers has twice as many sisters as he has brothers. How many sons and daughters do I have?"

He has to have at least two sons and four daughters, I thought. But that's not the answer, not yet.

"Oh God. Oh my God, Jack!"

Let's see. If she has as many brothers as she has sisters, and she is also someone's sister, then brothers equal sisters minus one (herself), or $B = S-1$.

"Jack, Jack, Jack, Jack, Jack."

Where is he? Can't he take care of her for once? It's not my fault. I didn't do it. I don't want to see her naked anymore, and she is going to be really mad at me, I don't want to I don't want to I don't want to . . .

"God help me God help me God help me."

Got it. So a brother has twice as many sisters as he has brothers, not including himself who is a brother. So two times the brothers minus one (himself) is the number of sisters. $2(B-1) = S$.

"Anne?" my father called. "Anne, what's going on?"

My stomach flipped and I grew cold. But he was not talking to me. My mother and I have the same name. She choked on her tears now and did not answer him. Neither did I.

He took the stairs two at a time. I counted his steps. I stopped breathing when he opened the bathroom door.

"What the hell?" He turned off the water.

"It hurts. Oh God, oh God, it hurts."

If you combine the two equations, $2S-4 = S$.

"I don't think we need to go to the hospital right now," he pronounced. We never went to the emergency room unless a doctor told us to. My mother whimpered something I couldn't hear.

"Anne can stay with Mark in the morning and we'll call Dr. Haase. Can you walk to the bed?"

If you divide 2S by S, you get $S = 4$. Four sisters. I had figured it out at the beginning! My heart jumped. I couldn't wait to see the faces of Danny and Matthew, the smart boys in class. We called Matthew "Encyclopedia Brown," because he always seemed to know everything. I never called him that. I knew a lot more than I ever told. And I knew this. The old man had four daughters and three sons, because $B = (S-1)$ or $3 = 4-1$ and my mother and father were safe in their bedroom. I fell asleep, my brain jangling and my heart jumping.

Since my mother fell on Friday night, my father spent the weekend circling around her while she mostly slept. Monday came and he went back to work. So, it was just my mother and me on those sun-hazy afternoons, the unwatched TV buzzing game shows in the living room. "Oh my God, how gauche," my mother would sniff, when she caught sight of a contestant, jiggling and breathless after having won a month's supply of dishwasher detergent. "She should use that money to buy herself a decent bra." And then her attention would turn back to me, and how I washed the clothes, and ironed the shirts, folded the laundry, and stripped the beds. My brother was allowed to go out and play. I changed her bandages.

My mother never asked me if I heard her. She knew I did, just as she knew my most shameful secret, the one I tried to deny for many decades: I had a mother who didn't love me. And so she never begged me to be gentle when I changed the bandages and sprinkled the foul-smelling white powder onto her weeping yellow flesh. She knew I did not go to her, or get my father, because at eleven, I finally hated her, too. And I think that was what she wanted. Because love can fade and disappear when you are fat, or crippled, or crazy. Hate is constant. Our bond was now beyond words: I would always hate her. And that hate was deeper, more powerful, and more vital than our love could ever hope to be.

Final: Comprehensive, Roughly

DESIRAE MATHERLY

"Often it is anxiety or pressure which pushes us to write from personal experience," observes Desirae Matherly. *"This particular essay emerged from fears surrounding my impending comprehensive exams."* Perhaps unsurprisingly, the essay, which first appeared in Fourth Genre, *takes the shape of an exam. This form may seem radical, yet it reflects the content of the piece and helps both the writer and the reader grapple with difficult philosophical questions.*

NAME _____
Final: Comprehensive, Roughly

I. Matching

Instructions: *Using what you know about words and the way they work, match the word in column A with the word in column B with which it shares the most in common. Write the matching word beside its mate in column A. If you suffer from test anxiety, go directly to Part IV.*

A		B
crypt	_____	bear
commentary	_____	stream
quality	_____	class
bare	_____	selection
soul	_____	quantity
Descartes	_____	momentary
current	_____	cryptic
election	_____	currency
channel	_____	sole
class	_____	Dehorse

II. Fill in the Blank

Instructions: *Fill in the missing word, number, or phrase.*

1. _____ is too much to pay for one week's worth of groceries.
2. I consider myself a(n) _____.
3. When I spin in place with my eyes closed, I feel _____.

III. True or False

Instructions: *With a magic marker, blot out the statements you consider to be true. In ten words or less, classify the statements you consider to be false in the space at the bottom of this page.*

You can't always get what you want.

I've been a miner for a heart of gold.

I was sinking deep in sin, far from the peaceful shore.

There's pow'r, pow'r, wonder-workin' pow'r in the blood of the lamb.

The fool on the hill sees the sun going down.

I'll fly away.

It took me four days to hitchhike from Saginaw.

You know me, I'm your friend, I'm your pusherman.

I've flown the house of freezing steel.

You've got to pick up every stitch.

I've seen him in the watch-fires of a hundred circling camps.

IV. Multiple Choice.

Instructions: *Choose the best answer.*

1. _____ A better title for this exam would be:
   a. Shaking the Tree of Knowledge, Seeing What Falls
   b. Literati Pedagogico: The Final Exam as Literary Genre
   c. _____

2. _____ Where is America?
   a. East of Eden
   b. Under the Table and Dreaming
   c. Below the Salt
   d. On Top of Old Smokey
   e. In a Prepositional Phrase
   f. Over the Edge
   g. $y = mx + b$

3. _____ The Poverty Line:
   a. divided an estimated 12.7 percent of the households in the United States from the other 87.3 percent in 2004.
   b. termed a *threshold,* is set at $9,570 per year in 2005 for one person living in the United States.

c. may lie close to what some Wal-Mart associates earn, after paying health insurance deductibles.
d. equates to $ 797.50 a month, $184.03 a week, $26.21 a day, or $1.09 per hour of life in a year.
e. is still more than what the majority of the world lives on, with poverty estimates worldwide usually measured as less than a U.S. dollar a day, relative to local economy.
f. is an abstraction, regardless of the Dept. of Health and Human Services and the Census Bureau.
g. is a convenient organizing concept for policy makers.
h. does not inspire compassion among those in the upper 87.3 percent.
i. is all of the above, and more.

4. _____ Art is:
a. true
b. beautiful

V. Translation

Instructions: *Working collaboratively, find the English equivalences of the following.*

1. à la belle étoile:
2. alter idem:
3. Selbstbildnis:
4. El llanto:

VI. Essay Response

Instructions: *Using yourself as primary source, and the lives of other people you love as secondary sources, construct a 3–5 paragraph response to three of the following questions. You may not use a separate* *sheet of paper, and your answer must appear directly below the question. Therefore, you must write tinily. Please don't ask me questions of clarification, as I feel that I have made this exam perfectly clear. In addition to the three elective responses, everyone must answer #4.*

1. I was in a high school trigonometry class when I first realized I had something on my mind that I needed to get down on paper. I had made the connection between two words: *Revolution* and *Evolution*. I spent the entire class covertly filling up the margins of a failed exam on the Cartesian coordinate system, explaining how the two words shared a connection deeper than nine letters. I don't know what I intended to do with my thought of that day, but I know that I did not perceive the writing of that moment as important enough for anyone else to read. Earlier that year I had begun to keep a journal, or more precisely a diary, whose pages I filled with utter drivel—"Went to the mall today, didn't see J. there," or "I love J.! I wish I could tell him how I feel." Now that J. exists only as a character I had mostly invented, I wish I could shake the sixteen-year-old me and explain to her the importance of time, and how little there is to write in. She should not have wasted those two years on a diary whose pages succumbed to the tortuous fancies of her teenage heart. She might have actually read that volume of Aristotle she checked out of the library, or she might have finished *War and Peace* and thought about it, or she could have at the very least noted some of her finer thoughts, which I am sure she must have had . . . the shape of her day, or the feeling of her body as it pressed out into the world. What are some of your finer thoughts for today, the ones which you will not write down?

2. We know that Montaigne read voraciously, and that his margins became overfilled, and it was because of their surplus ideas that his library's pages bred more pages, and his writing drifted from the margins into blank space, empty counties for his ideas, which were

utterly original hamlets. We value this originality, his commentary on the thinkers before and of his age, because we can only hope to experience the world as uniquely as he did, though most of us have no inclination to put down those thoughts which are profitless. But if we did record those profitless realizations, we might find something more valuable in them than either money or fame. If we were to follow the private thoughts of our days, we might find that they accrue into a sort of publication, and our words into a type of commentary. When we shout at the TV for showing us visions of idiocy or cruelty, when we mutter to ourselves about our neighbor's unkempt yard or barking dog, we are in the realm of our judgments, each active moment an evaluation of our experiences which we must have constructed in private, or with the help of those we converse with (that is, if we haven't simply bought them ready-made at the store of ideas). Somehow an inner dialogue is shaped that we appear to have no outlet for unless we channel it into our work. Ours is no less a philosophy because it is personal; the ideal is not so awfully separate from the practical. What better work then, than to be pundits of our own lives?

3. The day I began to set these thoughts down, I decided to not take a shower. I brushed my hair, which I never do, and tied it back in a scarf. I made oatmeal for my husband and myself while my son played on a bed blanket on the floor. We sliced up bananas to have on the oats, and sprinkled cinnamon, sugar, and raisins on top of that. This was a good moment, though I did listen to the news, to someone else's commentary on that day, which was *never* just about oatmeal and babies and cinnamon. While I ate, I philosophized at my husband, who patiently nodded without arguing with me. He went to work, and I washed dishes, did some light grading, and filed some papers away. But my most important act was the smallest, and took the lesser part of my morning. I took the scrap papers I had jotted spare ideas on, and recorded them in my journal—putting them back

for the lean times to come. Now my baby is a four-year-old child, my husband and I have divorced, and I live a day's drive, *three years away* (the greater distance) from that morning. Still, I have these notes. Can you describe the least wasteful process for cooking these ideas into a dish worth consuming?

4. The most important political act of any artist is to draw the middle edge of public opinion away from itself. Is this statement true? If you think so, explain in your own words how the homogenous compensate for their banality by creating the appearance of eating happiness, wholeness, difference, and creativity, and how poverty has become a romanticized ideal for those who collect raw and beautiful ideas. If it is not true that the artist draws the middle edge of public opinion away from itself, explain in 50 words or less why the only *safe* and ambitiously artistic citizen in a selfish society paints pretty pictures.

5. I used to believe that there was a hell in the center of the earth where people went when they were bad and died before apologizing. Since then, I have taken geology. Have you heard the story of the samurai who visits the Buddhist monk, and asks him where hell is?

   a. If you *have not* heard the story, tell me the joke about the man with the parrot who goes into the bar (you know, the one with the three blondes, the Catholic, the Jew, the black man, the Gypsy, the Indian chief, the Hindu, or the feminist) instead.

   b. If you *do know* the story about the samurai, relate to me the version you have heard, and be specific. In my version of the story, the monk scoffs at the samurai and says, "Why should I tell a stupid jackass like you where hell is?" to which the samurai rises, face on fire, drawing his sword. At this the monk says, "THAT is hell." As the samurai lowers his sword and sinks to his knees in realization, the monk quietly remarks, "and THIS is heaven."

6. Should Texas be granted diplomatic relations with (the) US?

7. One of the more serious and secretive responsibilities of the teacher is grading his or her students. I have always despised this aspect of my job. "Grading" is something we do for those things which are related to consumption: tobacco, dairy products, and restaurants. A friend of mine, a fellow essayist and teacher, introduced me to a Website called pickaprof.com. Myself and many other instructors I know are listed there, along with the averages of the grades we've given, reviews, and other tidbits interesting to students wanting information about professors in advance. For a long time I was one of only two English instructors at my school who had an average of 4.0 in the grades they give their undergraduate students. This fact still embarrasses me, and makes me feel that I have wronged my students by my acceptance of their work. Even though this representation of my grading history levels out A minuses, it is roughly true, though I know that a good deal of data has been omitted. Looking through my master file, I see that over a period of five years I distributed five F's, one D+, one C+, one C, and nine B-range grades. But I've always felt violated by Pick-A-Prof!'s evaluation of my teaching. Among the more private subjects people may keep to themselves—income, religion, politics, aesthetic desires, fears, regrets—how we evaluate the work we do must be the most private of all. Our labor transmits our secrets, if anyone would care to listen. My grading (of writing) is based upon originality, effort, sense of humor, serious revision, and philosophical maturity. These things are not quantifiable. To the contrary, when I taught Introduction to Logic as a graduate student in philosophy, my students' grades were like a bell-curve buffet. My grade book revealed A's as rare as chocolate-coated strawberries, B's like the wine that disappears early, C's like the cheese we expect. And the F's—try as I might, despite my elegantly honest multiple choice exams, even for a final that required them to demonstrate

an ability to complete logical proofs, my F's were like napkins that every one of my students carried discreetly beneath their plates, hoping no one would notice. And it could have been that there was only one way to classify categorical propositions, because no one real lived in them anyway; "Mexican Hat Dancers" were simply those nouns that lived in a Venn diagram to the exclusion of "Griffins" or "Unicorns," and these metaphorical populations would never mingle or converge except syntactically. (Choose C or D if A or B seems unlikely, True or False *can* answer your question, and yes, your grade will be expressed as a decimal.) Logic and math seem honest enough I suppose, at least going into them. Spelling was that way for me, long ago, until I learned about the effect of Norman French on Old English. But then, there is a decay in American English when we must rely on quantitative expressions to describe qualitative relationships between people, places, things, or ideas. When I say *class,* do you think of tax brackets, school divisions, or that certain strain of self-respect that was once believed to accompany nobility, but cannot be purchased for the love of money without cheapening it?

8. I spent seven years of my life in a trailer, three of those in Sinking Creek Trailer Park. Lot rent there was $75 a month. There were probably around 30 trailers in that park, and the landlord, Mr. Fisher, harvested almost $2,250 a month. Mr. Fisher lived behind the park, on the other side of his cornfield. He was a farmer, so he allowed his tenants some garden space, which in hindsight is remarkable. For three years I lived in Nelsonville, a mostly dilapidated Victorian town that chokes a major highway (Rt. 33) running between the Capit(o/a)1 of Ohio and the brick-street college town of Athens, which is 85.2 per percent "white" according to the 2004 census. There are few gardens in Nelsonville. Our house payment during that time was $373.21, something my husband and I could afford. It was $100 less than the two-bedroom apartment we used to rent in The Plains, which is

approximately seven miles southwest of Nelsonville. It seems ironic
to me that a house payment could be cheaper than rent, especially
since I estimate that I threw away $30,600 over the time I spent as a
renter before my marriage, which was about six years. That amount
was 72 percent of the cost of the house my husband and I lived in,
and I have nothing to show for those years, except expired leases that
outline what our finite freedoms were as renters. The people who
lived across the street (and beside us) were renters, among them the
bleached blond woman who was on a well-known talk show several
years ago. Her husband proposed to her after he had exposed his
butt-crack to national TV while pummeling her unfortunate
boyfriend on stage. This woman, and the family that lived next to her
in the duplex, were slovenly, loud, rude, vulgar, and not at all the
abstract and invisible "poor" that I like to imagine living in economic
theories I am sensitive to. Someone paid the rent, but who? I remember checking the HUD Website for income limits in Athens County,
Ohio, and finding that my husband and I were considered "very low
income." When I would peep out through the Venetian blinds at my
neighbors, I often wondered what made our families different, and
what "class" really must have meant to that sad, overripe Victorian
street. TWO-PART QUESTION: What is it about my former neighbors that I am trying to escape, and where is hell?

9. Sinking Creek Trailer Park was in Johnson City, Tennessee, about
one mile (as the crow flies) from the grocery store where we bought
our food, which is directly across from the controversial regional
landfill, which is five hundred yards away from the Hourglass Lounge
(a "gentlemen's" club, aka topless bar), which is five hundred more
yards away from the Keystone Projects, which is a good mile (the
crow tells me) from the ostensible center of Johnson City, whose
northern border has been developing rapidly for the past ten years or
more. Cow pastures have been parsed into luxury home lots to house

the influx of doctors into Johnson City, which grows because of the thriving medical industry there, and the lawyers are close behind, gypsies that they are. It seems that the only people who stay in one place are the people who are trapped where they began. But for the nomadic professional, compassion doesn't grow while just passing through, trying the dials on the radio to find something tolerably local. I might as well mention that the main radio station in Johnson City is WQUT (101.5 FM), a station that plays mostly classic rock from the seventies. My stepfather had a huge record collection from the seventies, so between WQUT and my stepfather, much of my musical education involved seventies rock. I still listen to seventies rock because it relaxes me. This is because I only remember the latter half of the seventies from the perspective of a young child, and the former half through my mom's high school memories. When I find myself humming songs to which I have forgotten the words, they are usually seventies tunes, and only recently eighties pop, or its short-lived inheritor/antithesis, nineties alternative. Despite this trans-decade auditory education, I only remember the words to Baptist hymns, as I was inundated with them for the first fifteen years of my life, until I became old enough to resist going to services and no one argued. Music is an art form available to everyone, so it must educate our aesthetic sensibilities in ways we rarely consider significant. For that matter, magazines must do the same, if only for their ubiquitous presences in the grocery lines where we find ourselves corralled for minutes every week (unless we pay someone to deliver our groceries, unless we go to the natural foods store or the farmer's market . . . *unless*). Magazines spread us out at the same time they spread themselves open for us. Do we take the test to see how sexy we are, do we measure up to the idols offered us, do we . . . but I get ahead of myself. THREE-PART QUESTION: When we reflect on what art most influenced us, what do we remember? Do we recall the Titians and the Bachs, or the *Vogues* and the Stones most, or, if it is holy art that we have a taste for, where are our stripes? Specifically, what are the best-dressed gods wearing this year?

10. A wise teacher once asked me, how would philosophy have been different if it had followed the manner of Montaigne instead of Descartes? Descartes' dualisms all arise from his ability to say "I think, therefore I exist." That he *can* say this referentially, of himself, amuses him enough to follow out the deductive consequences of this primal truth. We must have a mind and body that are separate. Not to belittle Descartes' realization, but big fucking deal. I have been realizing that "I exist" since grade school. Sometimes it would just hit me, in the schoolroom cafeteria, or in class, at my desk. I would suddenly feel unattached from my surroundings, look around, notice that everyone else was paying attention to the teacher, or doodling, or passing notes and whispering—and I would have my existential moment in utter loneliness and silence. I usually wanted to jump up and shout "Hey! I exist!" but the fear of punishment kept me quiet. In the lunchroom, when I would say, "I'm having the funny feeling like I'm alive," friends would roll their eyes and say I was weird. After high school, whenever I met a potential boyfriend, and we would be lying somewhere peaceful and sweet, I would ask him if he had ever felt himself existing, you know, in a *serious way.* (Like all time stops and everything in you becomes still though the rest of the universe keeps moving—and there you are, just existing along, and you can do anything you want to with this realization, anything at all.) A Buddhist might say to prolong this moment as long as possible, because it is a moment of pure and perfect clarity. If we could have this clarity with us all the time, the world would reflect the difference. What a much better form Descartes' realizations would have taken if he, like Montaigne before him, would have simply said, "I think, therefore I digress." Having no need then to posit any kind of truth beyond himself, he would have simply acknowledged his thinking as a movement

forward that cuts through the truth of the world like the bow of a ship, would have pressed aside all of the deep complexities that threatened to sink him (in effect being buoyed up by them), and skated across a significant volume of shit, that though truthful and logical, does not deserve to be pressed into service as philosophy, to be emulated by drones after him, like so many shakes of a bee's ass. Descartes might have found better uses for his time then, than nailing cats to tables by their paws that he could cut them up alive, and he might have recognized their agonized howls as something more than the sound a clock makes when hammered into a thousand pieces. Or maybe I would have had the opportunity read Spinoza instead of Descartes, or any number of neglected thinkers who had humbler truths to offer the world. *I have no need* for the truths of Descartes unless they exist in his mathematical principles, where lines can safely cross and uncross themselves like rapiers, or better yet, good Catholics, and put themselves to sleep with clean consciences. In the expression $y = mx + b$, what do we hear? Solve for m.

11. Aside from my concern that exams never accurately measure a student's range of knowledge (whether it be a five-week, ten-week, or sixteen-week course, or a degree-long adventure ending in a PhD, or that swampish range of time between birth and thirty years or so), there is something to be said for those most pious of pedagogical tools: the question and one's memory. Memory alone can only offer sensibility, so our answers count for something when they begin with a jerk and a rattle to move across a page like an old Ford Model T. But by the time we are going into our answers we wonder if we haven't left some integral piece behind. We want to be comprehensive in demonstrating that we have understood. But comprehensiveness is an impossibility, and only an impossible question can approach it. We could say, "There are three things you must understand before we

move on from here," or "It would be best if you read so-and-so on this matter," and finally, "Your test will cover all of chapter three," but we might as well be saying, "Reveal to me how much this matters to you, because if you do not see the value of knowledge in and of itself, then you have no right to claim it." (But we have already lost our way, and cannot tell the teachers from the students anymore. If we fail the Final, we have forfeited a wealth that cannot be taken away, and have assumed a poverty that will not wear off, be bought off, or stay secret for long. With a reading list as long as all our days and nights, we have no time to wonder whether the library has been exhausted. Having been born beautiful, rich, or sad will not keep us safe, and all the stars will turn their backs on us when it is time to turn in our answers.) TWELVE-PART QUESTION: Do we always think of hell as being exclusion or separation from God, or the good, or the beautiful/true, or do we sometimes simply say "hell" and mean someplace permanently uncomfortable? Is hell private or public, do we hide in it secretly or do others peek through their blinds at us in it, shamefully turning away when we look them straight in their eyes? Do we ever look at one another at all? Is there a brutal homogeneity overtaking the world, or is this a myth—that there is more evenness in the world than there actually is? How much of our thinking is thought out of us, before we ever ripen, before we ever make it to that final examination where we are classed and filed away? Or is knowledge fed on its own increase, like a viral pap sucking its own openings and closings and growing despite all weathers? When we examine ourselves in the Socratic manner, do we find our lives worth more? Or do we decrease and waste, Solomon-like, turning in the wind of our own pinings for some lovely innocence that died too long ago to even be lightly remembered? If dying people are burning libraries, why do we encrypt their final secrets instead of letting them waste in view? Do we know what happens to flesh or do we have it on good faith that it rots away, like paper rots, and plants rot, and pages too? Does our knowledge rot on the vine the longer we let it rest unharvested? Or do we care at all that our best minds fall quietly to the ground unnoticed by civilization, quieter for having not argued anything at all, softer for having always yielded, and closer to being gone than the sunlight at evening, when dusk thickens?

Here I Am in Bergdorf Goodman

SARAH MILLER-DAVENPORT

Mr. Beller's Neighborhood, *where this story first appeared, combines a magazine with a map and organizes stories geographically by setting. In the words of Thomas Beller, the site's editor, "It uses the external, familiar landscape of New York City as a way of organizing the wildly internal, often unfamiliar emotional landscapes of the city dweller."*

Here I am in Bergdorf Goodman, and not for the first time, holding up the left half of a pair of $900 boots with the kind of delicacy usually reserved for fine antiques and newborn babies. It's an exercise in frustration, a form of self-inflicted torture: I barely have $900 in the bank, let alone the kind of expendable income that allows for such a frivolous purchase. Plus, I tell myself, as I place the boot back on the display case, spending that kind of money on shoes is wrong. People are dying. And I haven't even made my annual contribution to public radio.

It is a beautiful boot, though—Marc Jacobs, in black pebble

leather with pinstriped suede trim and a small heel—and for a second or two I wonder what it would feel like to go into credit card debt for the sake of fashion. I glance around at the well-heeled women in the shoe department and try to conjure up a feeling of righteousness to ward off the sense of shame that kicked in as soon as soon as I passed through the revolving door downstairs. Shame over being trespasser, a class tourist in a rich-person's department store. Shame over caring what rich people thought of me. And shame at what my mother would think about the whole episode.

When I was growing up in New York City, my mother never took me into stores like Bergdorf's. We went shopping for shoes and nice dresses to wear to synagogue on the Lower East Side. That was where Jews went for shoes and nice dresses, even as late as the 1980s and even though the shoe store was next door to an empty lot piled with bricks and dirty needles.

The rest of my clothes came from Conway or other discount stores in Herald Square, or Macy's, if they were having a sale. My mother would go shopping on her lunch break and come home with bagloads of outfits for me to try on at home, returning what I didn't want the next day. I would model them for her in the living room and agonize over the prospect of offending the manufacturers of the items I had rejected. I must have known, through the fog of child-logic, that my feelings of guilt were completely misplaced, that what I was really afraid of was hurting my mother. That is how I ended up with a pair of pleated acid-washed jeans in the style of A. C. Slater from *Saved by the Bell,* worn once and then stuffed into the back of my closet.

A common refrain in my family, at least one spoken by me and my father, was, "We're not going to the poorhouse!" This was usually met with indignation by my mother, who would snap back, "You don't understand how little we live on. You don't pay the bills!" And both my dad and I would have to let it go since she was right—certainly about the bill-paying part.

Still, I was resentful, and felt downright deprived, when in the fifth grade she refused me a pair of metallic spandex leggings, which were deemed too expensive. As a consolation prize, I got some ribbed pseudo-leggings from Conway that were barely tight enough to fit into my slouch socks. (The socks were not quite right either.)

I should say here that we lived in a comfortable pre-war apartment on the Upper West Side of Manhattan. I grew up in relative privilege. We had a car, a dog, and went on the occasional family vacation. I went to private school, which was paid for by my grandmother. But money was always tight, and spending it was fraught with anxiety.

The department stores on the East Side—Saks, Bendel's, Bergdorf's, even Bloomingdale's—were off-limits. They were the bastions of the rich and insouciant, with snooty salespeople and spoiled customers, easier to scorn than to risk their rejection. My parents, liberal stalwarts in a time of Reagan-era excess, wore their fashion cluelessness like a badge of honor. They rooted for the downfall of Michael Milken and his cohorts in the savings and loan scandal, and cheered when Barney's was tarred by charges of racial discrimination.

In the ninth grade, when I transferred to an elite private school on the Upper East Side, my own fashion sense went a little haywire. Realizing there was no way I could keep up with my wealthier peers, I turned to buying all my clothes at the Salvation Army on Ninety-sixth Street and Broadway. I thought I had special skills when it came to spotting the best T-shirts—soft and worn, with some sort of ironic slogan or nonsensical text on the front—from among the rows of musty closet detritus. This, to my mother, was more economical and thus better than shopping retail, even though I went through most of high school wearing a hot-pink ski jacket as an overcoat.

That all changed once I had my own place in New York and a small but independently earned sum of money in my bank account. Shopping in New York is like a drug: the more money you spend, the more you want to spend. And once you pass your limit of what is an appropriate price for, say, a perfect black cotton top or a really, really great pair of flip-flops, it is hard to go back. Instead, I justify any extravagances with the argument that, for people like me, with no innate style, expensive clothes make us look better.

This doesn't mean that I won't immediately call my mother to confess when I spend too much money on a pair of shoes and then refuse to tell her how much they cost. When she asks me, with an innocence that verges on poignant, "Were they more than $75?" I realize that if she knew just how much more she might think less of me.

This is a woman whose own mother, two generations out of the shtetl, washed and reused tin foil—and not because she was an environmentalist. I am pretty certain my mother, who has lived in New York for four decades, has never seen the inside of Bergdorf's, the ultimate gatekeeper of the upper caste lifestyle. Bergdorf's radiates posh. It has soft, flattering lighting, and etched mirrors in the escalator shafts. It lacks the crushing din of manic shoppers looking for the sale rack. Even the shopping bags—lavender with indigo text in a deco font and a graphic of figures who look like they're on their way to a Jay Gatsby party—are a paradigm of high-class understatement. And although many of the customers are teenagers and women in their twenties wearing oversized sunglasses and skinny jeans, the whiff of old money in Bergdorf's is pungent.

Walking through the ground floor, past rows of jewels that cost as much as a car, I can't help but feel that being here is a small act of betrayal. This is a place where it is acceptable, in fact encouraged, to spend $900 on a pair of boots. Not that I ever have spent $900 on a pair of boots. But I plan to someday. Then I will call my mom.

Instead of the Rat Pack

GWENDOLYN KNAPP

In this essay, which first appeared in Hayden's Ferry Review, *Gwendolyn Knapp delves into the details of her family's tendency toward pack-ratting, a trait she tries to escape not only in real life but also in her writing. "After a lifetime of being surrounded by clutter, I feel the need to escape, and also to be released," she says. "I guess that's why I share my experiences rather than hoarding them away like I've been taught to."*

My mom has empty nest syndrome, though her nest is filled with more junk than you could nail to the walls of the world's Cracker Barrels. In the cement-block house with the raccoon infestation on Missouri Avenue in New Port Richey, Florida, my glorious southern mama works on her knack for collecting and preserving everything.

The woman has two storage spaces, one for fabrics only, which goes to show what happens when you buy bulk polyester in the seventies. She has enough stuff in her home so that when you go there she must guide you through the living room like a Seeing Eye dog: just cling to the back of her shirt as she pulls you through areas you can't navigate alone. Rest in peace if you knock over centuries of teacups and they crash to the terrazzo. My mom would kill you. And how could you sweep up all the broken pieces? Sheldon the Cat would walk on the shards and need expensive surgery.

Mom belongs to a club called Questers. This is a group of twenty-five or so women whose collective age adds up to the number of boxes in their living rooms. These women meet once a week to discuss pack-ratting.

"We're not pack rats," Mom always laughs, "We're Questers."

The quest itself is not to find a new knickknack—that's easy—but to find a space in your house where the knickknack will go. That is a long, arduous search.

My grandma was a Quester first. She was a lot of things first. I don't know any other woman in the world who shot a six- and seven-point buck with one bullet on the anniversary of her husband's death. That's another story though, and it involves too much venison. My granny hunted, fished, gardened, read romance novels, and bitched about Jeb Bush becoming governor of Florida until the day she died. She loved crosswords and saved stray kittens and squirrels and nursed them with baby doll bottles. She went to church religiously, cursed religiously, and collected used things like they were souls needing saving.

My mom learned everything about pack-ratting from Grandma. So did my sister and I. We'd go to her house every day after school, and each time there would be several new trinkets for her to show off. She often bought us stuffed animals at Goodwill and gave them to us when she picked us up in her giant wood-paneled wagon. I'd ride with my thrift-store teddy bear, crusty in parts, upon my lap. I'd pick at his fur until all the dirt nits were smoothed out, until he was *my* teddy. I loved every bear she got me. They all slept with me at night, dozens of them, and in the morning they'd be spread across the floor with their arms out like zombies.

"Hurry up, you old farts," Grandma would yell if we were behind a couple of blue hairs. *She* wasn't an old fart. She kept her hair long and dark blond and always tied it back with a ribbon that matched the color of her polyester pants and slip-on shoes. She ironed her hair ribbons every morning in her pink robe and curlers. It was her way.

"Try being dropped off at school every day of your life with the woman in her pink robe and curlers," Mom once told me. "One time she had to come inside the high school because our car broke down, and guess what she was wearing. I was mortified."

But guess who has that pink robe now? Guess who took all the curlers and put them in a storage space? Mom even has Grandpa's old chair; one summer a booger forest sprouted on the left side of it, and we vowed never to take his seat again.

Riding in the car with Grandma was like welcoming death with Clint Black on the radio. "Hold on," she warned when she gunned it past old farts, heading into oncoming traffic. I'd hold my new teddy up to see our ugly town out the window. It could be the last time we'd ever see it. My grandma drove like she was in her son's stock car. She was a stubborn woman too. One time, driving back from a family reunion in Ocala, the air-conditioning broke in her car, but she wouldn't admit it. She wouldn't let us roll the windows down. I about died from heat prostration by the time she dropped us off at home with her windows fogged up and all of us sweatier than glasses of ice tea. "Did the AC break?" she said. "I can't tell." That was the summer of "Achy Breaky Heart."

Grandma was a passionate pack rat. These were a few of her favorite things: braided rugs, blue glass pitchers, a yellow porcelain bird with an actual chip on its shoulder. She loved little bird figurines. She always put the birds on the television, which for many years rested atop another television, large and archaic—the television of my mother's youth, and here stacked upon it, the television of my day. It's like that Jeff Foxworthy joke about you might be a redneck if. You might be a redneck if you quote Jeff Foxworthy in a nonfiction essay.

ALL GOOD PACK RATS learn to stack from a young age. That's why a lot of parents buy their kids Legos. My mom also bought us Jenga, so we could see what happens when you take a piece away from its stack: everything falls apart. That's why you don't go throwing out the old couch with the rot-gut innards—which some vermin time-share with the roaches—in the garage. Because it is the foundation for the boxes of old *Vogue* magazines your mother hasn't read since the 1970s, around the same time she collected all that bulk polyester. Some day you'll need a place for your boxes of *Sassy Magazine* to go, and where would you put them if that couch wasn't somehow glued to the floor, Miss Jenga Expert?

Stacking is very important. I don't want to beat you over the head with this point like I could, with a golf club Mom uses to hit the ceiling of the garage to tell certain animals to shut the hell up while infesting the house up there. But when you run out of places to put things, you have to put some stuff away in boxes. Baskets work well too. You don't have to give things away. You never have to give away anything. Just stack it.

Much like life, if you start out with a bad foundation your stacks of precious things will fall over and be ruined. Look what happened to the Leaning Tower of Pisa. Sure they fixed it a little, but we don't have that fancy-shmancy Italian technology available at the house on Missouri Avenue. Where my mom has dedicated her life to building a nest of used furniture and piling it high with dead flowers and trunks of cloth diapers and baskets of baskets and lamp shades still in plastic, mounds of old pictures of relatives on land we no longer own—with nothing to show for it but more baskets and some exotic potted plants. Magazines: Mom's got piles of *Utne Reader*, *Marie Claire*, *Martha Stewart*, *Southern Living*, and surprisingly, *Yoga Life*. She's got a yoga DVD and a yoga mat, both stacked on the television along with the DVD player that's never been hooked up. On one bookshelf a rusty coronet and a Chia Pet bookend classic literature. On another, Easter Bunny, Dracula, and Little Drummer Boy point candles toward each other like light sabers. Seashell pictures from Big Lots with orange discount price stickers still on the front never make it to the wall. Dust bunnies hop around at your feet because they want your attention. They want to tell you a secret. *We're all going a little crazy here at the house on Missouri Avenue. Shhhhh.*

When an old relative dies, pack rats take in all they can from the person's home as if they're adopting abandoned children. It's their duty. It's horrible. All of those precious belongings are like children. Sometimes, when it involves good furniture, such as a used blue La-Z-Boy, possessions are more important than children.

"I need them. I'm not getting rid of them," Mom says of her inherited things. Pack-ratting is her way of grieving, her way of wallowing in the dirty quilts of the past. They are very worn, dirty, buggy quilts with holes that let in the cold, and still she wants them all.

MY GRANDMA DIED in November 2003. I wasn't there at her bedside like Mom was. I wasn't even in Florida. I was at my new home in North Carolina, about to drive to see this band, Crooked Fingers, play when Mom called to tell me. I was expecting it. Grandma had been moving in circles from her bed to the nursing home bed to the hospital bed with the tangles of white cords coming out of her like tiny waterslides, like maybe her brain tumor would come shooting down a tube one day screaming *yeehaw*. But the brain tumor was large and round like a golf ball and wouldn't budge. I never thought a brain tumor could be more stubborn than our sweet matriarch.

"It was peaceful," Mom told me, "I got to say goodbye to her, but we can't find Susie. We tried to call her and tell her it was Mommy's time, but we don't know where she is," Mom said.

"Oh," I said. What could I say about Aunt Susie? Maybe you should have called the one bar they got up in Dixie County instead.

"Go ahead to your concert," Mom told me. "Go be with your friends and then we'll get you a flight tomorrow. Okay?"

"Okay," I said. Except I didn't have many friends in my new town, and at the show the music was slow and quiet and the people all around drunk and loud. I couldn't hear the vocals at all. It was more difficult than listening to a twice-removed cousin's husband talk about gator hunting while your grandma sang along to "Winter Wonderland" at Christmas dinner. Except she always sang, "Walking 'Round in Women's Underpants."

WHEN GRANDMA DIED, unexplainable things happened. My cat jumped out the second-story window. My ovaries cramped so bad doctors thought I had appendicitis. Uncle Jack strangled Aunt Susie in Grandma's kitchen while I ate a piece of fudge. Forget I said that. It had more to do with Goldschlager and Susie's third husband, than with my grandma's death. The hair ribbons Grandma draped over her bedroom door seemed so young and strange then, as if they belonged on the door to some little girl's bedroom. Then they vanished. Everything in her house vanished. Plants in the backyard uprooted and hitched rides down Dixie Highway. There was nothing left of her house. Storage units and a parking lot are what the land became.

The house on Missouri Avenue suddenly looked different. The terrazzo disappeared altogether and the floor was made of cardboard that caved under footsteps. In parts, the floor was made of old fabric, flour sacks, serving plates, and starched white linens. My bedroom disappeared beneath a sea of unhung pictures that stared at walls of my old surfer posters in envy. Somewhere on the front porch a pumpkin rotted. Somewhere a fake frog went ribbit-ribbit beneath the box crushing him. Mom's boyfriend found a hole in the back bedroom, crawled into it, and found his bipolar disorder. Somewhere in this new inheritance, my mom sat and wept and blew her nose into Grandma's embroidered hankie.

FOR ALMOST TWO YEARS, my sister and I have avoided the house on Missouri Avenue. It's easy when you live in New Orleans or Wilmington. The rule is that we do Christmas at Mom's, but every other holiday is for the taking. We had Thanksgiving at my place this year. Then Molly tried to cop out of Christmas because of all the refugee travel she did when Hurricane Katrina hit. That's another story. She'd finally returned to the Crescent City and didn't want to leave.

"Oh no, you don't," I told Molly on the phone. "You get your ass to Florida. We're having an intervention."

Sounds fun, right? Well, Molly showed up anyways.

"We're gonna help you get rid of some stuff," was how we put it to Mom.

She went along with it. She was happy to hear it.

"Oh, wonderful," she even said when she saw us tiptoeing around boxes of fabric and hunchbacked furniture in my old room. "Yeah, if we get this room cleaned up I can do my yoga in here. And I'm hosting a Questers meeting next week, so I can move some stuff from the living room in here if we get it cleaned up."

I said, "You're having the meeting here? You're on crack. That living room is a nightmare."

"No it's not. It'll be fine. I just have to take the Christmas tree down."

In my life, the Christmas tree has never come down before Valentine's Day, so that we can thoroughly express our love for the tree each year. Dear dead, dead tree, be mine.

MOLLY AND I BUZZED around the bedroom. We cleaned out my old desk and closet. We had to work fast in the morning to get things thrown out while Mom busied herself with showering and getting dressed. No time to fawn over A+ algebra tests of the past. To run our hands over cotton ball artwork or taste what red ink on paper is like. We threw folders, pencils, papers, 1980s schoolwork into white garbage bags until the bags threatened to bottom out and spread the contents across the floor.

"*Macht schnell,*" we cried, "Get thee to a garbage can." If the bag bottomed out one could interpret it as a sign that God wanted those old papers to stay in the house forever. And Mom was lingering nearby, waiting for her chance to keep things.

We got in the closet, actually got in there. Nobody's been in there for a decade, what with the filing cabinet, basket of rugs, and dresser-turned-television-stand blocking it. Really, anything can work as a television stand.

You'd think this closet was the long lost gateway to hell or worse, say, 1990. Here, in flimsy boxes, we found a white leather purse, a faux gator-skin fanny pack, and various small baskets of beads and random Barbie heads, which we used to throw into the ceiling fan. It was our first ceiling fan and it was amazing. Today you shouldn't run the ceiling fan unless you want to know the speed it takes for the blades to snap off against mounds of boxes.

We piled crappy things in bags and put them outside the door. That's when Mom came to inspect the contents of these bags.

"You're not getting rid of this," she whined. "You can't get rid of this." Or this. Or this, this, this.

My dear mother with her orange kimono bathrobe and her head wrapped in a towel as if she were a living soft-serve ice cream cone. She looked at us like we were Grinches taking away her Who hash.

"You're not giving this stuff away," she told us, emptying the bags of stuff, and when that didn't work, yelling at us like we were adolescent turds again, not that we're so far from that at twenty-four and twenty-eight years old. Sweet Jesus, I thought, I hope she doesn't find out I just threw my math tests away.

"Why do you want to get rid of these plastic containers that fit inside your Caboodle?" She yelled at me, "You still have that Caboodle, don't you?"

"Yes," I mumbled.

"What?"

"Yes. I still have my Caboodle."

"Mom," Molly said, "Why don't you go blow-dry your hair and let us do this?"

"Fine."

Hi, I'm fourteen again. I feel the braces cutting the flesh of my mouth into streamers. Hey, there's a karaoke machine underneath this mound of shoes. Let's party.

Then at the bottom of another box in the closet, there are tiny rubber bands. We used these for Barbie hair ties. We were supposed to use these to harness our twisted, metal-covered teeth in place. Grades seven through twelve were a constant fear of opening my mouth wide enough for these rubber bands to break and snap against the roof of my mouth. Which means I kept my mouth closed tight while speaking too. I tried for years to convince schoolmates it was an Australian accent and not just me being a loser with rubber bands that could kill us all. Or even worse, fly out of my mouth and injure the face of Kyle Ulrichson, the hottest surfer known to mankind, or at least to my geometry class. If I'd been called on to recite the Pythagorean theorem in front of my peers, someone would have lost a blimey eye.

It took many years for my teeth to straighten up, because they were so hideously twisted and small. Before I had braces, my teeth overlapped in front. They stacked on top of each other because every part of me was made to work as a pack rat.

I've fought off my body's urge to turn pack rat. To stack. To collect things. Like cysts—my ovaries keep wanting to collect those. I'll toss ovaries into the ceiling fan like ugly Barbie heads. Or I could send them to the collection agency that says they're worth thousands of dollars. I'll pull out these teeth if they try to stack again. These cursed teeth, white trash teeth, some dangling today like sharp stalactites in the dank cave of my mouth. I should be thankful. I should be kneeling at the Christmas tree thanking the sweet lord for braces and a neon-yellow retainer with a frog sticker in it, though along with Mom's graduate classes my braces happen to be on a fifty-year payment plan.

Pack-ratting is something that is genetic, but also contagious. Most people are born with it in them. There's no way to avoid pack-ratting once you're born into a nest of the wolfish beasts and their scent is all over you. Not even killing yourself or being killed will help, because hell and heaven are stacked with pack rats and clouds are just dust bunnies that go on forever.

I'll tell you a secret: I have the special ability to find porcelain squirrels wherever I go. Which leads to collecting them, which leads to buying a small squirrel house or two for them to live in, which leads to people, like your friends, thinking you're crazy. Well, I do have a squirrel flag hanging up with the phrase *Welcome to the Nut House* scrawled across it.

If you are not a pack rat, you are probably the owner of some five hundred pairs of shoes including a pair of Birkenstocks you might wear with socks in winter, so I don't want to hear it. Or, like my mom, perhaps you have an old pair of ballet slippers you keep in the garage and sometimes you go out there and take them out of their box and rub the old satin of them, feel the days of your youth slip beneath your fingers like a long pink ribbon, so soft, you want to hold on to it forever.

When I was in sixth grade, my feet fit in Mom's slippers. Her feet were that small in college. Twiggy bird feet. I crammed my clumsy feet into the slippers and tried to go up on my toes as if I were meant to star in *Swan Lake*. I couldn't do it. It hurt so much. I couldn't take half the pain. I put the shoes away and pretended I'd never seen them. My toes bruised and I wore socks so Mom wouldn't see. She wanted her old things around, but she never wanted you to touch them.

"Do I go mess with all your things?" she'd ask me when she caught me dressed in her old purple hot pants or a velvet minidress, when I had out her old photo albums or her old records. She was a fashion designer for Frayne in the seventies and had, stuffed in drawers and closets, various artifacts of a previous, hipper life. I couldn't resist any of it.

BUT NOW SHE'S DIGGING around in all her mom's old things. Maybe things her mom wouldn't even want her to touch.

"What are you doing with all Grandma's things like this?" I ask during a low point in our intervention. "What do you want with all of this?"

This is how to upset your mom. This is worse than the time you all tried to play that *South Park* movie on Christmas Eve.

"You have a severe problem," Molly tells her.

"No. I. Don't," she says, and does her lip-pinch-like-a-butthole scowl. "I just can't let go of all this. I'm not ready."

"Mom, we're just trying to help."

"Shut up. I don't need help. Everyone acts like I'm crazy, and I'm not. I know I have a lot of shit, but so what? It's my life. It's not some joke, so stop laughing."

"I'm sorry," I say. I can't help but laugh. I'm standing in an empty box because it is the only place left for me to stand.

"Just close that closet back up and stop trying to go through everything. It's not helping," she says. She screams. She cries. She walks across boxes just to lie down on her childhood bed.

Molly and I shut the closet and sit in the living room, where the Christmas tree explodes from the corner and blocks half the television. On the Weather Channel, I can detect five days of the ten-day forecast. Nice Florida weather. Blue skies the color of La-Z-Boys.

"Hey, Mom. Why don't we get out of the house? The weather's great."

An hour later she emerges from her room.

"That's a great idea," she says. "Let me throw on some clothes and we can go shopping in Tampa. Did I tell you I won a gift certificate to Pier 1 at the Quester's meeting last week?"

MY GRANDMA GAVE ME a squirrel salt-and-pepper shaker when I was in high school. I wish I could show her my collection today. To let her touch all the pieces, and laugh at some and hear her say, *Ohhh, he's a handsome squirrel, isn't he, Dolly?* She always called me Dolly.

I forgot a squirrel picture at Mom's house after the Christmas of failed intervention, and she has yet to send it to me. I know she just stacked it on the dining table and walks by it every day. It is black and shiny, this squirrel picture. It's made of resin and painted wood, so you can see your reflection in it. She's looking at my squirrel every day and seeing herself in it. I'll never get it back.

MOLLY AND I FAILED. We just failed terribly like our family does at most things in life. How can you have any type of intervention with a woman who counts screaming as a hobby? We couldn't even touch

Grandma's things to move them out of the way to get to our things without Mom's face lighting up like a hot plate and shaking like a bobble-head Chihuahua. "Fine," we went around saying. "We won't touch anything. Just keep everything."

Surprise, Mom let us throw away the old bottle of Vanilla Fields perfume that had been rotting in a box in my closet since 1992. In middle school, I bathed in this vanilla scent, which must have killed off all the bedbugs and mites that nested in my old mattress, passed down from some ancient ancestor. I got scabies when I was in sixth grade, but nobody knew. Mom and Molly got them too. Scabies spread like pack-ratting through our house, infesting green carpet, white lace curtains, and the *Star Wars* sheets on our bunk bed. Mom was ashamed and cried. Molly laughed to her friends on the phone and said, "I knew we were white trash," then listened to Pearl Jam and cried. I just itched. I itched at scabies with my fingers, with my Barbies, with my hairbrush behind my knees. The walls of the house weren't rough enough for my back. I thought about heating the curling iron and burning out my armpits.

Not even this girl Carol Show who rode my bus and played French horn with me in band knew I had scabies because I wore more turtlenecks than an English teacher. At least my scabies went away. We washed everything in the house and stayed with Grandma. Carol Show got scabies in seventh grade and they lasted a whole year. I wasn't her friend. One day she told me, "You've turned into such a good horn player." She said this to sit next to me on the bus. She wanted me to give her compliments, but I didn't. She wore halter tops and high-heeled sandals.

When the bus drove past my house on Dixie Highway, because we looped past it twice before I got dropped off, naturally Carol Show said, "That's your house?"

She knew it was. Just like I knew she didn't live in a house at all.

"Yeah," I said.

"That's cool you guys have a fireplace."

"What?"

"Isn't that a chimney coming out the roof?"

"Oh yeah. We got a nice fireplace," I lied. That chimney was really some vent for the old brown kerosene heater that we never used except for stacking phone books on. If we used it, Mom swore, we'd burn the house down, so when it got cold we'd turn on several long brown space heaters from our collection and stand in front of them. The metal coils burned the hair off your legs if you stood too close.

"That's cool you got a fireplace," Carol Show said, and smiled. It wasn't comfortable to sit in a seat with two French horns and a girl who smelled like body odor, the type that doesn't belong to an eleven-year-old girl, the type that only rubs off on you if cheap men hug on you all the time.

"It's pretty useless," I said. "It doesn't get cold enough to use the fireplace, you know."

"Do you ever climb up inside it? I've heard about climbing up in one."

"No," I said, "there's bats in there."

"Bats?"

"Yes. A lot of bats," I said as she scratched at her arm. I'd heard bats in my grandma's chimney, before she smoked them out into the daylight and they showered the sky like flapping tar.

I didn't say anything about Carol Show's scabies. I didn't say, "Once I had scabies too, girl." Her scabies may have lasted longer than a year, but she stopped catching the bus and stopped going to school. She lived in the trailer park behind the Checkers where Molly later worked. Every day she got off the bus and lugged her French horn case down the highway toward home, strutting like a teen prostitute with a half-melted suitcase. Then one day she just disappeared. Maybe she went somewhere. Maybe she carried that horn to Vegas or New York or Tijuana. Maybe she carried that horn until her arm felt numb, and it must have been the best feeling. Do you know how that is, to not be itchy any more?

TODAY MOM HAS BITES on her body. They get worse every time I see her. First she blamed it on Aunt Susie and the strange things skin does because of Third Husband. Then she blamed it on camping and then on the house. Now she just curses her arms and legs and smears them with clear nail polish.

"You know that doesn't work, right?" I tell her.

"Well, it seems to be working." She shows me how the strange bite-rash on her arm has separated into colonies since she's used the nail polish.

"Perhaps they're getting ready to wage war on each other," I tell her.

"Stop being a smartass," she says.

She's always said life is not a sitcom, but here she is with bedbugs and not enough room to move a mattress in or out the door, any door. I can't help but want us to be a prime-time show. All they'd have to do is cast Barbara Streisand as Mom, Angelina Jolie as myself, and Lindsey Lohan as Molly, but only if Lohan lost a few more pounds and got a huge smooshed-fairy tattoo on her ass, so it looks like she sat on it. Instead of the Rat Pack, we can be the Pack Rat. One large mangy rodent. Nobody would mess with us.

"You need to get rid of that bed and get a new one," Molly says. "And by getting a new one, I don't mean one of the five mattresses you have in the garage either."

"I don't tell you what you need to get rid of," Mom says, as if the queen of telling you what to do has stepped down from her throne.

"Yeah freaking right," we say.

She doesn't continue this argument.

But she says "I can use these" about everything in the house. It's

like my dad's dad told him on my parents' wedding day: Why buy the
cow when you can get the milk for free?

The things Mom could not part with: a Dudley Do-Right mini
lunch pail that came with fake M&Ms candy in it as a 1997 stocking
stuffer; a manatee sweatshirt that was never cool, not even in 1991,
the year all middle schoolers said "Fuck you, whales," and moved on
to saving new sea creatures; a *Little Mermaid* sleeping bag (She was
my favorite cartoon, and alas, she too was a pack rat who wanted you
to look at her stuff. Isn't it neat—wouldn't you think her collection's
complete?); Molly's pink prom dress, size six with half the sequins
missing from Lord knows what type of dance action, which stays in
the closet; and the empty Wilson Phillips cassette holder Mom wants
to hold on (for one more day) to, in case she ever finds the actual
tape.

"Are you really that attached to Carnie Wilson?" I ask her, though
she doesn't hear. She's too busy going through a bag of my old track
T-shirts, yelling at me to keep them.

"Just give them to Goodwill already," I say, because I want to see
my precious things spread to people like a disease. I want to see a
mohawked hipster in tight jeans and a Gulf track shirt with KNAPP
on the back picking through the racks at a thrift store with his iPod
playing Nick Cave and the Badseeds. One day, I want to drive down
Dixie Highway and see a young girl wearing a Gulf High Cross-
Country dress with scabbed knees and a stick in her hand. *Hey,
Knapp,* her mom might yell from the back porch of their house,
which looks pink every evening because the sun sets that violently on
the Gulf. *Get your butt in here. Yeah, you better start running.*

The Art of Writing a Story about Walking across Andorra

ROLF POTTS

"I find that the creative nonfiction approach is a great way to tell certain stories that cannot exist within the orthodoxy of mainstream journalism," says Rolf Potts, whose assignments take him around the globe. "I often find myself utilizing creative nonfiction when my actual story assignment has finished, and I am looking to explore the emotional or philosophical heart of a given travel experience." Certainly there is nothing orthodox about this story, which first appeared online in World Hum; *in it, Potts satirizes the way travel stories are often constructed—though at the same time, readers will notice, he imparts a tremendous amount of traditionally journalistic information.*

I. Many Travel Stories Begin as an Attempt to Impress
   Pretty Women

   A. Once you have walked across the small Pyrenean nation of
      Andorra, you should proceed to Barcelona. Here, you will

look for a nightclub called L'Arquer. According to your guide-book, L'Arquer contains a fully functioning archery range, and you are intrigued by the idea that one can shoot bows and arrows inside a nightclub. As with Andorra, you are attracted by L'Arquer because you find it charming that such a place exists.

B. In actuality, of course, L'Arquer will not likely live up to your expectations. The archery range, for example, will probably be in a separate, cordoned-off area, and your fantasies of chugging beers while shooting arrows over crowds of drunken revelers will not come true. For this reason, you will not look very hard for L'Arquer, and you will end up settling for a pub called Shanghai. This way, L'Arquer will remain perfect in your imagination—unlike Andorra, the memory of which has now been tainted with jagged brown ridges, chintzy souvenirs, and drunken Scotsmen.

C. In the Shanghai pub, you will meet a Canadian woman named Lisa, who has come to Spain for two weeks of vacation. Eventually, she will ask you what you're here for, and you will tell her that you just walked across Andorra. Lisa isn't exactly sure what Andorra is, so the implicit gag (that Andorra is in fact a very small country, quite easy to walk across) is lost on her. Instead, she asks a neutral question: "How was it?" You reply that it was quite interesting.

D. After this, there will be a pause, which implies that Lisa wants you to elaborate. This is when the real Andorra story begins. What immediately follows the pause will not be the final and definitive story, but it will set the tone for how you'll remember Andorra in the future. This is where you begin to pick and choose, to play games with reality, to separate the meaningful from the mundane and hold it up for display. Later, when you are writing the story down, you will add details of history and culture—but for now you just want to hold Lisa's attention, because she has clear blue eyes and a captivating smile.

E. Skipping over the actual details of the hike, you tell Lisa about the Festa Major celebration in Andorra la Vella. Here, a group of mentally handicapped Andorrans singled you out from the crowd and cheerfully bullied you into joining them in a Catalan dance called the sardana. You choose to reveal Andorra through this story because it's funny and self-deprecating, and you want to single yourself out to Lisa as a charmed person who is instinctively adored by retards.

F. The story goes fairly well upon first telling, save for the facts that: (a) Lisa seems faintly offended when you use the word "retards"; and (b) you flub the phrasing near the end of the story, inadvertently implying (to Lisa's ears) that you were insensitive to the mentally handicapped Andorrans while you were dancing with them. You make a mental note to sharpen the clarity of your phrasing, since you were not, in fact, acting insensitive when it actually happened.

II. Historical Details Make It Look Like You Know What You're Talking About

A. After you have left Spain and returned to your home, you will decide you need to know more facts about Andorra before you properly begin to compose your story. Reference books and Web sites tell you that Andorra has sixty-seven thousand residents, only 33 percent of whom are Andorran citizens. Andorra has an area of 180 square miles. This is half the size of New York City, but two-and-a-half times larger than Washington, DC. Since you don't want to make your hike sound too easy, you will use the Washington comparison when composing your Andorra story.

B. You'll try to spruce up basic facts by clumping them together in a telling manner. Start by saying that Andorra has no airports, no trains, and no independent universities. Mention that Andorra's small army has not fought a war for seven hundred years, and that most of its ammunition consists of blank bullets used for public ceremonies. Point out that, while Andorra has a national automobile museum, it did not have substantial roads until the middle of the twentieth century. If possible, say: "More like a neighborhood than a country, Andorra's tourism boom has transformed it into a peaceful suburb of ski runs, luxury hotels, and duty-free shopping."

C. Touch on the history of Andorra, but—since this is primarily a travel story—try to deal with it in a concise manner. Write: "Andorra is the lone remaining legacy of Charlemagne's 'March States,' which were created to keep Muslim Moors out of Christian France in the ninth century." Then jump forward a few centuries to describe how, in the 1200s, a local power struggle between a French count and a Spanish bishop led to a compromise that made Andorra nominally sovereign. "Called the 'Pariatges,'" you will write, "this treaty plays French and Spanish influences off one another, and has insured Andorra's independence for centuries."

D. Mention that, to this day, power is officially shared by the president of France and the bishop of Urgell in Spain. Say: "Thus, Andorra has the current distinction of being the only nation in the world to have two heads of state—neither of whom lives in Andorra."

III. Editors Are Impressed by Tidy Narrative Formulas

A. Now that you have prepared the historical facts, you must choose a manner of storytelling. Were you writing a book about

Andorra, you might begin your story from a personal or emotional premise. You might say, for example, that your lover has just left you, and you resolved to walk across Andorra in an effort to heal your pain. Or you might say that your home was lacking in good taste or authenticity, and you walked across Andorra to discover an older and more genuine way of life. Or you might say that you've been fascinated with Andorra since childhood, and to walk its breadth would be to actualize a lifelong dream.

B. You are not, however, writing a book. Nor did you go to Andorra to heal your pain, seek a more genuine way of life, or actualize a lifelong dream. Rather, your Andorra sojourn was an extension of a trip to Paris, where you were teaching a seminar in (of all things) travel writing. As you walked across Andorra, in fact, your backpack contained a folder full of student papers. Every so often you took these papers out and wrote things like: "Show how the villagers act, don't tell." Or: "Establish that you are inside the castle before you introduce the janitor." Or: "Describe what the geishas looked like." Or: "Don't give away the samba dancer's secret at the beginning." Or: "Tell me more about the one-legged man with the sausage."

C. Regardless of what happened to you in Andorra, you must choose a template.

1. You could, for example, present yourself as a connoisseur who traveled to Andorra to sample *formatge de tupí* (a local specialty consisting of cheese fermented with garlic and brandy in an earthenware container).

2. You might present yourself as an avid hiker or skier, who came to compare the slopes of the Andorran Pyrenees with those of the French Alps. ("They are not as tall or dramatic," you might say, "but the casual lack of crowds lends a certain appeal.")

3. If you are good at humor, you could present yourself as a hapless wanderer in a tiny land full of baffling cultural differences and bizarre local folktales (be sure to mention the legend of L'Auvinyana, a feisty Andorran peasant who made her fortune as a prostitute in Barcelona and returned to her homeland, dressed in velvet and ostrich plumes, to seduce lumberjacks at gunpoint).

4. Another option is to follow in the footsteps of a famous historical, literary, or mythical traveler, making comparisons and contrasts as you go.

D. You are pleasantly surprised to find that a famous literary-historical traveler named Richard Halliburton walked across Andorra in 1921. "I wasn't sure whether the vaguely familiar word Andorra meant a fish or a fruit," Halliburton observed in his book *The Royal Road to Romance*, "until one day I ran across it by accident on the map, and found it was nothing edible, but an independent republic of six thousand people and one hundred seventy-five square miles, all lost for ten hundred years in the tops of the Pyrenees." Inspired, Halliburton traveled to the French border, rented a donkey named Josephine (which he promptly renamed Hannibal), and spent the next few days hiking the breadth of Andorra.

E. Thus, much as modern wanderers seek to follow the trail of Marco Polo across Asia, you decide that your Andorran journey took place in the footsteps of Richard Halliburton.

IV. When Bogged Down in Description, Trot Out Some Colorful Characters

A. Think back to the beginning of your Andorran experience. Like Richard Halliburton, you started on the French side, in a village called L'Hospitalet. You hiked all day, slept your first night at

Pedoures Lake, then crossed into Andorra at Ruf Peak, which is eighty-five hundred feet high. From there, you hiked down the Vall d'Incles into the heart of Andorra. As usual, you have difficulty describing this hike, because you feel there is a sameness to describing mountains.

B. You want to just say: "There were a few pines and far-off forests of beech-trees on some of the mountainsides. I climbed up and up and crossed another high Col, and I saw a whole new range of mountains off to the south, all brown and baked-looking and furrowed in strange shapes." This seems such a simple and appropriate way to describe hiking in the Pyrenees. Unfortunately, it happens to be a direct quote from Ernest Hemingway's *The Sun Also Rises,* which you read on a series of bus rides from Paris to L'Hospitalet.

C. You don't want to resort to the usual clichés, however—the "jagged ridges," the "crystal clear lakes," the "quaint chateaux perched on hillsides"—so you check your notebook. Here, you have scribbled observations from the hike, such as "yellow frogs, brown spiders, orange butterflies," and "French hikers carry what appear to be ski poles," and (to your own chagrin) "crystal clear mountain lakes perched below jagged brown ridges."

D. In general, you are insecure about this first portion of your Andorran journey, because all you have is background and description, and (as you told your students) travel stories work better when they include characters and dialogue. Thus, you should hurry your narrative hike to the ski-resort town of Soldeu, where you met a retired Scottish ski instructor named Morrie. Morrie was very friendly, very colorful, and (by the end of the night) very drunk. Morrie clapped you on the back, bought you beers, and took you on tours of recently built hotels and bars. Morrie pointed to the local elite and said: "Look at

that bugger. A generation ago he and his family were dirt farmers. Now they own half the hotels in Soldeu."

E. In one pub, Morrie introduced you to a number of British,
Spanish, and Argentine ski instructors. In your notebook, you
wrote: "Ski instructors arm-in-arm, singing along to 'Stuck in
the Middle With You,' by Stealers Wheel." Beside this entry, in
the margin of your notebook, you later added: "This could
almost be the Andorran national anthem."

F. As it turned out, the ski instructors didn't know much about
Andorra ("I think it became a country because France and
Spain didn't want it," one Brit suggested). The best information
you learned from these folks was that Andorra always wins lots
of medals in the "Little Country Olympics."

G. Now that you've have a chance to confirm this, you are pleased
to learn that there actually is a Little Country Olympics (officially called the "Games for the Small States of Europe"), which
pits Andorra against Cyprus, Iceland, Liechtenstein, Luxem-
bourg, Malta, Monaco, and San Marino. The Vatican, you are
somewhat disappointed to note, does not field a team.

V. Be Sure to Contrast the Purity of the Past with the
Superficialities of Today

A. Since the Little Country Olympics is a tangent at best, you go
back to your notes and scan for details about the hike from Soldeu to Canillo. "Trail to Canillo actually a thin path following a
stream near the highway," your notebook reminds you. "Ski lifts
and power wires. SUVs with French tags choking the highway."
There is not much drama here, so you decide to mention
smuggling.

B. Write: "Twisting down from the mountains, this trail is the
legacy of Andorra's time-honored smuggling tradition. Due to

her location between two larger neighbors, Andorra has always profited from monopolies and embargoes on both sides." Illustrate this with an example—say, the French match monopoly of the 1880s, when almost 2,000 pounds of matches were smuggled over from Spain each year.

C. Point out that the smuggling trade has given way to a somewhat bland trade in tourist souvenirs and duty-free goods. Say: "If a country expresses itself through its souvenirs, it's hard to tell what Andorra thinks it is." Describe how one can buy Scotch whiskey, Barcelonan newspapers, and even figurines of doobie-smoking Rastafarians (which, to your eye, look "disturbingly Sambo-like") in Canillo.

D. Imply that the superficialities of duty-free souvenirs in Canillo distressed you, and that you then had to find something authentic and redeeming. A church is always good for this. Our Lady of Meritxell would be ideal, since this is home to the patron saint of Andorra, who reputedly keeps her country safe from war and invasion. Unfortunately, you never visited this church.

E. Briefly consider pretending you went there, since you can easily patch together an account from tourist literature.

F. Choose instead, out of dull conscience, to describe St. Joan de Caselles, a twelfth-century Romanesque church that you actually did visit. Include the following phrases when describing the church: "rectangular nave with a wooden ceiling," "semicircular apse with a Lombard-style bell-tower," and "sixteenth-century Italian-German renaissance-style altarpiece, which includes scenes from the life of St. John." Embellish the sense of history this evokes.

G. Since the hike from Canillo to Andorra la Vella is largely suburban, make a quick transition to the capital. Use this 1921 Richard Halliburton quote: "There, on the hillside, was Andorra City, climbing slightly above the verdant floor of this sunlit garden—the most pathetic, the most miserable capital city of any nation in the world."

H. Contrast above passage with the comparative modernity of contemporary Andorra la Vella. Mention luxury hotels, Spanish tourists driving Opel station wagons, and French middle-class shopaholics, who swarm the duty-free stores.

VI. Don't Forget to Talk to a Local

A. Since it is bad form to write a story about Andorra without producing an actual Andorran, it is now time to bring out Ms. Roser Jordana. Mention that she was a small, sharp, no-nonsense woman. Recall how her pearls and rhinestones glittered as she fielded phone calls and answered your questions in the office of tourism.

B. As it is somewhat lame for the Andorran in the story to be from the bureau of tourism, boldly bring this irony into the foreground. Say: "Andorra's tourist economy has turned the nation into a country of visitors. So much so, in fact, that the first true Andorran I meet heads up the office of tourism in Andorra la Vella."

C. Scan your notes from Ms. Jordana's personal tour of the Andorran parliament house. Condensing facts, write: "About the size of a large dining room, the Andorran parliament chamber seats representatives from each of the country's seven parishes. Before the days of roads, this small building doubled as a hostel, and representatives would often sit in the kitchen to eat their sack lunches and discuss politics."

D. Though your notes say as much, it's best not to mention that Marc Forne, the current General Syndic of the Andorran parliament, looks a lot like the father from the 1980s American sitcom *Family Ties*.

VII. Public Festivals Are the Holy Grail of Any Travel Story

A. Festivals always lend color and climax to a travel story, so you should segue into the Catalan Festa Major, which you had the good fortune to experience on your second day in Andorra la Vella. Establish the scene: orchestras and fireworks, a medieval market, Spanish wine for a dollar a bottle, rowdy parades with huge-headed Catalonian "giant" puppets.

B. Describe the traditonal sardana dances in a square near the park: the old Andorrans dancing in perfect step-step-step, the Spanish oom-pah band under the gazebo, the pretty young women in short skirts, singing. Mention that, because of geographical access, Catalan Spain has had a stronger influence over Andorra than France.

C. You have no choice now but to deal with the mentally handicapped Andorrans. Recall how they began their sardana with inspiring concentration, but soon shook free of their minders and flapped across the plaza with ecstatic abandon. Each of them wore a name tag, so you know that it was a hefty fellow named Gordoneau who fixed you in his small-eyed gaze and yanked you out into the plaza to join the dance—which by that point was rapidly disintegrating into a gleeful mosh pit.

D. Jigging and swirling across the plaza, you slowly came to realize that the spectators regarded you and Gordoneau with the same bemused stare. When Gordoneau stopped at a plastic table and took a sloppy gulp of some stranger's beer, the old Andorran sitting there merely flinched and smiled up at you, as if you might do the same.

E. You think back to how you tried to explain this instant to Lisa two days later in Barcelona: how there was a wonderful freedom in the notion that—loosed of all expectations—anything you do in Andorra might be forgiven in advance. You intended no moral or quip-joke by saying this; you meant only to imply that one takes one's epiphanies where one can find them, and you were happy to be invited for a glimpse into Gordoneau's world.

F. You've since forgotten how long the dance went on before the harried minders corralled Gordoneau and his companions back into neat lines. No doubt it lasted mere minutes, but you realize that any accomplishment is relative, and that Andorra was somehow more knowable for the experience. What, after all, did Hillary know of Nepal? What did Armstrong know of the moon? More than most of us, perhaps—but neither of them had the chance to dance with Gordoneau along the way.

VIII. End with a Tidy Generalization, or Perhaps a Knowing Wink

A. Since esoteric digressions make editors nervous, you must find a more conventional way to end your story. Uncertain how else to proceed, you search the Internet for one last detail that might sum up what you experienced in Andorra.

B. Stumbling upon a random Web page about traditional Catalan nativity scenes, you read about a peculiar figure called the "caganer." The caganer is a harlequin of sorts, a grizzled old man who squats—trousers at his ankles, stogie in mouth—casually defecating in the background of the nativity. A sociologist, Xavier Fabregas, is quoted: "The caganer reminds us that even in the midst of the greatest mystery of humanity, the birth of the Redeemer, there are these ineluctable and physiological necessities."

C. It occurs to you that a travel writer is not unlike the caganer within his own narrative—an odd character, always squatting in the background, casually presuming the observer will ignore the fact that these brightly colored surroundings have been painted and positioned well after the events they represent.

D. Thus, from this metaphorical squat, you will write about how you packed your bags, bade farewell to Andorra la Vella, and made for the Spanish border.

E. You will write: "I know that I have only experienced the slightest taste of Andorra, but there is a certain joy in concise goals and knowable quantities—of entire nations that can be strolled across in the course of a long weekend."

Pursuing the Great Bad Novelist

LAURA SEWELL MATTER

"Since I've been starting with Facts, I think my writing has gotten better," says Laura Sewell Matter. *"I just have to wait for a Fact to provoke me (I am easily provoked), then I can follow it in search of more Facts. This part of the process is fun, but the peril is real: I sometimes come dangerously close to getting wrapped up in things that are Fascinating But Irrelevant."* This story, which first appeared in The Georgia Review, *is the writer's first published piece of creative nonfiction and chronicles her quest for more facts about an accidental find on an Icelandic beach.*

On a cold spring day in 2002, I found a damp and crumpled piece of paper on a beach near Reykjavík, Iceland. Unwadding it, I discovered it was a single page torn from a book. It was brownish, about five inches by seven, with typeset Icelandic words on both sides, and page numbers: 17 and 18. I had been studying the language for almost a year and had attained a level of competency that enabled me to read books (slowly, painstakingly, with a dictionary at hand), but the paper was too wet and matted with seaweed to decipher.

I decided to keep it. Nearby, I came upon another small clump of pages that appeared to be from the same book: pages 19 through 22 and 27 through 30. I collected these, too.

When I got back to my apartment, I spread the pages out to dry on the shelf beneath the window, and a decaying, fishy smell filled the room. In one sense, I had picked up some trash from the beach. But I couldn't help taking a more romantic view of the situation. Somehow these pages had ended up in the ocean, where by rights they ought to have disintegrated in the water or been bleached by the sun, yet they came back to land whole. A mystery. Maybe that's why I found the story they told so compelling, even though I recognized, from the moment I began reading, that I had found something amazingly, almost unbelievably, bad:

"Oh, I hope that isn't true. You have been—been so good to me," she said, and her beautiful eyes showed sincere affection.

"You have been like a good daughter to me," he said and smiled a dull smile. "You have been very good to me."

She let her eyes rest on the embers in the fireplace for a moment, and then looked back at him.

"Why are you so proud?" she asked quietly and sensitively.

The earl laughed a cold laugh.

"Come, Veronica. You know my pride is nothing compared to your own. Oh, don't be so contrary! It's the family shortcoming. I've paid attention to you. It's a fault, isn't it, Bolton?—The fault follows you. I have no son." A weakness came into his voice for a moment, but then it became hard and unfeeling again. "I don't care about my cousin Talbot. Wayneford—it was my mother's property—I want to have a good and competent house manager. Dear Veronica, I am naturally too sensitive. You

don't need to make up your mind right now. You can think
about it until the morning."

She made a movement with her hand so similar to the one
the earl had done before she entered that Mr. Bolton was quite
amazed.

"Thank you both, I can decide now," she spoke, smiling, and
directed her words at Mr. Bolton. "I knew poverty. I sat beside
my father's deathbed. Poverty is horrible." Her eyes became wet
with tears and her lips trembled. "I know the power of wealth.
So I never have to marry."

"What do you decide then?" asked the earl sharply.

"I decide," she said, and stood up straight and proud, "to
accept these conditions."

"Excellent," said the earl, and appeared more jovial. "Now
you can leave us, Veronica."

The earl was near the door and opened it for her. She nodded
and left. The aged and grumpy lawyer thought that when she
left the hall some of the daylight left with her.

His Highness took a seat in his old chair again.

"I knew I could rely on her," he said, and the old hateful
sneer settled on his lips. "Compose the will, Bolton, I'll sign it
tomorrow."

—pages 17–18 [author's translation]

The whole story unfolded before me, even though I had only ten
pages.

After agreeing to honor Lord Lynborough's conditions (whatever
they were), Veronica goes out riding across the moors, contemplating
the difference between her bleak apartment in Camden Town and her
uncle's beautiful Devonshire estate. Suddenly, she nearly tramples a
puppy with her horse, but it is snatched to safety just in time by a
mysterious man who happened to be lolling about in the heather
through which she is galloping.

Then there are four missing pages (23 through 26), which the ocean kept from me.

When the story resumes, Lynborough has appeared on the scene in his carriage, and Veronica is trying to persuade him to give the heroic puppy rescuer a job on his estate. The earl asks the man for his name. He is Ralph Farrington, of Australia. The earl tells him to report to the gamekeeper for work. The chapter concludes with the departure of the earl and a bit of foreshadowing about what is to befall young Veronica: "She did not know that the stage was set and the tragedy of her life was about to begin."

Tragedy? Pshaw. Though I couldn't read beyond page 30, it was obvious what would happen: a happy future awaited Veronica and Ralph as mistress and master of Wayneford, while the earl, who sneered and glared, would be punished for his sinister nature and other crimes as yet unnamed. This was melodrama. As with most Hollywood movies, the outcome was never in doubt. It wasn't a question of "How will it end?" but "What will blow up along the way?"

At the time that I found the pages, I had been in Reykjavík for eight months on a Fulbright scholarship, studying Icelandic language and literature. I had come with the intention of applying to doctoral programs in Scandinavian literature the following year; I already had a master's degree in medieval philology with an emphasis in Old Norse. (People often react with amused surprise when I tell them this. Philo—*what?* In Old Norse? I can never truly explain.) When I began graduate school, I planned to study Middle English literature, having long been attracted to chivalric romances and Arthurian mythology. But instead of devoting my attention to tales about knights errant, I had, at my professor's behest, spent months poring over dialect atlases of fourteenth-century England in an attempt to determine the geographic provenance of a manuscript containing a religious allegory about bees. I thought about quitting entirely, then decided to just change my emphasis. At least in Norse literature there are dwarves, and no bees. I loved the Icelandic sagas: stories not of knights but of farmers who ride around braining each other with axes. Even so, I was not a dedicated scholar.

When my classes at the University of Iceland ended in May, I had spent the last of my scholarship money but decided to stay in Reykjavík anyway. I wanted to experience the Icelandic summer, and I had no pressing reason (no job, no specific obligations) to return to the States. I passed the mornings writing fiction and the afternoons reading popular Icelandic novels, newspapers, or even gossip magazines with a dictionary in hand. I had decided that if I was going to make a contribution to the world of literature, it would not be as a scholar. I would write my own books instead.

This proved more difficult than I anticipated—which is to say, the novel I began writing that summer in Reykjavík was *bad*. Almost nothing happened in it. The protagonist (a young man much like me in all respects except gender) went around experiencing angst. I knew it was no good, but I didn't know what to do about it. I couldn't let go of the concept (something about global politics as experienced by an expatriate American in the post-9/11 environment). I cringe when I think of it now. At the end of the summer I would toss the entire novel into the garbage, but at the time I fiddled with it endlessly.

When I got bored, I wrote about Veronica and Ralph instead. If I couldn't finish reading their story, I could invent it. Perhaps it was something like this: Ralph is working as a groundskeeper at Wayneford. One day, he sees smoke rising from the house and realizes it's on fire. He runs into the flaming building to see if anyone needs rescuing. Veronica's mentally retarded cousin Talbot is in there, hiding beneath the harpsichord. Ralph tries to grab him and pull him to safety, but Talbot is strong and stubborn. Ralph must grab a vase from the mantel and crack Talbot on the head to render him unconscious before dragging him to safety. When Ralph emerges, Veronica is there and swoons with relief as she recognizes the depth of her feelings for him. Meanwhile, Lynborough perishes in the conflagration. Veronica inherits the estate and marries Ralph, and they go on honeymoon to Torquay—which, unfortunately, has just been beset by pirates.

WHEN THE SUMMER finally ended, I returned home. By then it was clear that I couldn't (emotionally) commit to pursuing a career in academe, but I also couldn't (financially) continue to live solely as a reader and writer of bad novels. I didn't have a wealthy uncle from whom to inherit an estate to finance my career as an aspiring writer. I needed a job.

My old college roommate worked at a large Silicon Valley technology company (best left nameless) that was searching for a new administrative assistant. The office was quiet, with comfortable chairs and free coffee. The responsibilities were minimal. This seemed compatible with my interest in reading and writing, both of which could be accomplished surreptitiously in the office, so I applied.

At that desk, I began work on a new novel featuring a young man (much like me in all respects except gender) who found some mysterious pages from an unknown novel on a beach and became obsessed with them. I called it *The Water's Edge*. I had no idea how it would end. The protagonist experienced angst about his inability to figure out what the pages meant. There was very little in the way of plot.

Still, I had Ralph and Veronica. Why I continued thinking about them, a year after I first discovered those bits of a bad novel, is difficult to explain. Certainly it was not because I admired what I had read. The characters were caricatures; the plot, such as I knew it, was ludicrously improbable. I was not a reader of romances (unless you count the chivalric medieval variety). I suppose I wanted to keep reading that book because I wanted confirmation that I had correctly inferred what would happen to Veronica and Ralph, but I also wanted to be amazed to learn how they would achieve this. I wanted both the expected outcome and surprise: I wanted *melodrama.*

Admittedly, in other circumstances the story alone would not have warranted my fascination. Had I found the book on a shelf, I probably wouldn't have opened it; if I had, I soon would have set it down again. But because I found it on a beach, I *had* to read it. The discovery of the pages was melodrama itself. Like a man lying about the moors to prevent the unconscionable trampling of innocent, free-roaming puppies, these pages were lying on the sand that day for a reason; though they could not know it, they were destined to be there, waiting for the girl—me—to wander into sight.

I decided to search for the book. Possibly, I thought, I might track it down. I had only ten pages, but I knew the principal characters' names and the Devonshire setting; on the basis of these facts, I suspected the novel was a translation from an English one, and I suspected that it was old—perhaps Victorian—on the basis of the pages themselves. In the course of my studies, I had read enough books of hundred-year-old scholarship to know this almost by feel, but the signature mark "2" stamped at the bottom of page 17 was concrete evidence that this was not a recent publication. In bygone days, printers used signature marks to indicate the gathering of leaves in which a page was to be bound, but this hasn't been common practice for decades.

And so I began searching. Admittedly, this was partly an evasion strategy to get out of working on my second bad novel, which was stagnating and showing no more promise than the first. The search was also a distraction from my mundane job. But I convinced myself that if I could figure out what the pages on the beach were all about, I would have something to write about. I would have material for my novel.

But, first, I had to find the book. I looked in character encyclopedias; I searched the proper names as subjects in library catalogs; I looked for books on Devon; I Googled passages from the Icelandic text; I posted messages on romance novel forums on the Internet; I talked to a town librarian; I talked to a Stanford University librarian; I e-mailed the Library of Congress. Every librarian I spoke with was sympathetic, but nobody could provide definitive advice. Nobody responded to my online postings. Finally, I decided to e-mail the National Library of Iceland, in case my assumption that it was an English novel was mistaken. I attached a picture of one of the pages I had found and asked if they had suggestions for locating the book.

I received a terse response from an Icelandic librarian a few days later. She provided no suggestions or explanations. She simply wrote, "The page is from this book," and pasted in index details from the library catalog. The book was indeed a translation from English, published in Icelandic under the title *Veronika* (which, I assume, was the critical clue that enabled her to match the page to its source). It had also been published in another Icelandic edition under the title *Úrskurður hjartans*—a direct translation of the English title: *The Verdict of the Heart*. The author was one Charles Garvice.

Knowing all of this proved insufficient. I still had to locate a copy. I tried first with used book dealers on the Internet. Though many of them had other books by Garvice—a shocking number of books, in fact—nobody had this one. I did a global library catalog search and discovered two copies: one at the University of Minnesota and another at the British Library. Neither was a circulating copy, so I would have to make a trip. Off-season airfares to London were scarcely more than fares to Minneapolis, and, in another fortunate plot twist, a friend of mine from graduate school had moved to London and was living a half mile from the British Library. He would be happy to give me a patch of floor space to sleep on if I came to visit—so London it was. I would fly eight thousand miles to read a bad book.

When I asked for a week off work on short notice for a trip to London, my boss (a Brit himself) wanted to know why; when I told him that I was going to the British Library, he had to know what for; when I explained that I was trying to track down an obscure book, he wanted to know what book it was. There was no way around it: I had to tell him.

"It's this . . . romance novel," I said.

A few days later at lunch, when I mentioned to some other coworkers that I would be taking a vacation, my boss added, with a bemused grin, "She's going to the library." The others (software engineers who probably read potboiler fantasy novels and *Star Trek* fan fiction if they read for pleasure at all) shook their heads at the absurdity of it. They had no literary pretensions, so were not inclined to be dismissive of the fact that I was traveling overseas to read a romance novel. What amazed them was the fact that I was planning my vacation around any book at all.

I WENT FOR the simple reason that I wanted to know what would happen next. But not just to Veronica and Ralph. I told myself that finding out what happened in the book would tell me what should happen next in the novel *I* was writing—but that too was absurd. Though I wouldn't have put it this way at the time, I really wanted to know what would happen next *to me.*

Something had to happen. I was in my midtwenties; I had finished as much schooling as I cared to, and I no longer had a distant graduation date to serve as goal; I had settled down in a long-term relationship; I had taken a job that I continued to think of as a temporary step, but toward what I could not say—certainly I had no immediate plans to leave it, because I didn't know what I would leave it *for.* I was not unhappy, but I had no sense of momentum, no sense of forward propulsion. I had no significant life goal in mind. Tracking down the book about Veronica and Ralph may have been an arbitrary goal, but it was a goal nonetheless. It gave me a sense of plot—a path to follow, one thing leading to the next, proceeding to some climax and (I could only hope) resolution. The pursuit made me feel that I was making some sort of progress in my life. And my goal was no more silly, for crying out loud, than the goals of an Arthurian knight—to track down some mysterious knave in green tights, or to find out "what women want." Quests are usually about the desire to seek; the things sought are mere pretext.

Alfred Hitchcock (a melodramatist of sorts himself) had a word for the object of a hero's quest. It could be a briefcase, some jewels, a puppy—anything that would motivate action. What it was didn't matter. He called it a MacGuffin. *The Verdict of the Heart* was mine.

ON THE DAY I arrived in London, I went straight to the library, roller bag in tow. I hadn't anticipated that getting a reader's pass would be difficult. I thought it was something like a public library card, available to all comers—until I looked at the application form. They wanted me to list my publications and current academic affiliations, but of course I had none. As I sat waiting for my number to be called, I saw a man dressed in Muslim clerical garb withdraw angrily from the counter, his application refused. I grew concerned. I understood why the British Library would be protective of its collection, and why the materials must be intended mostly for purposes of serious scholarship, but all the same, I couldn't help but wish for a more welcoming atmosphere. The situation was pointedly clear: dilettantes and delinquents might tour the gift shop, but in the reading rooms they would be unwelcome. I began to prepare my appeal to pity. If deemed unworthy based on my credentials, I would explain that I had come all the way from California because *I had to read this book*—I would tell them about what had happened on the beach in Iceland and how I had used half of my annual vacation days for this trip—and how this was one of only two copies of the book that I could locate in the whole world. I was aware of how silly all of this sounded.

Fortunately, the situation did not come to that. On the form, when I explained the purpose of my research, I did not write "unaccountable desperation." Instead, I said that I was writing a book—which was sort of true, if you counted the rotten, half-done, plotless novel. When the woman who processed my application asked if I had any evidence of prior publication to corroborate the fact that I was a "writer," I replied in the most confident tone I could muster: "Not yet." She said that I could be granted only a one-month pass, under the circumstances. If I were published, she explained, I could be granted a three-year pass.

"One week would do it," I said. She took an unflattering mug shot, printed out my reader's pass, and sent me off to the reading room.

The afternoon was nearly gone. I put in my order right away, but the book would not be available until the following morning. I had an hour to kill before I could meet my friend at his flat and sleep off my jet lag, so I wandered the library until I came across a small art exhibition in a back corridor. I can't remember the name of the artist or the content of the images in great detail—all I can recall are washes of blue and fragments of verse interspersed with the images—but I remember the title of the exhibit: *The Water's Edge.* Coincidence or sign? I didn't know. At that moment, I was just annoyed that my title was "taken." I despaired of ever having an original thought to convey. I just wanted to lose myself in the story of Veronica and Ralph.

The next morning, I held the book in my hands at last. Even as a physical object, it was flimsy. Unlike the Icelandic edition, which had

been printed on paper substantial enough to withstand the tides, this
was a cheap, mass-market paperback; each brittle page was reinforced
with a sheet of translucent, gauzelike adhesive. I looked at the picture
of the rosy-lipped young woman on the cover and wondered what
the real scholars (most of whom hunched over thick tomes, and
many of whom were *really wearing tweed*) would think of me as I sat
among them with this tawdry little book.

The Verdict of the Heart was everything I expected it to be. There
were unambiguous villains. Ralph and Veronica were good. Ralph did
indeed rescue someone from a house fire, and justice prevailed in the
end. I was wrong about Lord Lynborough, though: he was gruff but
fair. Cousin Talbot (not retarded) turned out to be the bad guy. Alas,
one of my favorite lines—the one about how the tragedy of Veronica's
life was set to begin the day Ralph rescued the puppy—was missing
from the original. (The Icelandic translator must have taken a little
liberty there.) But the important thing is that it all ended happily for
Veronica and Ralph.

I kept flipping back to the cover. Above the illustration was a bit of
marketing copy that boldly claimed this to be the work of the world's
bestselling author. I had realized the writer was prolific when I saw
the long list of titles beneath his name in the library catalog, but it
had never occurred to me that he could have been so popular. I wondered: how could Charles Garvice have been the bestselling author in
the world less than one hundred years ago if I had never heard his
name before the Icelandic librarian's e-mail? Could the claim be as
empty as those about "Dr. J. Collis Browne's Chlorodyne," advertised
on the back cover, which promised to cure coughs, colds, bronchitis,
asthma, diarrhea, dysentery, spasm, palpitations, hysteria, neuralgia,
rheumatism, gout, and toothache?

When I returned to California, the marketing copy on the cover was
what stuck with me. Of course, I was satisfied by my ability to correctly
predict the outcome of a formulaic romance novel—I have seldom felt

quite as tickled with delight as I did during those two days in the library—but the buzz was short-lived. The mystery of Charles Garvice supplanted the mystery of Veronica and Ralph in my imagination.

In spite of my curiosity, I did not pursue the question at first. Instead, I wrote a few more chapters of *The Water's Edge*, which were just as pointless as the ones that preceded them. A month or so later, I tossed this second novel into the garbage and decided to do more research. The Internet was no help this time. I was driven back into the bowels of the library to track down other obscure books and microfilms of magazines, most of which had been out of print for decades.

CHARLES GARVICE *was* the bestselling English author of the early twentieth century. His fame spread beyond Britain to North America and Australia. His works were translated into numerous languages, including French, German, Spanish, Dutch, and of course Icelandic. He published more than one hundred novels, selling over seven million copies worldwide by 1914. His name became a metonym for the volumes he produced: throughout England, "Garvices" were traded like gossip. He made enough money to buy back the copyright to all of his own early serialized stories by acquiring the periodicals—not just the copies in which his work appeared, but whole publishing enterprises—and then reissuing the stories in new book versions, bringing in more money with every edition. According to Garvice's sometime agent, Eveleigh Nash, his books became "as numerous in the shops and on the railway bookstalls as the leaves of Vallombrosa." Considering sales like these, you could argue that Garvice was one of the greatest bad novelists ever.

It is hard to imagine how a writer could be so prolific and widely read less than a hundred years ago and so utterly forgotten today.

Regardless of whether he was good, he was immensely popular. Where did all those readers—and all those books—go? "I might say that I began, wedged into the angle of a playground wall at a certain preparatory school at Bexley Heath, with Dickens' *David Copperfield* on my knees," Garvice told a journalist from *Bookman* magazine when asked about his early life. According to the few limited accounts of his childhood, Garvice was born in or around Stepney, England, in about 1850, just when *David Copperfield* was first appearing in serial installments. Professionally, Garvice would have a lot in common with Dickens: both got their start as journalists and learned the craft of fiction by writing for periodicals; both enjoyed popular success in their lifetimes and were consequently accused of mercenary motives; both had a certain penchant for the melodramatic and a tendency to use more words than necessary (both were paid by the word).

But Garvice was no Dickens. He didn't offer challenging insights or social critique; he just pandered to the popular taste for exciting stories with happy endings. He never felt that there was anything inherently filthy about lucre. In later life, he proudly told his friend Douglas Sladen that when he sold his first story, at the age of nineteen, he realized "a mine of wealth lay glittering at my feet."

Fortune did not follow immediately upon this youthful realization. His first novel, *Maurice Durant,* was not a success when it was published in 1875. It had been reasonably successful as a serial, but when it was published in volume form, sales were weak. Garvice blamed the failure not on the book's lack of literary merit but on the way it was marketed. The book did not sell because it was too long and too expensive for popular sales, he reasoned. He learned quite early in his career that writing was a business like any other.

Garvice spent the next twenty-three years cranking out serials for the periodicals of American publisher George Munro, who later repackaged and resold them as novels with titles like *A Modern Juliet,*

Woven on Fate's Loom, and *Just a Girl.* The latter, which came out in 1898, was Garvice's greatest popular success to date in America, selling more than one hundred thousand copies. The accompanying publicity was enough to attract the notice of the British public. *Just a Girl* was a bestseller in Garvice's native country—an achievement matched by every subsequent novel he published. In 1913, his annual sales for all titles combined stood at 1.75 million copies, worldwide. He continued more or less apace for the rest of his life.

The critics were merciless. His work was routinely dismissed by highbrow publications such as the *Athenaeum,* which snidely acknowledged Garvice's success: "The very thickness with which the colours are laid on will make the novels popular in circles which know nothing of artistry."

The question that concerned the critics was not whether Garvice's work was high art—it patently was not—but whether he was a calculating businessman who condescended to write for the newly literate feminine masses or a simpleton who believed in the sort of twaddle he peddled. A fool or a cormorant. Either way, he was damned.

I began to collect Garvice novels—*On Love's Altar, His Love So True, A Relenting Fate.* I could never get through any of them, other than *The Verdict of the Heart.* Little beyond the particulars of the heroines' hair color differentiates one from another, and without seaweed stuck to the pages, the stories were stripped of mystery. They bored me.

I did manage to get through Garvice's one nonfiction book, *A Farm in Creamland,* which he referred to in its introduction as a "useful" book about agriculture. He conceived it as a guide for would-be gentleman farmers, so that they might learn from his experiences after he moved his family in 1904 from London to Devon to enjoy a pastoral life.

"I shall ramble at my own sweet will," Garvice wrote in the preface, "incidentally recounting certain happenings, pathetically or comically humorous, in the locality in which this farm is situated." Ramble he did—about his farm and his children and his chickens and pigs. "Certain happenings" included the day in 1905 when Garvice took the bus to the neighboring town of Ridgeford for a haircut and was asked by a fellow passenger for his opinion on the new artificial manure, which he happily and expansively provided.

The book is not useful at all, unless you are interested in understanding the man who peddled romantic tripe to the masses. Garvice was a fool for Devon and the charms of country living. His farm was *not* the glittering mine of wealth that his novels were; it was losing money. He kept at it, he said, because he wanted to work the land in "the genuine, dirty, Devonshire fashion." He wanted what the characters in his novels could have: a Wayneford of his own. This idea lends credence to the notion that his novels were not born entirely of condescension. In writing, perhaps he was not simply pandering to popular taste but indulging his own desire to live happily ever after. He seemed to believe in the possibility of living the dream that his books described.

Garvice did not stop writing during the years on the farm, but his literary output decreased. After publishing twelve novels in 1902 and five in 1903, he averaged only three a year between 1904 and 1907. But he could not give it up entirely. His writing was financing the romance of farming.

By that point in his career, he knew his material well; he had been putting out the same stories over and over since the 1870s. Whenever a new novel was in order, he lit his pipe, called in his secretary, Miss Johnston, and began to dictate. Miss Johnston was a "clever and highly cultured young woman" who had once worked for Ford Madox Ford. Garvice had poached her away from Ford to have someone to help him elevate his style a bit, figuring she might have picked up a thing or two from her former employer. He could joke about his lowbrow reputation with fellow "cash authors" at his club in London, but perhaps he really was sensitive to the charges of the critical establishment. Not that their relentless criticism had any impact on his commercial success.

Not even the Great War could diminish his sales. In fact, women began sending their Garvices to soldiers in the trenches, and the world's bestselling novelist found a new category of readers. The *English Review* (a highbrow journal that, incidentally, was founded by Ford) took note. As Thomas Moult reported, Garvice's books enjoyed a favor in the trenches surpassed by none and equaled only by that accorded Jack London. However, Moult could not resist adding that "it requires the extraordinarily attenuated state of things . . . for the average healthy male to even think of turning to [Garvice], let alone reading him and asking for more."

The critics do have a point. I look at the awkward punctuation in *The Verdict of the Heart*—the excessive and awkward use of dashes—and I see a man pausing to puff on his pipe. I see why his prose ends up sounding so bad, the cleverness and cultivation of his secretary notwithstanding. I understand why he engendered so much antipathy from his contemporaries on the literary scene, who may well have nurtured similar fantasies about fame and sales and what they could do with these, and who must have been frustrated that such awful writing was so richly rewarded. And I recognize that most people would find it difficult to have sympathy for a man whose fortune in modern currency would make him a millionaire—a man who wanted to use this fortune in pursuit of something resembling a feudal lordship over the colorful and charming local peasants. And yet, I feel bad for him. He endured more public ridicule than any decent human being deserves.

What Moult and the other critics failed to acknowledge, but what Garvice knew and honored, are the ways so many of us live in emotionally attenuated states, during times of peace as well as war. Stories like the ones Garvice wrote may be low art, or they may not be art at all. They may offer consolation or distraction rather than provocation and insight. But many people find provocation enough in real life, and so they read for something else. One cannot have contempt for Garvice without also having some level of contempt for common humanity, for those readers—not all of whom can be dismissed as simpletons—who may not consciously believe in what they are reading, but who read anyway because they know: a story can be a salve.

CHARLES GARVICE SUFFERED a cerebral hemorrhage on 21 February 1920. He lay in a coma until his death, eight days later.

The London *Times* offered the following anecdote in Garvice's obituary:

> It cannot be said that his work was of a high order; but criticism is disregarded by his own frank attitude towards the possibility of the permanence of his literary reputation. His answer to a captious friend who seemed solicitous to disabuse him on this score was merely to point with a gesture to the crowds on the seaside beach reading. "All my books," he said: "they are all reading my latest." It was a true estimate.

The "captious friend" had a point. Garvice *has* been forgotten, notwithstanding the occasional editions of his work that have been reissued, like the 1980 Bantam edition of *Only a Girl's Love*—a mass-market paperback that was sold as part of "Barbara Cartland's Library of Love"—or the 2007 trade paperback edition of *At Love's Cost* published by Dodo Press, which seems to specialize in out-of-copyright canonical "classics." Those critics who found his work so risible that they would rather rend the pages from the spine and toss them into the drink than sit on the beach reading them have had their way in the end.

The formula that Garvice so successfully exploited—virtuous heroines overcoming numerous obstacles to attain happiness—is a predictable one, which any author might employ. His readers are now dead, and their Garvices—if they exist at all—molder in the attics of the Western world while books much like them, by authors who have learned the same lessons and applied the same patterns to their fiction, are being read on the beach today.

Poor Garvice, I sometimes think. But there was nothing poor about him. He knew what he was doing. He understood the value of a well-placed puppy; he could tell a story that millions of people were delighted to read. As a bad novelist myself—with deficiencies in exactly the areas where Garvice had strengths—I can see the virtue in this.

I'll never know who decided to toss that copy of *Veronika* into the ocean. An Icelandic fisherman? An unlikely beach reader in Reykjavík? I like to think of a rebellious granddaughter—a student of literature perhaps—who found the book in an attic. Did she tear the pages from the spine herself to express her scorn, or did the ocean dissolve the glue? Did she stand on the beach and release the paper to the wind? She must have been so filled with contempt for the silly stuff, so appalled that people can nurture such absurd hopes and expect to find them fulfilled in the pages of a book. She could not have imagined another reader would find what she cast out and be moved to go to the far side of the earth just to see what would happen next.

Works Cited

"Death of Mr. Garvice." *Times* (London), March 2, 1920.

Garvice, Charles. *A Farm in Creamland: A Book of the Devon Countryside.* London: Hodder & Stoughton, 1911.

———. *The Verdict of the Heart.* London: Newnes' Sixpenny Copyright Novels, 1912.

——. *Veronika: skáldsaga.* Reykjavík: Bókaútgáfan, 1942.

Moult, Thomas. "Outside Literature: A Note on the Late Mr. Garvice." *English Review* 30 (April 1920): 373–76.

Nash, Eveleigh. *I Like the Life I Lived.* London: John Murray, 1941.

"Our Library Table." *Athenaeum* 3817 (December 22, 1900): 825.

Rutland, Arthur. "Charles Garvice." *Bookman* 46 (September 1914): 233–39.

Sladen, Douglas. *Twenty Years of My Life.* London: Constable & Company, 1914.

Moby-Duck

or, The Synthetic Wilderness of Childhood

DONOVAN HOHN

"I originally intended to reconstruct the journey of the toys in the omniscient third person," says Donovan Hohn about this story, which appeared in Harper's. *"At first it seemed like bad luck that my reporting coincided with my wife's due date. The entire time I was on the road I was worried that I wouldn't make it home in time. . . . A journalist would have had to leave that personal experience out, but as an essayist I could turn an obstacle into an advantage. In retrospect, it's clear that my impending fatherhood—the anxieties, the guilt, the anticipatory joy—is what animated this material for me, probably from the start. That's what I love most about this form: that traffic between the ocean and the lab, that osmosis between the self and the world."*

We know exactly where the spill occurred: 44.7°N, 178.1°E. We know the day, January 10, 1992, but not the hour. Neither do we know the name of the ship nor of its captain nor of the shipping magnate who owned it. We do know the harbors from which it sailed (Hong Kong) and to which it was headed (Tacoma). We know that despite its grandeur, when rocked by forty-foot waves, the colossal vessel, a floating warehouse weighing fifty thousand deadweight tons or more and powered by a diesel engine the size of a barn, would have rolled and pitched and yawed about like a toy in a Jacuzzi.

We know that twelve of the colorful containers stacked above deck snapped loose from their moorings and tumbled overboard. We can safely assume that the subsequent splash was terrific, like the splash a train would make were you to drive it off a seaside cliff. We know that each container measured forty feet long and eight feet wide and may have weighed as much as fifty-eight thousand pounds, depending on the cargo, and that at least one of them—perhaps when it careened into another container, perhaps when it struck the ship's stays, perhaps as it descended to high-pressure depths—burst open. We know that when it left port, this ill-fated container had contained seventy-two hundred little packages; that, as the water gushed in and the steel box sank, all or most of these packages came floating to the surface; that every package comprised a plastic shell and a cardboard back; that every shell housed four hollow plastic animals—a red beaver, a blue turtle, a green frog, and a yellow duck—each about three inches long; and that printed on the cardboard in multicolored lettering were the following words: FLOATEES. THE FIRST YEARS. FROM 6 MONTHS. EXPERT DEVELOPED ♥ PARENT PREFERRED. 100% DISHWASHER SAFE.

From a low-flying plane on a clear day, the packages would have looked like confetti, a great drift of colorful squares, exploding in slow motion across the waves. Within twenty-four hours, the water would have dissolved the glue. The action of the waves would have separated the plastic from the cardboard. There, in the middle of the North Pacific, in seas almost four miles deep, more than six hundred miles south of Attu Island, the western extreme of the United States, more

than a thousand miles east of Hokkaido, the northern extreme of
Japan, and more than two thousand miles west of Sitka, Alaska, 28,800
plastic animals produced in Chinese factories for the bathtubs of
America—7,200 red beavers, 7,200 green frogs, 7,200 blue turtles, and
7,200 yellow ducks—hatched from their plastic shells and drifted free.

ELEVEN YEARS LATER, more than seven thousand nautical miles
to the east, an anthropologist named Bethe Hagens and her
boyfriend, Waynn Welton, a retired digital cartographer, spotted
something small and bright perched atop the seaweed at the southwest end of Gooch's Beach near the entrance to Kennebunk Harbor
in Maine. They stopped and crouched. Its body was approximately
the size and shape of a bar of soap, its head the size of a Ping-Pong
ball. A brand name, THE FIRST YEARS, was embossed upon its belly.
The plastic was "white, incredibly weathered, and very worn," Hagens
would later recall. Welton remembers it differently. It was, he insists,
still yellow. "Parts of it had started to fade," he told me. "But not a
great deal. Whatever they'd used for the dye of the plastic had held up
pretty well." Yellow or not, the thing looked as though it had crossed
the ocean; on that Hagens and Welton agree. It was fun to imagine, a
lone duck, drifting across the Atlantic, like something out of a fairy
tale or a children's book—fun but also preposterous. Sensibly, they
had left the toy where they found it and walked on.

The classified ads in the July 14, 1993, edition of the Sitka *Daily
Sentinel* do not make for exciting reading, though they do convey
something of what summertime in Alaska's maritime provinces is
like. That week, the Tenakee Tavern "in Tenakee" was accepting appli-
cations "for cheerful bartenders." The Baranof Berry Patch was buying berries—"huckleberries, blueberries, strawberries, raspberries."
The National Marine Fisheries Service gave notice that the winners of
the 1992 Sablefish Tag Recovery Drawing, an annual event held to

encourage the reporting of tagged sablefish, would be selected at 1:00 P.M. on July 19 at the Auke Bay Laboratory. "Tired of shaving, tweezing, waxing?!" asked Jolene Gerard, R.N., R.E., enticing the hirsute citizens of Alaska's panhandle with the promise of "Permanent hair removal." Then, under the ambiguous heading of "Announcements," between "Business Services" and "Boats for Sale," an unusual listing appeared.

> ANYONE WHO has found plastic toy animals on beaches in Southeast please call the Sentinel at 747–3219.

The author of the ad was Eben Punderson, a high school teacher who moonlighted as a journalist. On Thanksgiving Day, 1992, a party of beachcombers strolling along Chichagof Island had discovered several dozen hollow plastic animals amid the usual wrack of bottlecaps, fishing tackle, and driftwood deposited at the tide line by a recent storm. After ten months at sea, the ducks had whitened and the beavers had yellowed, but the frogs were still as green as ever, and the turtles were still blue.

In subsequent weeks beachcombers on other islands found more of the toys, and new ones kept washing ashore. Laurie Lee of South Baranof Island filled an unused skiff with the horde she'd scavenged. Signe Wilson filled a hot tub. Betsy Knudson had so many to spare she started giving them to her dog. It appeared that even the sea otters of Sitka Sound were collecting them: one toy had been plucked from an otter's nest. On a single beachcombing excursion with friends, Mary Stensvold, a botanist with the US Forest Service who normally spends her days hunting rare varieties of liverwort, gathered forty of the animals. Word of the invasion spread. Dozens of correspondents answered the *Sentinel's* ad. Toys had been found as far north as Kayak Island, as far south as Coronation Island, a range of tide line extending for hundreds of miles. Where had they come from?

Eben Punderson was pretty sure he knew. Three years earlier, in May of 1990, an eastbound freighter, the *Hansa Carrier*, had collided with a storm five hundred miles south of the Alaskan peninsula. Several containers had gone overboard, including a shipment of eighty thousand Nikes. Six months later, sneakers began washing up along Vancouver Island. The story had received national attention after a pair of oceanographers in Seattle—Curtis Ebbesmeyer, a scientist with a private consulting firm that tracked drifting icebergs for the oil industry, and James Ingraham of the National Oceanographic and Atmospheric Administration (NOAA)—turned the sneaker spill into an oceanographic experiment. By feeding coordinates collected from beachcombers into NOAA's Ocean Surface Current Simulator, or OSCURS, a computer modeling system built from a century's worth of Navy weather data, Ebbesmeyer and Ingraham had reconstructed the drift routes of some two hundred shoes. In the process the basement of Ebbesmeyer's bungalow had become the central intelligence headquarters of what would eventually grow into a global beach-combing network. Would a similar accident account for the appearance of the bath toys?

Punderson had one lead. The ducks—and for some reason only the ducks—had been embossed with the logo of their manufacturer, The First Years. A local toy store was unable to find the logo in its merchandise catalogues, but the director of the Sheldon Jackson College Library traced the brand back to its parent company in Massachusetts, Kiddie Products. Punderson spoke to the company's marketing manager, who confirmed the reporter's speculations. Yes, indeed, a shipment of Floatees had been lost at sea. "Solved: Mystery of the Wandering Bathtub Toys," ran the headline in the *Sentinel*'s Weekend section a month after Punderson's ad first appeared. And that is where the story should have ended—as an entertaining anecdote in the back pages of a provincial newspaper. Mystery solved. Case closed. But then something unexpected happened. The story kept going.

In part the story kept going because Ebbesmeyer and his beach-combers joined the hunt, in part because the toys themselves kept going. Years later, new specimens and new mysteries were still turning up. In the autumn of 1993, Floatees suddenly began sprinkling the shores of Shemya, a tiny Aleutian island that lies about 1,500 miles closer to Russia than to Sitka, not far from the site of the original spill. In 1995, beachcombers in Washington State found a blue turtle and a sun-bleached duck. Dean and Tyler Orbison, a father-son beach-combing team who every summer scour uninhabited islands along the Alaskan coast, added more toys to their growing collection every year—dozens in 1992, three in 1993, twenty-five in 1994, until, in 1995, they found none. The slump continued in 1996, and the Orbisons assumed they'd seen the last of the plastic animals, but then, in 1997, the toys suddenly returned in large numbers.

Thousands more were yet to be accounted for. Where had they gone? Into the Arctic? Around the globe? Were they still out there, traveling the currents of the North Pacific? Or did they lie buried under wrack and sand along Alaska's wild, sparsely populated shores? Or, succumbing to the elements—freezing temperatures, the endless battering of the waves, prolonged exposure to the sun—had they cracked, filled with water, gone under? All 28,800 toys had emerged from that sinking container into the same acre of water. Each member of the four species was all but identical to the others—each duck was just as light as the other ducks, each frog as thick as the other frogs, each beaver as aerodynamic as the next. And yet one turtle had ended up in Signe Wilson's hot tub, another in the jaws of Betsy Knudson's labrador, another in the nest of a sea otter, while a fourth had floated almost all the way to Russia, and a fifth traveled south of Puget Sound. Why? What tangled calculus of causes and effects could explain—or predict—such disparate fates?

There were other reasons why the story of the toys kept going, rea-sons that had nothing to do with oceanography and everything to do with the human imagination, which can be as powerful and as inscrutable as the sea. In making sense of chaotic data, in following a slightly tangled thread of narrative to its source, Eben Punderson had set the plastic animals adrift all over again—not upon the waters of the North Pacific but upon currents of information. The Associated Press picked up the *Daily Sentinel*'s story. Newspapers across the country ran it. The Floatees eventually made brief appearances in *The Guardian* and *The New York Times Magazine,* and a considerably longer appearance in *The Smithsonian.* Like migrating salmon, they returned almost seasonally to the pages of *Scholastic News,* a magazine for kids, which has reported on the story seven times. They were spotted in the shallows of *People* and MSNBC, and in the tide pools of *All Things Considered.* They swirled around the maelstrom of the Internet and bobbed up in such exotic waters as an oceanography textbook for undergraduates and a newsletter for the collectors of duck-themed stamps.

These travels wrought strange changes. Dishwasher safe the toys may have been, but newspaper safe they were not. By the time they drifted into my own imagination, the plastic animals that had fallen into the Pacific in 1992 were scarcely recognizable. For one thing, the plastic had turned into rubber. For another, the beavers, frogs, and turtles had all turned into ducks. It had begun the day Eben Punderson published an unusual ad in the pages of the Sitka *Daily Sentinel*—the metamorphosis of happenstance into narrative and narrative into myth.

FAR ACROSS THE ocean, in a toy factory made of red brick, a pinkly Caucasian woman in a brick-red dress and a racially ambiguous brown man in a sky-blue shirt work side by side at an assembly line. From a gray machine, yellow-beaked and lacking irises in the whites of their eyes, rubber ducks emerge, one by one, onto a conveyor belt.

Chuckedy-chuckedy-chuck goes the rubber duck machine. As the ducks roll past, the woman in the brick-red dress paints their beaks brick red with a little brush. The man in the sky-blue shirt paints their irises sky blue. It is beautiful, this unnamed country across the sea. Green grass grows around the factory. The people who work there clearly enjoy making rubber ducks. They are all healthy, well rested, and smiling. At the end of the assembly line another racially ambiguous brown man, lighter and yellower than the first, packs the ducks, ten to a cardboard box, onto a grass-green truck that carries them to a waiting ship named the *Bobbie*. The *Bobbie*'s crew consists of a racially ambiguous stevedore in a hard hat and a pinkly Caucasian, white-bearded captain whose blue cap matches his blue coat. There are two gold stripes around the cuffs of the coat and two red stripes around the smokestack of the ship. A few decades ago the captain would have been smoking a pipe. Now he waves jauntily from a porthole. Above him, a white puff rises from the smokestack into a sky-blue sky.

Away the *Bobbie* chugs, carrying five cardboard boxes across a blue-green sea, a white streamer of smoke trailing behind it. Smiling overhead is an enormous sun the color of a rubber duck. Then a storm blows up. Waves leap. The *Bobbie* tosses about. The captain cries and throws his hands in the air. Down goes a cardboard box. Ducks spill like candy from a piñata. The sea calms. Slowly, the ducks drift apart, across the ocean, to diverse and far-flung ecosystems. One duck frolics with a spotted dolphin. A second receives a come-hither look from a blueberry seal in a lime-green sea. A polar bear standing on an ice floe ogles a third. And so their journeys go, each duck encountering a different picturesque animal—a flamingo, a pelican, a sea turtle, an octopus, a gull, a whale. Finally, who should the tenth rubber duck meet but a brood of real ducks. "Quack!" says the mother duck. "Quack! Quack! Quack!" say the ducklings. "Squeak," says the rubber duck. "Press here," says a button on the rubber duck's wing, and when you do, a battery-powered computer chip embedded in the back cover of Eric Carle's *10 Little Rubber Ducks* emits what to my admittedly untrained ear sounds like the cry of a cormorant tangled in fishing line.

Published in the spring of 2005, shortly after my own duckie hunt began, Carle's picture book was inspired by a newspaper article, titled "Rubber Ducks Lost at Sea," that he'd happened upon in 2003. "I could not resist making a story out of this newspaper report," a brief author's note explains. "I hope you like my story." Beautifully illustrated with Carle's signature mix of paint and paper tearings, the book is hard not to like. Studies have shown that the primary colors, smiling faces, and cute animals with which *10 Little Rubber Ducks* abounds—and of which the rubber duck may well be the consummate embodiment—have the almost narcotic power to induce feelings of happiness in the human brain. The myth had at last found if not its Aesop, then at least its Disney.

"THE LOSS OF fantasy is the price we have paid for precision," I read one night in an outdated *Ocean Almanac* while investigating the journey of the Floatees, "and today we have navigation maps based on an accurate 1:1,000,000 scale of the entire world." Surveying the colorful, oversized landscape of my *National Geographic* atlas, a cartographic wonder made—its dust jacket boasted—from high-resolution satellite images and "sophisticated computer algorithms," I was unconvinced; fantasy did not strike me as extinct, or remotely endangered. The ocean is far less fathomable to my generation of Americans than it was when Herman Melville explored that "watery wilderness" a century and a half ago. Most of us are better acquainted with cloud tops than with waves. What our migrant ancestors thought of as the winds we think of as turbulence, and fasten our seat belts when the orange light comes on. Gale force, hurricane force—encountering such terms, we comprehend only that the weather is really, really bad and in our minds replay the special-effects sequences of disaster films or news footage of palm trees blown inside out like cheap umbrellas. In growing more precise, humanity's knowledge has also grown more specialized, and more fantastic, not less: the seas of my consciousness teem with images and symbols and half-remembered trivia as fabulous as those beasts frolicking at the edges of ancient charts. Not even satellite photographs and computer algorithms can burn away the mystifying fogs of ambient information and fantasy through which from birth I have sailed.

Not long ago on the op-ed page of the *New York Times*, the novelist Julia Glass worried that her fellow Americans, "impatient with flights of fancy," had lost the ability to be carried away by the "illusory adventure" of fiction, preferring the tabloid titillation of the "so-called truth." Perhaps, concluded Glass, "there is a growing consensus, however sad, that the wayward realm of make-believe belongs only to our children." By the spring of 2005, I had reached different conclusions. Hadn't we adults, like the imaginative preschoolers Glass admires, also been "encouraged"—by our government, by advertisers, by the fabulists of the cable news—"to mingle fact with fiction"? Hadn't millions of adults bought the illusory adventures of both Frodo Baggins and Donald Rumsfeld? Medieval Europeans divided the human lifetime into five ages, the first of which was known as the Age of Toys. It seemed to me that in twenty-first-century America, the Age of Toys never ends. Yes, stories fictional and otherwise can take us on illusory adventures, but they can also take us on disillusory ones, and it was the latter sort of adventure that I craved.

I TRACKED DOWN a phone number for Curtis Ebbesmeyer and asked him how the journey of the castaway ducks had ended. I'd read that some toys were supposed to have crossed the Arctic, reaching the

North Atlantic by the summer of 2003. Had they made it? Oh, yes, Ebbesmeyer assured me, yes, they had. Right on schedule, he'd received a highly credible eyewitness report from a trained anthropologist in Maine, which he'd published in his quarterly newsletter, *Beachcombers' Alert!* He promised to send me a copy. But—he added—if I really wanted to learn about things that float, then I should join him in Sitka that July. "You can't go beachcombing by phone," he said. "You have to get out there and look."

Since 2003, Sitka has played host to an annual Beachcombers' Fair over which Ebbesmeyer—part guru, part impresario—presides. Beachcombers bring him things they've scavenged from the sand, and Ebbesmeyer illuminates these discoveries as best he can. "Everything has a story," he likes to say. When an object mystifies him, he investigates. At this year's fair, a local fisherman would be ferrying a select group of beachcombers to the wild shores of Kruzof Island, where some of the toys had washed up. Ebbesmeyer, who would be leading the expedition, offered me a spot aboard the boat. Alaska—snow-capped mountains, icebergs, breeching whales, wild beaches bestrewn with yellow ducks. There was only one problem. The Beachcombers' Fair ended July 25, and my wife and I were due to have a baby on August 1, which was cutting it pretty close.

Soon thereafter an envelope with a Seattle postmark arrived. Inside, printed on blue paper, were a half-dozen issues of *Beachcombers' Alert!* Thumbing through this digest of the miscellaneous and arcane was a bit like beachcombing amid the wreckage of a storm. Alongside stories about derelict vessels and messages in bottles, the oceanographer had arrayed a photographic scrapbook of strange, sea-battered oddities, natural and man-made—Japanese birch-bark fishing floats, the heart-shaped seed of a baobab tree, land mines, televisions, a torn wet suit, a 350-pound safe. Many of these artifacts had accumulated colonies of gooseneck barnacles. Some were so encrusted they seemed to be made of the creatures: a derelict skiff of barnacles, a hockey glove of barnacles. A disconcerting number of the photographs depicted the plastic heads of mannequins and dolls, including the head of a plastic infant impaled like a candy apple on a stick.

At the end of an article titled "Where the Toys Are," Ebbesmeyer had published Bethe Hagens's letter. "You won't believe this," she'd written after hearing about the castaway toys on NPR, "but two weeks ago, I found one of your ducks." In fact, Ebbesmeyer *had* believed her, or wanted to. The details of her description matched the profile of a Floatee perfectly. Because Hagens had neglected to keep the evidence, however, her testimony remained in doubt. Accompanying the article was a world map indicating where and when the toys had washed up. Off the coast of Kennebunkport, Ebbesmeyer had printed a pair of question marks the size of barrier reefs.

There are two ways to get to the insular city of Sitka—by plane and by boat. In my dreams, I would have picked up the frayed end of that imaginary, seven-thousand-mile-long trail that led to Gooch's Beach and followed it, Theseus-style, to its source—sailing back across the Gulf of Maine, back through the Northwest Passage, that legendary waterway which the historian Pierre Breton has described as a "maze of drifting, misshapen bergs," a "crystalline world of azure and emerald, indigo and alabaster—dazzling to the eye, disturbing to the soul," a "glittering metropolis of moving ice." To Lieutenant William Edward Parry of the British Navy, who captained the *Alexander* into the maze in 1818, the slabs of ice looked like the pillars of Stonehenge.

By the summer of 2005, global warming had gone a long way toward turning that metropolis of ice into the open shipping channel of which Victorian imperialists dreamed. That September climatologists would announce that the annual summer melt had reduced the floating ice cap to its smallest size in a century of recordkeeping. Nevertheless, even a transarctic journey aboard a Coast Guard icebreaker was out of the question if I wanted to make it to Sitka and back before the birth of my first child. Instead I booked passage on the M/V *Malaspina,* part of the Alaskan Marine Highway, which is in fact not a highway at all but a state-operated fleet of ferries. Sailing from Bellingham, Washington, the *Malaspina* would reach Sitka five days before the Beachcombers' Fair began. If I flew home as soon as the fair ended, I would be in Manhattan a week before the baby arrived—assuming it did not arrive early, which, my wife's obstetrician warned us, was altogether possible. My wife was not at all happy about my plan, but she consented on one condition: that if she felt a contraction or her water broke, I would catch the next flight home, no matter the cost.

ON MY WAY to Bellingham I stopped in Seattle to visit Curtis Ebbesmeyer. I met him at home, in a quiet neighborhood near the University of Washington, where he had earned his Ph.D. Navy blue awnings overshadowed the porch of his bungalow, and peering into the semidarkness I could see four matching Adirondack chairs, lined up, side by side, as if to behold the vista of the lawn. Ebbesmeyer himself greeted me at the door. "Come in, come in," he said.

His face was familiar to me from photographs I'd seen in the press and in the pages of *Beachcombers' Alert!,* where he makes frequent cameo appearances, displaying a water-stained basketball, hoisting a plastic canister that was supposed to have delivered Taiwanese propaganda to the Chinese mainland, gazing down deifically at the four Floatees perched upon his forearm. He has a white beard, a Cheshire grin, and close-set eyes that together make his face a bit triangular. Since Ebbesmeyer likes to wear Hawaiian shirts and a necklace of what appear to be roasted chestnuts but are in fact sea beans, the waterborne seeds of tropical trees that ocean currents disseminate to distant shores, pictures of him often bring to mind cartoons of Santa Claus on vacation.

He brewed us each a cup of coffee and suggested we adjourn to the backyard, which he refers to as his "office." Passing through his basement, I saw many of the objects I'd read about in *Beachcombers' Alert!* Piled high on a bookshelf were dozens of Nikes. Some of them had survived the 1990 container spill—the first Ebbesmeyer ever investigated—in which eighty thousand shoes had been lost. Others came from later accidents: eighteen thousand Nike sneakers fell overboard in 1999; thirty-three thousand more in December 2002. In January 2000, some twenty-six thousand Nike sandals—along with ten thousand children's shoes and three thousand computer monitors, which float screen up and are popular with barnacles—plunged into the drink.

Nike's maritime fortunes are not unusually calamitous; as many as ten thousand containers spill from cargo ships annually. But few commodities are both as seaworthy and as traceable as a pair of Air Jordans, which conveniently come with numerical records of their provenance stitched to the undersides of their tongues, and which— submerged up to the ankle, laces aswirl—will drift for years. It helps, too, that Ebbesmeyer learned the serial numbers for all the shoes in the 1990 spill. In his basement, Ebbesmeyer selected a high-top at random and taught me how to "read the tongue." "See the ID?" he asked. " '021012.' The '02' is the year. '10' is October. '12' is December. Nike ordered these from Indonesia in October of 2002 for delivery in December."

Next he pulled down a black flip-flop, and then a matching one that he had sliced in half. Inside the black rubber was a jagged yellow core resembling a lightning bolt—a perfect identifying characteristic. If Ebbesmeyer had discovered the coordinates of this particular spill, the sandals would have provided a windfall of valuable data. Unfortunately, the shipping company, fearing legal liability, had "stonewalled" him, "like usual."

It took Ebbesmeyer a year of diplomacy and detective work to find out when and where the Floatees fell overboard. Initially, the shipping company stonewalled him, like usual. Then one day he received a phone call. The container ship in question was at port in Tacoma. On the condition that he never reveal its name or that of its owner, he was welcome to come aboard. For four hours, Ebbesmeyer sat in the ship's bridge interviewing the captain, a "very gracious" Chinese man who had a Ph.D. in meteorology and spoke fluent English. The day of the spill the ship had encountered a severe winter storm and heavy seas, the captain said. The readings on the inclinometer told the story best. When a ship is perfectly level in the water, its inclinometer reads 0°. If a ship were keeled on its side, the inclinometer would read 90°. Containers begin to break loose when a ship rolls more than 35°, Ebbesmeyer has found. When this particular spill occurred, the inclinometer would have registered a roll of 55° to port, then a roll of 55° to starboard. At that inclination, the stacks of containers, each one six containers tall, would have been more horizontal than vertical. Perhaps Dr. Ebbesmeyer would like to have a peek at the log book, the captain discreetly suggested. He'd already opened it to January 10, 1992. There were the magic coordinates.

OSCURS COULD NOW reconstruct, or "hindcast," the routes various toys had traveled, producing a map of erratic trajectories that appeared to have been hand drawn by a cartographer with palsy. Beginning at the scattered coordinates where beachcombers had reported finding toys, the lines wiggled west, converging at the point of origin, not far from where the International Dateline crosses the forty-fifth parallel. The data that Ebbesmeyer's beachcombers had gathered also allowed NOAA's James Ingraham to fine-tune the computer model, adjusting for coefficients such as the height at which the toys rode in the water (an object with a tall profile will sail as well as drift). The toys, it turns out, rode high, skating across the Gulf of

Alaska at an average rate of seven miles a day, twice as fast as the currents they were traveling. Among other things, the simulation revealed that in 1992 those currents might have shifted to the north as a consequence of El Niño.

OSCURS could forecast as well as hindcast, and in this respect, Ebbesmeyer and Ingraham were like clairvoyant meteorologists of the waves. OSCURS was their crystal ball. To the eyes of a driftologist, even the most state-of-the-art globe is in one respect as fabulous as the cartographic dreamscapes of the past. No clouds swirl across a map's invisible skies. The painted topography of its empty seas are not troubled by the wind. The polar ice does not thicken and thin with the seasons and the ages. There is no sign of "thermohaline circulation," the vertical movement of water layers caused by variations in density and temperature. A globe is a static illusion of permanence because it lacks a crucial dimension, the dimension that OSCURS was programmed to map—time.

By simulating "long-term mean surface geostrophic currents" (those currents that flow steadily and enduringly, though not immutably, like rivers in the sea) as well as "surface-mixed-layer currents that are functions of wind speed and direction" (those currents that change as quickly as the skies), OSCURS could project the trajectories of the toys well into the future. According to the simulator's predictions, some of the animals would drift south, where they would either collide with the coast of Hawaii in March 1997, or, more likely, get sucked into the North Pacific Subtropical Gyre.

" 'Gyre' is a fancy word for a current in a bowl of soup," Ebbesmeyer likes to say. "You stir your soup, it goes around a few seconds." The thermodynamic circulation of air, which we experience as wind, is like a giant spoon that never stops stirring. Comprising four separate currents—the southerly California Current, the westerly North Equatorial Current, the northerly Kuroshio Current, and the easterly North Pacific Drift—the North Pacific Subtropical Gyre travels from the coast of Washington to the coast of Mexico to the coast of Japan and back again. Some of the toys would escape the gyre's orbit, spin off toward the Indian Ocean, and, eventually, circumnavigate the globe. Others would drift into the gyre's becalming center, where a high-pressure system has created what Ebbesmeyer calls "the garbage patch"—a purgatorial eddy in the waste stream that is approximately the size of Texas. "It's like Jupiter's red spot," says Ebbesmeyer. "It's one of the great features of the planet Earth, but you can't see it."

A similar high-pressure calm at the center of the North Atlantic Gyre gave rise to the legend of the Bermuda triangle as well as to the Sargasso Sea, named for the free-floating wilderness of sargasso sea-weed that the currents have accumulated there. A *Sargasso of the imagination,* I thought to myself as I listened to Ebbesmeyer describe the garbage patch. The phrase comes from a scene in *Day of the Locust* in which Nathanael West is describing a Hollywood backlot jumbled with miscellaneous properties and disassembled stage sets.

THE ATLANTIC IS far shallower and narrower than the Pacific, and upwellings of cold, nutrient-rich water nourish the sargasso forest and the marine life that inhabits it. The center of the North Pacific Subtropical Gyre, which circles around the deepest waters on the planet, is, by contrast, a kind of marine desert. If you go fishing in the garbage patch, all you're likely to catch aside from garbage is plankton.

In 1998, with help from Ingraham and Ebbesmeyer, a researcher named Charlie Moore began collecting water samples from the eastern edge of the North Pacific garbage patch, trawling along a 564-mile loop encompassing exactly one million square miles of ocean. Approximately 800 miles west of California, where the wind speed fell below ten knots, drifts of garbage began to appear. The larger items that Moore and his crew retrieved from the water included polypropylene fishing nets, "a drum of hazardous chemicals," a volleyball "half-covered in barnacles," a cathode-ray television tube, and a gallon bleach bottle "that was so brittle it crumbled in our hands." Most of the debris that Moore found had already disintegrated. Caught in his trawling net was "a rich broth of minute sea creatures mixed with hundreds of colored plastic fragments."

OSCURS's simulations predicted that relatively few of the bathtub toys would have contributed to this "plastic-plankton soup," as Moore calls it. The majority would have stayed well to the north, closer to the site of the spill, caught in the Sub-Polar Gyre, which travels counterclockwise between the coasts of Alaska and Siberia. Smaller and stormier than the North Pacific Subtropical Gyre, the Sub-Polar Gyre does not collect vast quantities of trash at its center. Here, the Floatees would have remained in orbit, completing a lap around the Gulf of Alaska and the Bering Sea once every three years, until a winter storm blew them ashore or they strayed onto one of the northerly currents flowing through the Bering Strait. There, OSCURS lost them. Ingraham had not programmed his model to simulate the Arctic. To follow the animals into the ice, Ebbesmeyer had to rely on more primitive oceanographic methods. He went to a toy store and purchased a few dozen brand-new Floatees to use as lab animals in various experiments. Several specimens he subjected to the frigid conditions inside his kitchen freezer in order to find out whether cold would make them crack (it didn't). Others he bludgeoned with a hammer to see what it would take to make them sink (a lot). Even breeched and taking on water, they kept afloat. Able to withstand fifty-two dishwasher cycles, the toys, Ebbesmeyer concluded, could also survive a ten-year voyage through the ice. Using data collected from transarctic drift experiments conducted in the late 1970s, he calculated that, once beset, the toys would creep across the North Pole at an average rate of a mile per day. When they reached the North Atlantic, the ice would melt and set the Floatees loose upon the waters east of Greenland. Some would catch the Gulf Stream to Europe. Others would ride the cold southerly longshore current that flows past Gooch's Beach.

ALTHOUGH HIS LIBRARY of shoes may suggest otherwise, Ebbesmeyer has not amassed a museum of flotsam in his basement. He collects stories and data, not things. Fat, three-ring binders occupy most of the shelf space. They contain "a small portion" of the studies he has conducted over the years. I saw binders labeled FISH-ING FLOATS and VIKINGS, PHYTOPLANKTON and DRIFTING COFFINS, EDDIES and ICEBERGS. There was an entire binder devoted to Isis and Osiris, the star-crossed Egyptian gods. Ebbesmeyer told me the tragic ending of their tale: "Osiris's brother killed him, put his body in a coffin, put the coffin in the Nile River, and it washed up three hundred miles to the north of Lebanon. His wife, Isis, went to find it, and she did. That's the first documented drift of an object between point A and point B that I know of."

In the backyard, seated on the patio, where a string of rubber duckie Christmas lights festooned a grape arbor and wind chimes made mournful noises on the breeze, Ebbesmeyer waxed ecclesiastical. "There's nothing new around," he said. Take Osiris. Even today, when the Nile floods, flotsam follows that same route. Not even pollution is new. He told me to think of volcanic eruptions, of the tons of pumice and toxic ash an eruption throws into the sea. No, when you studied the history of flotsam long enough you realized that only one thing was fundamentally different about the ocean now, only one thing had changed since the time of the ancient Egyptians. "See, pumice will absorb water and sink," he said. "But 60 percent of plastic will float and the 60 percent that does float will never sink because it doesn't absorb water; it fractures into ever smaller pieces. That's the difference. There are things afloat now that will never sink."

Ebbesmeyer went inside and returned a moment later carrying what at first glance appeared to be exotic produce—a new, flatter variety of plantain or summer squash, perhaps. He spread these yellowy lozenges out on the patio table. "Remnants of high-seas drift-net floats," he said. There were four of them, in varying stages of decay. The best-preserved specimen had the hard sheen of polished bone. The worst was pocked and textured like a desiccated sponge that had been attacked with a chisel. Ebbesmeyer picked up the latter float. "This is a pretty cool old one," he said. By "cool" he meant that it told the story of drift-net floats particularly well.

"High-seas drift nets were banned by the United Nations in 1992," his version of this story began. "They were nets with a mesh size of about four inches, but they were, like, fifty miles long. The Japanese would sit there and interweave these for fifty miles. There were something like a thousand drift nets being used every night in the 1980s, and if you do the math they were filtering all the water in the upper fifty feet every year. Well, they were catching all the large animals, and it clearly could not go on."

According to Ebbesmeyer, those high-seas drift nets had not gone away, and not only because pirate drift netting still takes place. Before the moratorium, fishermen had lost about half of their nets every year, and those lost nets were still out there, still fishing. "Ghost nets," they're called. When he tells stories like this, Ebbesmeyer will punctuate the most astonishing facts with his eyebrows. He'll say something like, "What happens is, the nets keep catching animals, and then the animals die, and then after a while, the nets get old, and they roll up on a coral reef, and the waves roll it along like a big avalanche ball, killing everything in its path." Then his bushy eyebrows will spring up above his glasses and stay there while he looks at you, wide-eyed with autodumbfoundment.

And killer drift-net balls are genuinely dumbfounding, like something from a B horror movie—so dumbfounding that, smelling a hyperbole, I later checked Ebbesmeyer's facts. A ghost net may not kill everything that crosses its path, but it sure can kill a lot. News reports describe nets dripping with putrefying wildlife. Just three months before I showed up on Ebbesmeyer's doorstep, NOAA scientists scanning the ocean from the air with a digital imaging system had spotted a flock of 100 or so ghost nets drifting through the garbage patch. When they returned to fetch them, they found balls of net measuring thirty feet across. "There is a lot more trash out there than I expected," one of the researchers, James Churnside, told the Associated Press. A few years earlier, Coast Guard divers had spent a month picking 25.5 tons of netting and debris—including two four-thousand-pound, fifteen-mile-long, high-seas drift nets—out of reefs around Lisianski Island in the North Pacific. They estimated that there were six thousand more tons of netting and debris still tangled in the reefs when they left.

In Ebbesmeyer's opinion, ghost nets may pose a still greater danger once they disintegrate. While we were conversing on his patio, he handed me the oldest of the drift-net floats. "Hold this a minute," he said. It weighed almost nothing. "Now put it down and look." On the palm of my hand, the float had left a sprinkling of yellow dust, plastic particles as small as pollen grains in which, if you believe Ebbesmeyer, the destiny of both the Floatees and of the ocean could be read.

Out on his front lawn, as I was leaving, I asked him what he thought of *10 Little Rubber Ducks*. Despite the gloomy future he glimpsed in that handful of plastic dust, he thought Carle's cheerful picture book was "delightful," especially that little squeaker in the back, and he hoped that it would "make the ocean fun to kids." He did have one criticism. He couldn't figure out why Carle along with just about everyone else seemed compelled to turn the four Floatees into rubber ducks. Coverage of the story in newspapers and magazines almost always showed a picture of a solitary rubber duck, and usually not even the right kind of duck. What was wrong with the other three animals? "Maybe it's a kind of racism," Ebbesmeyer speculated. "Speciesism."

The Floatees are no longer on the market, but before I left, Ebbesmeyer loaned me a set that had survived his experiments, to be returned when I was done with them. I have been carrying them around with me ever since, and they are at present perched before me on my desk as I write. Monochromatic and polygonal in a Bauhaus sort of way, they bear little resemblance to the rubber ducks in Carle's book or, for that matter, to any other plastic animal I've ever seen. Although blow-molded out of a rigid plastic (probably polyethylene), they look whittled from wax by some artisanal tribesman. The frog's four-fingered hands (the left smaller than the right) seem folded in prayer. The limbs of the turtle are triangular stubs. The duck's head, too large for the flat-bottomed puck of a body it sits upon, is imperfectly spherical, the flat plane of its beak continuing like a crew-cut mohawk over the top of the skull. Poke an axle through the duck's puffed cheeks and its head would make a good wheel. Wildly out of scale and dyed a lurid, maraschino red, the beaver seems altogether out of place in this menagerie, a mammalian interloper from somebody's acid trip. A seam left by the split mold bisects all four animals asymmetrically, and there's a little anal button of scarred plastic where the blow pin, that steel umbilicus, withdrew.

"WHY DO PRECISELY these objects we behold make a world?" Thoreau wonders in *Walden*. "Why has man just these species of animals for his neighbors; as if nothing but a mouse could have filled this crevice?" Since Thoreau's time, ecologists have explained why that mouse filled that crevice, and since then Walden woods have grown far less bewildering. For Thoreau the distinction between the natural world and the man-made one matters less than that between the subjective experience within and the objective world without. For him, both rocks and mice are objects that he perceives as shadows flickering on the walls of his mind. For him, anthropomorphism is inescapable. All animals, he writes, are "beasts of burden, in a sense, made to carry some portion of our thoughts."

The word "synthetic" in its current sense of "chemically unnatural" would not appear in print until 1874, twenty years after the publication of *Walden* and five years after the invention of celluloid, the first industrial synthetic. In its 137-year history, the synthetic world has itself grown into a kind of wilderness. With the exceptions of our fellow human beings and our domestic pets, the objects that make the worlds we behold today are almost entirely man-made. Consider the following: In nature, there are 142 known species of Anatidae, the family to which ducks, swans, and geese belong. Of those species only one, the white Pekin duck, a domesticated breed of mallard, produces spotless yellow ducklings. Since the invention of plastic, four known species of Anatidae have gone extinct; several others survive only in sanctuaries created to save them. Meanwhile, by the estimates of one collector, the makers of novelties and toys have concocted more than five thousand different varieties of novelty duck, nearly all of which are yellow, and most of which are not made in fact from rubber but from plasticized polyvinyl chloride, a derivative of coal. Why has man just these species of things for his neighbors, a latter-day Thoreau might ask, as if nothing but a yellow duck could perch on the rim of a tub?

Let's draw a bath. Let's set a rubber duck afloat. Look at it wobbling there. What misanthrope, what damp, misty November of a sourpuss, upon beholding a rubber duck afloat, does not feel a Crayola ray of sunshine brightening his gloomy heart? Graphically, the rubber duck's closest relative is not a bird or a toy but the yellow happy face of Wal-Mart commercials. A rubber duck is in effect a happy face with a body and lips—which is what the beak of the rubber duck has become: great, lipsticky, bee-stung lips. Both the happy face and the rubber duck reduce facial expressions to a kind of pictogram. They are both emoticons. And they are, of course, the same color—the yellow of an egg yolk or the eye of a daisy, a shade darker than a yellow raincoat, a shade lighter than a taxicab.

Like the eyes of other animals (rabbits, for example, or deer) and unlike the eyes of a happy face, the rubber duck's eyes peer helplessly from the sides of its spherical head. Its movement is also expressive— joyously erratic, like that of a bouncing ball, or a dancing drunk. So long, that is, as it doesn't keel over and float around like a dead fish, as rubber ducks of recent manufacture are prone to do. It's arguable whether such tipsy ducks deserve to be called toys. They have retained the form and lost the function. Their value is wholly symbolic. They are not so much rubber ducks as plastic representations of rubber ducks. They are creatures of the lab, chimeras synthesized from whimsy and desire in the petri dish of commerce.

Apologists for plastics will on occasion blur the semantic lines between the antonyms "synthetic" and "natural." Everything is chemical, they rightly say, even water, even us, and plastic, like every living creature great and small, is carbon-based and therefore "organic." But to my mind the only meaningful difference between the synthetic and the natural is more philosophical than chemical. A loon can symbolize madness, and a waddling duck can make us laugh. But the duck and the loon exist outside of the meanings with which we burden them. A loon is not really mad. A duck is not really a clown; it waddles inelegantly because its body has evolved to swim. A rubber duck, by comparison, is not burdened with thought. It is thought, the immaterial made material, a subjective object, a fantasy in 3-D.

ONE NIGHT, DURING the thirty-third week of her pregnancy, my wife and I attended a practicum in infant CPR. With the other expectant parents, we sat around a conference table set with babies—

identical, life-size, polyethylene babies, lying there on the formica like lobsters. The skin of these infantile mannequins was the color of graphite. Even their eyeballs were shiny and gray. Their mouths had been molded agape, so that they seemed to be gasping for air. To dislodge an imaginary choking hazard, you were supposed to lay the baby facedown over your left forearm and strike its back with the heel of your right hand. If you struck too hard, its hollow head would pop from its neck and go skittering across the linoleum. The morning after my visit with Ebbesmeyer, hurtling up the eastern shore of Puget Sound aboard the Amtrak Cascades bound for Bellingham, it occurs to me that "garbage patch" sounds like "cabbage patch," and for a moment I am picturing a thousand silvery, gape-mouthed heads bobbing on the open sea.

The old woman across the aisle, a retired high school chemistry teacher from Montana, tells me that she and her husband are traveling the globe. They have been to every continent but Antarctica. She teaches me how to say "I don't have any money" in Norwegian. She tells me about the mural she saw in Belfast depicting a masked man and a Kalashnikov. She tells me about her nephew, who has in fact been to Antarctica. He spent a night dangling from the ice shelf in something like a hammock. *National Geographic* named him one of the top mountain climbers in the world, she says. Then he died in an avalanche in Tibet. Left three little boys. She smiles as she says this. In the window behind her, the blue waters of Puget Sound flash through the green blur of trees.

The train groans into a curve. Suddenly there are green and orange and blue containers stacked atop flatbed train cars parked on a neighboring track. The polyglot names of shipping companies speed by: Evergreen, Uniglory, Maersk. Then, at a clearing in the trees, the great brontosaural works of a gantry crane loom up above a Russian freighter loaded with what looks like modular housing. PORT OF SEATTLE, a sign on the crane reads.

We are somewhere east of the Strait of Juan de Fuca—Juan de Fuca, whom I read about in one of my books. He was a Greek sailor in the Spanish navy whose real name was Apostolos Valerianos. He claimed to have discovered the entrance to the Northwest Passage at the forty-seventh parallel in 1592. The transit from the Pacific to the Atlantic had taken a mere twenty days, he reported, and the northern lands between these oceans were filled with riches. Despite how familiar this tale must have sounded, for centuries people actually believed him. Although no one knows for certain whether the Greek sailor ever even visited the North Pacific, his description of the entrance to the passage, then known as the Strait of Anian, bears a superficial resemblance to the entrance of Puget Sound, and so the Strait of Juan de Fuca memorializes the pseudonymous perpetrator of a hoax.

Viewed from the patio of the Bellingham ferry terminal, the M/V *Malaspina* is a splendid sight, its white decks gleaming, a yellow stripe running the length of its navy-blue hull, its single smokestack painted in the motif of the Alaskan state flag—gold stars of the Big Dipper and the North Star against a navy-blue sky. All the motor vessels in the Alaska Marine Highway system are named for Alaskan glaciers, and the *Malaspina* is named for the largest, a fifteen-hundred-square-mile slow-moving mesa of ice, which is in turn named for an eighteenth-century Spanish navigator, Alejandro Malaspina, whose search for the Northwest Passage ended in 1791 at the sixtieth parallel, in an icy inlet that he christened *Bahía del Desengaño*, Disappointment Bay. When I wheel my suitcase down the gangway that evening, the splendor of the M/V *Malaspina* diminishes with every step. The ferry is, I see upon boarding it, an aging, rust-stained hulk, repainted many times. Posted in a display case of documents near the cocktail lounge one can read a disconcerting open letter in which "past and present crew members . . . bid farewell to this proud ship." Queen of the fleet when it was first launched in 1962, the *Malaspina*, the letter explains, "will cease scheduled runs of Alaska's Inside Passage on October 27, 1997." Why the old ferry is still in service eight years later the documents in the display case do not say.

The *Malaspina*'s diesel engines rumble to life. I am going to sea! Who can resist an embarkation? The thrill of watery beginnings? Not me. The evening is cool and exhilarating, the sky clear save for a distant, flat-bottomed macaroon of a cloud. The wavelets on Bellingham Bay are as intricate as houndstooth, complicated by cross breezes and by ripples radiating from the hulls of anchored boats. The dock falls away. I stand at the taffrail and think to myself, *taffrail*, enjoying the union of a thing and its word. Out on the sundeck, at the mouth of the Plexiglas solarium where I will spend the next three nights sleeping for free in a plastic chaise lounge, backpackers are pitching their tents, duct-taping them down so that the wind doesn't toss them overboard. Soon a rustling nylon village of colorful domes has sprung up. "Tent city," the veteran ferry-riders call it. On the forested hills of Bellingham, the houses face the harbor. How festive the ferry must look from up there! As the ship turns and slithers toward the horizon, the low sun moves across the windows of the town, igniting them one by one.

During the middle of the first night, off the eastern shore of Vancouver Island, the temperature drops, a fog shuts down, and my cell phone loses reception. So much for daily phone calls to my pregnant wife. A plastic deck chair, it turns out, makes for a miserable mattress. Cold air seeps between the slats. The government-issue cotton blanket I rented from the ship's purser for a dollar is far too thin. Some of my neighbors in the solarium move inside to sleep like refugees on the carpeted floor of the recliner lounge. I rent a second blanket for the second night, but it hardly makes a difference. Shivering in a fetal position, I think about that mountain climber dangling from the Antarctic ice shelf in a hammock and feel faintly ridiculous. After two nights in the solarium of a cruise ship—a state-operated, poor man's cruise ship, but a cruise ship nonetheless—I have already had my fill of adventuring.

WHAT IS CHILDHOOD? Developmental psychologists will tell you that infancy and toddlerhood and childhood and adolescence are neurologically determined states of mind. Sociologists and historians, meanwhile, tell us that childhood is an idea, distinct from biological immaturity, the meaning of which changes over time. In his seminal, 1960 study of the subject, French historian Philippe Ariès argued that childhood as we know it is a modern invention, largely a byproduct of schooling. In the Middle Ages, when almost no one went to school, children were treated like miniature adults. At work and at play, there was little age-based segregation. "Everything was permitted in their presence," according to one of Ariès 's sources, even "coarse language, scabrous actions and situations; they had heard everything and seen everything." Power, not age, determined whether a person was treated like a child. Until the seventeenth century, the European idea of childhood "was bound up with the idea of dependence: the words 'sons,' 'varlets,' and 'boys' were also words in the vocabulary of feudal subordination. One could leave childhood only by leaving the state of dependence." Our notion of childhood as a sheltered period of innocence begins to emerge with the modern education system, Ariès argues. As the period of economic dependence lengthened among the educated classes, so too did childhood. These days education and the puerility it entails often last well into one's twenties, or longer.

Twenty-two years after Ariès published his book, media critic Neil Postman announced in *The Disappearance of Childhood* that modern childhood as Ariès described it had gone extinct, killed off by the mass media, which gave all children, educated or otherwise, premature access to the violent, sexually illicit world of adults. Children still existed, of course, but they'd become, in Postman's word, "adultified."

I was ten years old when Postman published his book, and in many respects my biography aligns with his unflattering generational portrait. In Postman's opinion the rising divorce rate indicated a "precipitous falling off in the commitment of adults to the nurturing of children." My parents divorced just as the American divorce rate reached its historical peak. After my mother moved out for good, my brother and I came home from school to an empty house where we spent hours watching the sorts of television shows Postman complains about (*Three's Company, The Dukes of Hazzard*). Reading Postman's diagnosis, I begin to wonder if he's right. Maybe my childhood went missing.

But then I think of Joshua the Mouse. One day at the school where I teach I stopped to admire a bulletin board decorated with construction paper mice that a class of first graders had made. Above one mouse there appeared the following caption: "My mouse's name is Joshua. He is 20 years old. He is afraid of everything." I love this caption. I love how those first two humdrum sentences do nothing to prepare us for the emotional revelation of the third. And then there's the age: twenty years old. What occult significance could that number possess for Joshua's creator? When you are six, even eight-year-olds look colossal. A twenty-year-old must be as unfathomable as a god. And contemplating poor, omniphobic, twenty-year-old Joshua, I am convinced that children may impersonate adults but they will never become them. I doubt that childhood has ever been the safe, sunlit harbor adults in moments of forgetfulness dream about. I suspect that it will always be a wilderness.

"For as this appalling ocean surrounds the verdant land," Ishmael philosophizes midway through his whale hunt, "so in the soul of man there lies one insular Tahiti, full of peace and joy, but encompassed by all the horrors of the half known life. God keep thee! Push not off from that isle, thou canst never return!" We canst never return, but oh, how we try, how we try.

Postman does not only argue that television produced "adultified children"; paradoxically, it also produced "childified adults." As evidence, he points to the absence on television of characters who possess an "adult's appetite for serious music" or "book-learning" or "even the faintest signs of a contemplative habit of mind." One wonders what he would have made of the popular culture of centuries past—the pornographic peep-show boxes, the slapstick vaudeville acts, the violent and salacious Punch and Judy shows, the bearbaitings and cockfights, the dime novels and penny weeklies. The great difference to me seems one not of quality but of quantity: entertainment has become so cheap and ubiquitous that it is inescapable. Even the material world has become a "Sargasso of the imagination." Life is still half known.

THE ALASKAN STRETCH of the Inside Passage snakes through the Alexander Archipelago, a chain of one thousand or so thickly forested islands, some as small as tablecloths, some as large as Hawaii. These are, in fact, the tops of underwater mountains, part of the same snowcapped range visible on the mainland to the east. Most rise steeply from the water and soar to cloudy heights. Before going there, I expected southeast Alaska to feel like a giant outdoor theme park— Frontierland—and the shopping districts of the resort towns where the gargantuan cruise ships dock confirm my worst expectations. Cruise-ship companies now own many of the businesses in those districts and may soon be able to "imagineer" (as the folks at Disney call it) every aspect of your vacation experience. But the backwaters of the Inside Passage, too narrow and shallow for the superliners to enter, contain lost worlds.

In the narrowest of the narrows, it feels as though we are motoring down an inland river rather than along the ocean's edge—some Amazon of the north. Although this is the Pacific, the water doesn't

look, smell, or sound like the sea. Neither waves nor flotsam get past
the outer islands to the placid interior. In the summer, streams of
glacial melt freshen the channels, and in places the minerals those
streams carry turn the channels a strangely luminous shade of jade.
The banks sometimes loom so close you could play Frisbee with a
person standing on shore. Hours go by when we see no other ships,
or any sign of civilization besides the buoys that mark the way
among the shoals.

Early in the morning, fog rises here and there from the forests of
hemlock, cedar, and spruce. It is as if certain stands are burning,
except that the fog moves much more slowly than smoke. On the far
side of one mountain, a dense white column billows forth like a
slow-motion geyser that levels off into an airborne river flowing
into a sea of clouds. I've begun to notice currents everywhere, a universe of eddies and gyres. Phytoplankton ride the same ocean currents that carried the Floatees to Sitka. Zooplankton follow the
phytoplankton. Fish follow the zooplankton. Sea lions, whales, and
people follow the fish. When, at the end of their upriver journey,
salmon spawn and die en masse, their carcasses—distributed by
bears, eagles, and other scavengers—fertilize the forests that make
the fog, which falls as rain, which changes the ocean's salinity. All
deep water travels along what oceanographers call the "conveyor
belt," which begins with warm water from the Gulf Stream draining into the North Atlantic, where evaporation increases the salinity and makes it sink to the ocean floor, where it creeps south to
the Antarctic circumpolar stream. After a thousand years—a
millennium!—the conveyor belt ends here, in the North Pacific,
where the ancient water wells up, carrying nutrients with it.
Oceanographers learned much of this from studying radioactive iso-
topes released into the sea as fallout from nuclear tests. I'm becoming a devout driftologist. The only essential difference between rock,
water, air, life, galaxies, economics, civilizations, plastics—I decide,

standing on the *Malaspina*'s deck, totally sober, watching the fog make pretty shapes above the trees—is the rate of flow.

EVERYWHERE THEY LOOK, archaeologists find them—buffalo sprayed with pigments onto the walls of caves, killer whales cut from cedar or stone, horses molded from terra-cotta or plaited out of straw. Our primal fear of predators and our hunger for prey cannot alone account for this menagerie. Three thousand years ago in Persia, someone carved a porcupine out of limestone and attached it to a little chassis on wheels. Four thousand years ago in Egypt, someone sculpted a mouse and glazed it blue. Why blue? Whoever heard of a blue mouse? Is this the forebear of the red beaver and the yellow duck? In fact, many of the figurines that look to us like toys turn out to have been totemic gods or demigods, used in religious ceremonies or funerary rites. To make the archaeological record all the blurrier, some totems in some cultures were given to children as playthings once the festivities had ended. One thing is clear: animals held an exalted position in the lives of both children and adults. Even after the missionaries came and cleansed them from the temples, the animistic gods survived, adapting to the altered cultural landscape. In Europe of the Middle Ages, one of the most popular books after the Bible was the *Bestiary,* a kind of illustrated field guide to the medieval imagination, wherein the animals of fable and myth were reborn as vehicles of Christian allegory. From the *Bestiary* came the idea that after three days a pelican could resurrect a dead hatchling with her blood, and from the *Bestiary* we learned that only a virgin girl can tame a unicorn. Even Aesop, that pagan, remained a favorite with old and young alike well into the seventeenth century.

Gradually, as allegory gave way to zoology and farming to industry, we decided that animals were for kids. "Children in the industrialised world are surrounded by animal imagery," notes John Berger in "Why Look at Animals?" Despite the antiquity of zoomorphic toys and the "apparently spontaneous interest that children have in animals," it was not until the nineteenth century that "reproductions of animals became a regular part of the decor of middle-class childhoods—and then, in [the twentieth] century, with the advent of vast display and selling systems like Disney's—of all childhoods." Berger traces this phenomenon to the marginalization of animals, which the age of industrialism either incarcerated as living spectacles at the public zoo, treated as raw material to be exploited, processed as commodities on factory farms, or domesticated as family pets. Meanwhile, "animals of the mind"—which since the dawn of human consciousness had been central to our cosmologies—were sent without supper to the nursery. Animals both living and imaginary no longer seemed like mysterious gods. They seemed, increasingly, like toys.

Go bird-watching in the pre-industrial libraries of literature and myth, and you will find few ducks, which is puzzling, considering how popular with the authors of children's books ducks have since become. Search, for instance, the fields and forests of Aesop, whose talking beasts are the ancestors of both Chanticleer the Rooster and Walter the Farting Dog, and you will meet ten cocks, a cote of doves, several partridges, a caged songbird, six crows, three ravens (one portentous, another self-loathing), a dozen or so eagles, five jackdaws (one of whom wishes he were an eagle), many kites, flocks of cranes, two storks, three hawks, a cote of pigeons, three hens, a sparrow with a bad case of schadenfreude, five swallows, many peacocks, a jay who wishes he were a peacock, many swans, two nightingales, two larks, two owls, a gluttonous seagull, a thrush ensnared in birdlime, and nary a single duck.

Aesop's fables exhibit considerable ornithological knowledge, but their primary aim is to transmute animal behavior into human meaning—to burden them, as Thoreau would say, with some portion of our thought. "The lot of each has been assigned by the will of the Fates," the god Juno explains to an insecure peacock in one fable, "—to thee, beauty; to the eagle, strength; to the nightingale, song; to the raven, favorable; and to the crow, unfavorable auguries." The closest to ducks that Aesop gets is geese, which invariably end up on dinner plates.

Even Aesop's most famous goose, the one who lays the golden egg, succumbs to the carving knife. In a Kashmiri version of the same tale, Aesop's barnyard variety Anatidae becomes the Lucky-Bird Humá, a visitor from the magical avian kingdom of Koh-i-Qáf. A Buddhist version of the tale replaces the egg-laying goose with one of the only mythical ducks I have found, a mallard plumed in gold, which turns out to be a reincarnation of the Bodhisattva.

In all three versions of the fable, the human beneficiaries sacrifice their magically profitable waterfowl on the altar of their greed. The farmer kills the goose, cuts it open, and finds no eggs. Dreaming of rupees, a Kashmiri woodcutter accidentally asphyxiates the Lucky-Bird Humá while carrying him to market in a sack. A family of Brahmin women decide to pluck out all of the Bodhisattva's golden feathers at once; they turn into the feathers of a crane. Unlike the others, the Buddhist version tells the fable from the bird's point of view, and for that reason it is peculiarly affecting. Both Aesop's fable and the Kashmiri one show us the folly of human desire, and it is satisfying, reading them, to watch our wicked, bumbling protagonists endure dramatically ironic reversals of fortune. The Buddhist fable shows us the folly of human desire, but it also makes us experience that folly's cost, the debt of suffering our appetites can incur. The tone of the final sentences is more sorrowful than ironic. Trying to escape, the once-golden mallard stretches his plucked wings but, featherless, finds he cannot fly. His captors throw him into a barrel.

With time, his feathers grow back, but they are plain white ones now. He flies home, never to return.

ON THE MORNING that I disembark from the *Malaspina* at Sitka, Tyler and Dean Orbison are just returning from a two-week, three-hundred-mile beachcombing expedition to Latuya Bay and back. They go on such expeditions every summer, traveling farther and farther afield every year, poking around in bunkers abandoned at the end of World War II, walking beaches where the only footprints in the sand are animal tracks. They have a cabin cruiser big enough to sleep in and a skiff for going ashore. From the cruiser, they look for V-shaped coastlines that funnel the tides, and they look for "jack-straw"—driftwood logs jumbled like a pile of pick-up-sticks—and, most important of all, like prospectors panning in the tailings, they look for "good color," their term for plastic debris visible from afar. Where there's some color, there's sure to be more. Their style of beachcombing is by necessity a two-man job. One person has to stay in the skiff to keep it from foundering on the rocks while the other person wades in and combs. They take turns. Dean prefers to hunt high up, in the purple fireweed, where storms will throw objects out of the reach of tides. Tyler, Dean's son, is "a digger." Like a human metal detector, he's learned to divine the location of buried objects by reading the terrain. This year, for the first time, Tyler and Dean started combing in seaside caves where tangled driftwood will form a kind of flotsam trap. It's dark in the caves. You have to beachcomb with a flashlight. It's also cold, but the labor of log-lifting keeps you warm. The effort's worth it. Every cave the Orbisons searched contained a farrago of wrack—a Dawn dish detergent bottle, glass fishing floats, Floatees. Half a water pistol turned up in one cave, the other half in another. By far the most common objects the Orbisons find are polyethylene water bottles. They have begun keeping the screw-tops, cataloguing the varieties. On this last trip they identified seventy-five different brands, many of them foreign in origin. Up in Latuya Bay they saw a black wolf and the bones of a whale, and they picked wild strawberries, and when their cooler ran out of ice they floated alongside a glacier and broke off a chunk.

Now, at the end of my first day ashore, they've fetched me from my hotel. "Growing up here, I mean, there's nothing," Tyler tells me from the backseat of his father's truck while we're waiting for his parents to emerge from Sitka's only supermarket. "I mean we don't even have a mall. So I took to the outdoors pretty hard." It is clear that Tyler has never given much thought to the marginalization of animals. You wouldn't either if you'd grown up in southeast Alaska, where bears make off with household pets, and ravens alighting on transformers cause power outages, and bald eagles sometimes come crashing through dining room windows. If anything, it's the people who occupy the margins here. Just look at a map: Sitka perches on the coastal brink of Baranof Island, wedged between mountainous wilderness to the east and watery wilderness to the west. Sitkans share their island with an estimated twelve hundred grizzly bears—more than are found in all of the lower forty-eight states combined. In May and June, eagles and ravens—the supreme deities in the pantheon of the native Tlingit—wheel overhead. In July and August, the creeks grow dark with spawning sockeye and chum. In November, the whales and the whale-watchers arrive. People like me may feel sorry for the 1.2 million sea otters that the Russian American Company parted from their pelts in the early 1800s, but Sitka's otters have replenished themselves with such procreative gusto that local fishermen now regard them as pests—crop-thieving, net-wrecking vermin of the sea.

Like most beachcombers of the Pacific rim, the Orbisons started out collecting Japanese fishing floats, the glass balls that you sometimes see hanging in nets from the ceilings of seafood restaurants, or decorating the window displays of maritime boutiques. The popularity of glass floats owes partly to their delicate, soap-bubble beauty, partly to the Kuroshio Current that sweeps them across the Pacific and bowls them up the beaches of the American west coast, and partly to Amos L. Wood, an aeronautics engineer and beachcombing enthusiast whose books *Beachcombing for Japanese Floats* and *Beachcombing the Pacific* have become to beachcombers what Audubon guides are to bird-watchers.

A century and a half ago, beachcombers tended to be transcendental weirdos like Ellery Channing and Henry Thoreau. Back then, much of New England's shoreline was as wild as Alaska's is today and more treacherous to passing ships. Just before Thoreau arrived at Provincetown in 1849, a ship carrying Irish immigrants sank off Cohasset. The bodies of the drowned lay strewn along the beach, torn asunder by the surf and fish. "There are more consequences to a shipwreck than the underwriters notice," Thoreau observed. "The Gulf Stream may return some to their native shores, or drop them in some out-of-the-way cave of Ocean, where time and the elements will write new riddles with their bones." Even where no shipwrecks had occurred, a Cape Cod beach in 1849 was "a wild rank place" littered "with crabs, horse-shoes and razor clams, and whatever the sea casts up—a vast *morgue,* where famished dogs may range in packs, and crows come daily to glean the pittance which the tide leaves them."

Still a recent coinage, the word "beachcomber" in 1849 meant approximately what we mean by "beach bum"; it evoked a character like the narrator of Melville's *Omoo,* a transient ne'er-do-well who'd fled from civilization hoping to sample tropical women and tropical fruits and loaf around beneath the blowsy palms. "Idle, drunken, vagabond," Edward Wakefield wrote in 1845, "he wanders about without any fixed object, cannot get employed by the whaler or anyone else, as it is out of his power to do a day's work; and he is universally known as 'the beach-comber.'" The local Cape Codders whom Thoreau met on his seaside rambles usually took him for a traveling salesman. What other explanation could there be for a vagabond with a walking stick and a knapsack full of books?

THE ORBISONS GAVE up collecting for driftology in the summer of 1993, when they began discovering bath toys. Tyler was just twelve at the time, but he was the one to find their first toy, a beaver, and he remembers the moment vividly. "We were on Kruzof Island, looking for glass balls," he says. "We didn't really know what else to look for. It was beautiful weather; the reason we went to Kruzof is because it's really hard to get ashore, and that's where we go when the weather's good. We were up beyond the high-tide line. It was in the drift a ways. It had been there for a little bit. And I thought, This is cool. It was bleached out, exactly like the beavers we find now. I would say it had been there since the winter storms."

They assumed that their beaver was a solitary castaway, but when they arrived back in town, talk of the mysterious invasion was in the air. Dean and Tyler went looking for more plastic animals, and found them. They started keeping meticulous records, treating the Floatees as data, which they eventually reported to Ebbesmeyer. About three years later, the oceanographer began publishing *Beachcomber's Alert!,* and the Orbisons were among his first subscribers. They own every issue. "Curt tells us what to look for, and we go out there and find it," Dean explains. This year, at Ebbesmeyer's bidding, they searched for and found a computer monitor, Japanese surveying stakes, hockey gloves, "antisandals" (a sheet of rubber from which flip-flop-shaped blanks have been stamped), part of a naval sonar buoy, and six new Floatees, including a turtle they'd chiseled from the ice. After cataloguing the junk on their porch and showing it to Ebbesmeyer, they'll take most of it to the dump.

———

BACK IN THE 1970s, when I was a child, rubber ducks were wilder than they are now. There was nothing iconic or nostalgic about them. Some rubber ducks of the Nixon era were white, some were calico. Some had swan-like necks and rosy circles on their cheeks. Some came with rococo feathers molded into their wings and tails. No one used them to sell baby clothes or soap. Normal adults did not give them to one another, or decorate their desks with them. As far as I can remember, no one I knew even owned a rubber duck. I did own one, however, on account of the pet name my mother had given me: Donovan Duck. My duck was a somewhat hideous specimen, with white plumage, a green topcoat, a big head, and the posture of a penguin. It resembled a Hummel figurine that had sprouted a beak.

Not long ago, my mother sent me a photograph in which, naked, eight months old, sitting in the bath across from my brother, I appear to be attempting to gnaw through my rubber duck's skull. The picture is dated January 1973. Most exotic varieties of rubber duck have since gone extinct—they are the dodos and carrier pigeons of the nursery—and what new ones have evolved share a single, yellow ancestor whose pop-cultural apotheosis was by January 1973 already underway. It had begun three years earlier, in 1970, when an orange puppet named Ernie appeared on PBS and said, "Here I am in my tubby again. And my tubby's all filled with water and nice, fluffy suds. And I've got my soap and washcloth to wash myself. And I've got my nifty scrub brush to help me scrub my back. And I've got a big fluffy towel to dry myself when I'm done. But there's one other thing that makes tubby time the very best time of the whole day. And do you know what that is? It's a very special friend of mine. My very favorite little pal"—at which point Ernie reaches into the suds and, brandishing his yellow duck, bursts into song.

You can watch a video clip of the number online. A pink towel hangs from a wooden post at the left edge of the frame. The post looks like something out of an old Western. There is no other scenery to speak of. Behind the bathtub—which is huge, presumably claw-footed, and decorated with three pink daisies—hangs a sky-blue backdrop. Bubbles of the sort you blow with a wand come floating up from the bottom of the screen, and the gurgle of water accompanies the music. Although I watched my share of *Sesame Street* as a child, I far preferred Super Grover's mock-heroic pratfalls to Ernie's snickering bonhomie, and I have no memory of the rubber duckie number. My wife, on the other hand, still knows the song by heart.

"Rubber Duckie, joy of joys," Ernie sings. "When I squeeze you, you make noise, / Rubber Duckie, you're my very best friend, it's true." It's all so synthetic, so lonely, so imaginary, so clean. And apparently children loved it. In the 1969 pilot episode of *Sesame Street,* in which a version of the rubber duckie song appeared, children in the test audience responded so enthusiastically to Ernie and Bert and so tepidly to segments featuring the live actors that the show's creators redesigned it, giving the puppets a starring role.

However novel the medium, however inventive Jim Henson's puppetry, Ernie's bathtub serenade draws upon a history of representation that can be traced back to the eighteenth century, when British portraitists stopped painting children as diminutive adults and turned them into puppy-eyed personifications of Innocence. In the Romantic era, no longer was innocence merely the antithesis of guilt; it was also the antithesis of adulthood and modernity. Children became little noble savages and childhood became a place as well as an age—a lost, imaginary, pastoral realm.

It is striking how much the modern history of childhood resembles that of animals. "In the first stages of the industrial revolution," John Berger writes, "animals were used as machines. As also were children." In the latter stages of industrialism, poor children who escaped the factory often took to the street, where they formed what social historians call "child societies," gangs of urchins who—like feral cats—invented a social order all their own. Partly in fear of child societies, middle-class parents of the Gilded Era began treating their children increasingly like pets. Nurseries and playrooms became more common, and toy chests began to overflow.*

In 1869, a printer from Albany, New York, named John Wesley Hyatt mixed ground camphor with nitrocellulose, thereby inventing celluloid. In 1873, the first Pekin ducks were imported to the United States from China. And in the 1880s, bathtubs began appearing in middle-class homes along with indoor plumbing. Celluloid eventually evolved into the plastics industry. The Pekin duck eventually became the preferred species of American duck breeders, making yellow ducklings a familiar symbol of birth and spring. And the average American bathroom, which had once consisted of a washtub and an outhouse, was consecrated as a temple of cleanliness. Much as the modern nursery sheltered children from the social contamination of the street, so the modern bathroom protected their naked, slippery bodies from germs. In the first decades of the twentieth century, public-health campaigns and soap advertisements—usually illustrated with pudgy little tots—exhorted parents to bathe their children often. Little boys, the thinking went, were naturally indisposed to bathing. Bath toys not only made hygiene boyishly fun; they helped overcome the naughty urges that bathing tended to arouse: "The baby will not spend much time handling his genitals if he has

*Teddy bears and other stuffed animals, Peter Stearns explains in *Anxious Parents: A History of Modern Childrearing in America*, "were widely appealing at a time when parents were trying to facilitate new sleeping arrangements for babies and also to guard against unduly fervent emotional attachments to mothers. The decline in paid help for young children also opened the door to the use of toys as surrogate entertainment." One commentator at the time speculated that toy animals helped children overcome primal fears of scary predators, turning lions and tigers and bears into snuggly sidekicks. Perhaps the most astute psychological profile of the child consumer appeared in *Playthings*, the trade journal of the American toy industry, which in 1913 was predicting that "the nervous temperament of the average American child and the rapidity with which it tires of things" would guarantee a never-ending bull market in toys.

other interesting things to do," one government-issue child-care manual advised in 1942. "See that he has a toy to play with and he will not need to use his body as a plaything." Enter the rubber duck.

Ducklings are the aquatic equivalent of kittens and bunnies. In fact, it's hard to think of a smaller, cuddlier animal that can swim. Most of the frogs and turtles of children's literature are middle-aged men, whereas even in nature ducklings are model offspring: obedient, dependent, vulnerable to predation, clumsy, soft, a little dumb. Just think of them waddling in a train behind a mother duck, a familiar image memorialized by Robert McCloskey's bestselling children's book *Make Way for Ducklings*. McCloskey's baby mallards, penciled in black and white, look like real baby mallards—a little stylized, but real. Like the ducks depicted in other venerable children's books, they bear little resemblance to Ernie's Day-Glo squeak toy. Beatrix Potter's Jemimah is a white Pekin duck in a bonnet and shawl. Donald Duck, the most famous water fowl at mid-century, was also a white Pekin, and the most common toy duck was still the ancient bird-on-a-leash, a wooden pull-toy with wheels instead of feet. Before the rubber duck could eclipse it, plastic had to replace wood as the preferred material for toys, which, following the technical innovations spurred by World War II, it did.

McCloskey published his book in 1941. That same year, at the beginning of the war, two British chemists, V. E. Yarsley and E. G. Couzens, prophesied with surprising accuracy and quaintly utopian innocence what middle-class childhood in the 1970s would be like. "Let us try to imagine a dweller in the 'Plastic Age,'" they wrote in the British magazine *Science Digest*.

> This creature of our imagination, this "Plastic Man," will come into a world of colour and bright shining surfaces, where childish hands find nothing to break, no sharp edges or corners to cut or graze, no crevices to harbour dirt or germs, because,

being a child his parents will see to it that he is surrounded on every side by this tough, safe, clean material which human thought has created. The walls of his nursery, all the articles of his bath and certain other necessities of his small life, all his toys, his cot, the moulded perambulator in which he takes the air, the teething ring he bites, the unbreakable bottle he feeds from . . . all will be plastic, brightly self-coloured and patterned with every design likely to please his childish mind.

Here, then, is one of the meanings of the duck. It represents this vision of childhood—the hygienic childhood, the safe childhood, the brightly colored childhood, in which everything, even bathtub articles, has been designed to please the childish mind, much as the golden fruit in that most famous origin myth of paradise "was pleasant to the eyes" of childish Eve. Yarsley and Couzens go on to imagine the rest of Plastic Man's life, and it is remarkable how little his adulthood differs from his childhood. When he grows up, Plastic Man will live in a house furnished with "beautiful, transparent, glass-like materials in every imaginable form," he will play with plastic toys (tennis rackets and fishing tackle), he will, "like a magician," be able to make "what he wants." And yet there is one imperfection, one run in this nylon dream. Plastic might make the pleasures of childhood last forever, but it could not make Plastic Man immortal. When he dies, he will sink "into his grave hygienically enclosed in a plastic coffin." The image must have been unsettling, even in 1941; that hygienically enclosed death too reminiscent of the hygienically enclosed life that preceded it. To banish the image of that plastic coffin from their readers' thoughts, the utopian chemists inject a little more technicolor resin into their closing sentences. When "the dust and smoke" of war had cleared, plastic would deliver us "from moth and rust" into a world "full of colour . . . a new, brighter, cleaner, more beautiful world."

For new parents who had themselves grown up during the Depression and the war, the fantasy of childhood as consumer paradise exerted a powerful appeal. Browsing through issues of *Parents Magazine* from 1950, I came upon an ad campaign for Heinz baby food ("Scientific Cooking Gives Finer Flavor, Color and Texture to Heinz Strained Carrots"). In one Heinz ad, targeted at new mothers, cartoon butterflies, fairies, and dolls encircle the photograph of a baby girl. "Wee elfin creatures go riding on butterfly wings," the copy reads, "dolls speak in a language all their own and something altogether new and wonderful happens everywhere a baby looks . . . your child lives in a magic world where everything's enchanted." Then came television, enchantment in a box. Annual toy sales in America shot from $84 million in 1940 to $1.25 billion in 1960. Peg-and-socket pop beads sold to girls as costume jewelry consumed forty thousand pounds of polyethylene resin per month in 1956. In 1958, "twirling hoops" consumed fifteen million pounds of the stuff. Polystyrene replaced balsa wood as the material of choice for model cars and planes. Plasticized polyvinyl chloride, the material from which the brand new Barbie doll was made, provided a cheaper, more durable alternative to latex rubber, rendering traditional molded rubber animals and dolls obsolete except in name.

Not long after PBS first broadcast it, Ernie's rubber duckie song went to number sixteen on the *Billboard* charts. Radio stations were playing it, adults were buying it. And, unlike the other *Sesame Street* characters, Ernie's rubber duck could not be licensed. Producers had picked up the prop at a local dimestore, which meant that even as it became a recurring character and a pop music phenomenon, it remained in the public domain, free for the taking, no fees required. Does that mean that if Ernie had gone bathing with a white duck or a green one, our iconic ducks would be white or green? I'm not sure. The threads of chance and meaning are hard to disentangle. On the album cover of the single of the song, Ernie, for some reason, is holding a different duck, a white one with burnt-orange spots. Perhaps there is more to the message in this particular bottle than the medium. Perhaps Ernie alone does not explain the yellowness of the duck.

"Ideals of innocent beauty and the adorable have changed little in a hundred years or more," the historian Gary Cross writes. "Many today share with the Victorian middle class an attraction to the blond, blue-eyed, clear-skinned, and well-fed child and are appalled by, uninterested in, and even hostile to the dark, dirty, and emaciated child. Even when humanitarian groups try to shame us into giving money to support poor peoples far away, they usually show us an image of a smiling olive-skinned (not black) girl, a close copy of our ideal of innocence." So maybe it's just as Curtis Ebbesmeyer suspected. Maybe there is a racial bias at play. Is it too much of a stretch to see in the yellowness of the rubber duck a visual reminder of that well-fed, blue-eyed, clear-skinned, yellow-haired Victorian ideal? After all, real ducklings have black, beady eyes, not blue ones like the ducks in Eric Carle's book. The lyrics to Ernie's serenade show just how childlike his rubber duckie is. "Every day when I, / Make my way to the tubby," the song's chorus goes, "I find a little fellow who's / Cute and yellow and chubby!" Chubby versus well-fed, blond versus yellow, what's the difference?

Tuesdays during the seventh month of her pregnancy, my wife and I attended a prepared childbirth class on the maternity ward of our hospital. On one wall of the classroom hung a poster of an egg, mid-hatch. Contemplating it during the long, tedious hours of instruction, I began to wonder why this particular poster had been hung before our eyes. Was it meant to comfort us? Did we prefer the clean, white orb of an egg to the bloody, mammalian mess of one body gushing forth from the wounded nethers of another? On the opposite wall of the classroom hung an enlarged, sepia photograph of naked, racially diverse babies; aligned firing-squad style along a fence over which they appeared to be attempting an escape, they displayed their wrinkly bums for our delight. Children are fundamentally the same, such images suggest, as indistinguishable as ducklings despite the color of their skin. They inhabit a world before sex, before race, before history, before self, before humanity. Children, then, are beasts of burden, too—ducklings and bunnies of burden—asked to carry the needful daydreams of adults. The apotheosis of the rubber duck wouldn't be truly complete until the children who had watched that 1970 episode of *Sesame Street* grew old enough to look back forgetfully with longing and loss.

WE ARE GOING beachcombing. We are going beachcombing on Kruzof Island, along a pumice beach at the mouth of Fred's Creek, which originates high on the perennially snow-capped slopes of Mount Edgecumbe and empties into Sitka Sound. Curtis Ebbesmeyer is here, aboard the *Morning Mist,* wearing his sea-bean necklace and a baseball cap decorated with stickers from Seattle coffeehouses. Dean Orbison is here, in his customary plaid woodsman's shirt and a pair of Sitka sneakers—the local name for knee-high rubber boots. Tyler Orbison is not here; sadly, he had to work. Piloting the *Morning Mist*—a white, twin-engine troller with outrigging as tall as flagpoles and orange floats the size of beach balls dangling like ornaments from its rails—is Larry Calvin, a spry, white-haired fisherman in suspenders.

A self-employed, left-wing entrepreneur who subsidizes his fishing with profits earned in the building-supply business, Calvin embodies an old brand of American individualism that seems to flourish in the strange demographic conundrum that is maritime Alaska, a place both rural and coastal, both red and blue, Western and Tlingit, industrial and aquacultural and wild. On Calvin's black ball cap a fish leaps above the words ABSOLUTE FRESH.

With us aboard the *Morning Mist* are a dozen or so scholars—oceanographers, archaeologists, anthropologists, linguists, historians—who have come to Sitka for the annual Paths Across the Pacific Conference, an academic symposium scheduled to coincide with the Beachcombers' Fair. The organizing theory of the conference is this: People started crossing the Pacific Ocean by boat tens of thousands of years ago, far earlier than was previously thought. Some Asian immigrants sailed to America by mistake when blown astray. Some came on purpose, paddling along the coast of the Beringian ice shelf, traveling a little farther east with every generation. Comparatively little is known about these ancient migrations, and on the way to Kruzof Island, an oceanographer named Thomas Royer tells me one reason why. Sea levels have risen so much since the last ice age that the earliest settlements in Alaska are now one hundred meters underwater.

Another passenger, an archaeologist, interrupts to contest Royer's figures. Sedimentation adds about a centimeter a year to the ocean floor, this archaeologist says, which means you'd have to dig deeper than one hundred meters. You'd have to dig about four hundred meters to find any artifacts.

Most of the chitchat aboard the *Morning Mist* is similarly quibbling, interdisciplinary, and esoteric. When did people first begin using boats—forty thousand years ago? Fifty thousand years ago? What does it take to start a migration—a critical mass, or a few individuals with the itch to explore? Why did people migrate in the first place—the profit motive? hunger? exile? Ebbesmeyer and Ingraham's computer simulations may help these marine archaeologists reconstruct the routes of those transoceanic migrations, the history of which is inseparable from the history of global climate change. In other words, it is humanity's own past and future that the oceanographers are scrying in the tangled drift routes of the toys.

Looking out from the cabin of the *Morning Mist,* Royer teaches me how to read the surface of the sea. "You see that smooth area there?"

he asks. "Either temperature or the salinity will change the surface tension of the water, so the same wind will ruffle the water in one spot but not in another." All variations in the surface are the effects of hidden causes. What to me looks simply like an expanse of water is in fact a kind of shifting, aquatic topography, like an enormous lava lamp, only far more complex and subtle. Instead of one liquid suspended in another, there are slopes of dense, salty water and rivers of light, brackish water, and all of it, over the course of centuries, will eventually intermingle. As in all complex systems, minute changes to the ocean—in salinity, in temperature, in air pressure—can entail grand and unpredictable climate events. Because of melting glaciers, for instance, the salinity in the 18-mile-wide coastal current that flows north along the Alaskan seaboard is presently decreasing, making the water fresher and lighter. Counterintuitively, however, sea levels in Alaska are falling—or so it seems—because the land, relieved of the weight of ice, is lifting, the way an air mattress resumes its shape after you stand up.

In the half hour or so it takes us to get to Kruzof, centuries seem to recede. Sitka disappears into a blur of blue horizon. The world out here would not have looked much different a millennium ago, I think to myself. It resembles the opening verses of Genesis. There is only the land, the water, the trees. And then, at the edge of my peripheral vision, an orange figure swoops and dives. It's a kite. A kite shaped like a bird, and there on the beach below it are three figures, a father and his children, dressed in colorful swimsuits. They have rented one of the four rustic cabins that the National Forest Service maintains on Kruzof Island. The cabin itself becomes visible now, tucked back into the trees. Here, in the forest primeval at the foot of a dormant volcano, is a scene from the New Jersey shore. Larry Calvin anchors the *Morning Mist* well away from the rocky shallows and ferries us in several at a time aboard his aluminum skiff. The father flying the kite hollers hello, the children eye us warily. Ebbesmeyer hands out white plastic garbage bags in which to collect our discoveries. Dean Orbison will lead one beachcombing party to the south. I join Ebbesmeyer's party, headed north.

I try to remember what the Orbisons and Amos Wood have taught me. Up ahead, where the beach curves and tapers into a sickle, there's lots of jackstraw and even a little color—a fleck of blue, a daub of red. To get there we have to cross Fred's Creek, which spills down through the trees over terraces of rocks before carving a delta of rivulets and bluffs through the sand. The delta is perhaps a dozen yards wide, and those of us without Sitka sneakers have trouble getting across. I manage to leap from rock to rock. Curtis Ebbesmeyer, who ambles along somewhat effortfully, is in no state to go rock jumping. He hikes up into the trees and crosses where the creek narrows. Reuniting on the far shore, we make our way down the beach in a line, scanning the sand. Ebbesmeyer launches into one of his litanies of facts. Bowling balls float, he informs us, or rather the nine-, ten-, and eleven-pounders do. Heavier ones sink. And did you know that the valves of clams are not symmetrical? A colleague of his once surveyed the clamshells along a mile of beach. "At one end of the beach, it's mostly rights, and at the other end it's mostly lefts." The currents can tell the difference.

In *Beachcombing the Pacific,* Amos Wood tells us "to keep looking out at the horizon and not continuously at the sand, for after a few hours this can be tiring on the neck"—advice that I am all too happy to follow. For the first time since I entered Alaska aboard the *Malaspina* a week ago, the rain clouds have cleared. A strong breeze is blowing inland across the sparkling waves. To our right, there is the sound of the surf; to our left, the soughing of the trees. Peering into them, I see only shadowy depths of green. The beach here is more gravelly than sandy. It's like walking over peppercorns. Our boot soles crunch, and I fall into a kind of trance. No matter how crappy a pittance the tide leaves, no matter how darkly ominous the riddles in the sand, beachcombing has its delights. There is pleasure in setting your senses loose. At the sight of something half-buried, the eye startles and the imagination leaps. At the edge of the waves flickers a silver flame. A hundred yards off, from beneath a pile of driftwood, glows a small, fallen sun. Then, at the moment of recognition, there is a kind of satisfying latch. The silver flame? An empty bag of Doritos, torn open. The small sun? A red, dog-chewn Frisbee. The strange becomes suddenly familiar once again, though never quite as familiar as before. Occasionally the object you've inspected is unrecognizable or exotic or mysteriously incongruous. Occasionally that surf-tossed bottle turns out not to have been left by a camper but tossed from a Malaysian shrimp boat crossing the Andaman Sea.

It occurs to me that this is what I have been pursuing these past months, this is what I found so spellbindingly enigmatic about the image of those plastic ducks at sea—incongruity. We have built for ourselves out of this New World a giant diorama, a synthetic habitat, but travel beyond the edges or look with the eyes of a serious beach-comber, and the illusion begins to crumble.

According to Ebbesmeyer, the beachcombing this year has not been good. It all depends on the winter storms. But to me the junk seems abundant. I clamber over the jackstraw, finding there a pre-dictable assortment of water bottles, but also a polystyrene ice cream tub, a plastic length of hose, nylon nets, huge cakes of Styrofoam, all of which I dump into Ebbesmeyer's bag.

"Aw, man," Ebbesmeyer says of the Styrofoam. "That'll break up into a billion pieces. That's the worst stuff. In Seattle you can't recycle Styrofoam. Pisses me off. So what do you do with it? See all those lit-tle cells? The irony is, it's made of polystyrene, which sinks, and they foam it to make it into something that floats. That's what I think of when I see that stuff, all the windrows of Styrofoam, coffee cups with barnacles growing on them. You say you'd love to get it off the beach, but there's no way." He tells me about a container that spilled a shipment of filtered cigarettes. "There are about ten thousand polymer fibers per butt—that's, what? Ten to the order . . . about ten billion fibers for just one container." His eyebrows spring up above his glasses.

This, then, is the destiny of those toy animals that beachcombers fail to recover: baked brittle by the sun, they will eventually disintegrate into shards. Those shards will disintegrate into splinters, the splinters into particles, the particles into dust, and the dust into molecules, which will circulate through the environment for centuries. The very features that make plastic a perfect material for bathtub toys—so buoyant! so pliant! so smooth! so colorful! so hygienic!—also make it a superlative pollutant of the seas. No one knows exactly how long a synthetic polymer will persist at sea. Five hundred years is a reasonable guess. Globally, we are presently producing two hundred million tons of plastic every year, and no known organism can digest a single molecule of the stuff, though plenty of organisms try, including many of the friendly organisms depicted in Eric Carle's *10 Little Rubber Ducks*.

Luckily for them, none of Carle's ducks runs into a Laysan albatross. The encounter would not be pretty. The Laysan albatross is probably the most suicidally voracious plastivore on the planet. Although the bird prefers squid, it will scarf up almost anything colorful that it sees on the ocean's surface. Albatross nesting grounds in the North Pacific are littered with the plastic debris that the birds have crapped out intact. Three to four million cigarette lighters have been collected from seabird rookeries on Midway. Albatross chicks have been known to starve to death on the plastic their parents regurgitate into their mouths, and the intestines of the adult birds can handle only so much before a fatal case of indigestion sets in. Naturalists recently found seven hundred different plastic items inside the feathery carcass of an albatross found in the Pacific. After cataloging this scrap, they assembled it into a mosaic, a great technicolor mandala of detritus, that is a marvel to behold. The other day, during a lecture he gave at a Rotary Club luncheon in Sitka, Ebbesmeyer showed a slide of the thing. Backlit against a white screen, it at first calls to mind stained glass. Then, as you look closer, you start spotting familiar objects strewn amid the shrapnel. Two cigarette lighters and a dozen-odd bottlecaps appear to be as good as new. Somewhere among those seven hundred items may be the remains of a Floatee.

Where does all that plastic come from? Container spills, fishing boats, and recreational beaches, but also sewers and drainage systems that empty into the sea. Bottlecaps are especially abundant in the North Pacific because they are small enough to slip through grates. The lost Super Balls of my childhood may now be abob in the garbage patch. The California Coastal Commission, an independent, quasi-judicial state agency, estimates that there are forty-six thousand pieces of visible plastic floating in every square mile of the ocean, never mind the invisible pieces Charlie Moore has gone trawling for. Based on the samples he collected, Moore calculates that in the North Pacific Subtropical Gyre there are now six pounds of plastic for every one pound of zooplankton. Zooplankton such as salps, a kind of chordate jellyfish that feed by pumping sea water through their gelatinous bodies and straining out the nutrients, ingest bits of plastic far too small to catch an albatross's eye. But the journey of the toys won't end there, in the watery belly of a salp. Long after my own organic chemistry has fertilized leaves of grass, the pulverized, photo-degraded remains of that hollow duck of mine will, chemically speaking, live on, traveling through the food chain, scattering toxins in their wake.

We find the remains of a derelict motorboat, a Bayliner. The boat was here last year, Ebbesmeyer says, marooned but intact on the beach to the south. A year's worth of wave and wind action has torn its fiberglass hull asunder. It looks as though someone blew it up. We find one big blue shard of fiberglass and then, fifty feet farther, another piece. I would like to place a time-lapse camera on a beach like this and watch what happens over the course of a year, watch the giant logs jump around and the flotsam explode. Not far from the Bayliner's gas tank, we find a child's baseball mitt that looks as good as new, and then, not far from the glove, in the damp sand at the edge of the ebbing surf, we come upon the fresh footprints of a bear. The beach ends, the shoreline giving way to a labyrinth of wave-washed boulders into which the footprints continue. "Stonehenge for bears," says Michael Wilson, a Canadian geoarchaeologist who later this week will deliver a lecture titled "Natural Disasters and Prehistoric Human Dispersal: The Rising Wave of Inquiry."

Wilson leads us into the boulders, talking loudly. The wind is behind us, and we assume that the bear will keep its distance, but you can tell that Ebbesmeyer is feeling nervous. I am, too. We both start glancing into the trees. Wilson's spotted something, something big and blue, and runs ahead to see what it is. It turns out to be an empty plastic barrel with the word "toxic" printed on the lid. It appears to be watertight. Wilson thumps it like a drum, then hoists it up above his head and roars like one of the apes in *2001*. We'd like to take it back with us rather than leave it here to decompose, but the damn thing is just too big, and we end up abandoning it there, among the rocks. As we turn to retrace our steps, I think of Wallace Stevens's anecdotal jar: *The wilderness rose up to it, / And sprawled around, no longer wild.*

ANOTHER INCONGRUITY: in 1878, nine years after the invention of celluloid, a sales brochure promoted it as the salvation of the world. "As petroleum came to the relief of the whale," the copy ran, so "has celluloid given the elephant, the tortoise, and the coral insect a respite in their native haunts; and it will no longer be necessary to ransack the earth in pursuit of substances which are constantly growing scarcer." A hundred years later, in the public mind, plastic had gone from miracle substance to toxic blight. In 1968, at the dawn of the modern environmental movement, the editor of *Modern Plastics* argued that his industry had been unfairly vilified. Plastic was not the primary cause of environmental destruction, he wrote, only its most visible symptom. The real problem was "our civilization, our exploding population, our life-style, our technology." That 1878 sales brochure and that 1968 editorial were both partly, paradoxically, right. Petroleum did save the whale, plastics did save the elephant, not to mention the forest. Modern medicine would not exist without them. Personal computing would not exist without them. Safe, fuel-efficient cars would not exist without them. Besides, they consume fewer resources to manufacture and transport than most alternative materials do. Even environmentalists have more important things to worry about now. In the information age, plastics have won. With the wave of a magical iPod and a purified swig from a Nalgene jar, we have banished all thoughts of drift nets and six-pack rings, and what lingering anxieties remain we leave at the curbside with the recycling.

Never mind that only 5 percent of plastics actually end up getting recycled. Never mind that the plastics industry stamps those little triangles of chasing arrows into plastics for which no viable recycling method exists. Never mind that plastics consume about four hundred million tons of oil and gas every year and that oil and gas may very well run out in the not-too-distant future. Never mind that so-called green plastics made of biochemicals require fossil fuels to produce and release greenhouse gases when they break down. What's most nefarious about plastic, however, is the way it invites fantasy, the way it pretends to deny the laws of matter, as if something—anything—could be made from nothing; the way it is intended to be thrown away but chemically engineered to last. By offering the false promise of disposability, of consumption without cost, it has helped create a culture of wasteful make-believe, an economy of forgetting. The flotsam Ebbesmeyer and his beachcombers find is not only incongruous, it's uncanny, in the Freudian sense—a repressed fact breaking forth with the shock of strangeness into our conscious minds. As he, Charlie Moore, and other oceanographers can tell you, the ocean does not so easily forget. Chemically, it remembers. An environmental geochemist at the University of Tokyo has shown that on the open sea polyethylene acts as a toxin sponge, attracting and concentrating free-floating, non-water-soluble chemicals such as DDT and PCB, and plastics themselves contain a host of known carcinogens, including PCBs, that are safe only as long as they remain inert. Some of these compounds have also been recently identified as "gender-bending" endocrine disruptors. The American Plastics Council has called such findings "fascinating" but inconclusive, and many concerned scientists agree. A PVC duck in the bathtub may well be harmless to your child, but no one yet knows how post-consumer plastics that escape the landfill are altering the chemistry of the environment. The experiment, which began a century or so ago, is ongoing. In the meantime, Ebbesmeyer worries that plastics could do to our civilization what lead did to the Romans. He thinks the garbage patch may betoken nothing less than "the end of the ocean." The seas have become synthetic. The planet is sick. It can no longer recycle its ingredients, or purge itself of pollutants.

Some of the archaeologists in our beachcombing expedition have studied the midden heaps of shells that prehistoric seafarers left around the Pacific Rim. Garbage often outlasts monuments, and if ten thousand years from now archaeologists come looking for us, they will find a trail of plastic clues. It will be easy to date us by our artifacts. At the rate we're burning and extruding fossil fuels, the age of petrochemical plastics promises to be relatively short.

I have yet to reach the end of my own trail of clues. I'd like to go farther. I'd like Larry Calvin to ferry me two thousand miles west, to that spot in the middle of the North Pacific where thirteen years ago a container of bath toys tumbled into the sea. I'd like to ride a container ship through a winter storm and return with it to Guangdong Province, where low-wage factory workers manufacture 70 percent of the toys we Americans buy—about $22 billion worth—71 percent of which are made of plastic. I've read disturbing reports about the Chinese toy industry, and now when I read Eric Carle's *10 Little Rubber Ducks*, which was itself manufactured in China, and come to the scene of the woman in the brick-red dress painting brick-red beaks with her little paintbrush, I can't help but think of Huangwu No. 2 Toy Factory, where, according to the nonprofit China Labour Watch, in order to earn the legal minimum wage of $3.45 for an eight-hour day, a piece-rate worker in the spray department "would have to paint 8,920 small toy pieces a day, or 1,115 per hour, or one every 3.23 seconds."

Did workers make the Floatees under similar conditions? Before leaving for Sitka, I called The First Years, Inc., which has recently been bought out. The current management seemed to know less about the Floatees than I did, or pretended to. There was no way they could tell me which factory produced that yellow duck of mine, they said. I would like to know the provenance of everything. I would like to follow the duck back into the blow molding machine, back into the resin extruder, back to the petroleum refinery, back to the oil field or coal mine whence it came. But for now, it's time to give up the chase. In 1827, returning from another failed attempt to find the Northwest Passage, Lieutenant Parry, upon learning that he was to become a father, sent a letter home to his pregnant wife: "success in my enterprize is by no means essential to our joy, tho' it might have added something to it; but we cannot, ought not to have *everything* we wish. . . ."

On Kruzof Island, I find that for the first time since Bellingham my cell phone is picking up a signal. I call my wife and tell her I've decided to fly home sooner than planned, just to be safe. A week after my return, following a difficult, thirty-hour labor, my wife will give birth to a son, the sight and touch of whom will dispel my usual, self-involved preoccupations and induce a goofy, mystical, sleep-deprived euphoria. My wife will cry, and when she does so will I. These will be tears of joy, of course, but also of exhaustion and of awe and, truth be told, of sadness. Holding my son for the first time, I will feel diminished by the mystery of his birth and by the terrible burden of love, a burden that, requiring hopefulness, will feel too great to carry, but which I will take up nonetheless.

In the meantime, back on Kruzof Island, there is Fred's Creek to cross.

Tired, loaded down with our plastic bag of scavengings, Ebbesmeyer is having a hard time fording the stream. He picks his way carefully up into the trees, places his foot on a partially submerged rock, but hesitates. His breath is short and his footing poor. The rest of our party has continued on without us. I wait. "Throw me the bag," I call to him, and he does. It lands with a splash at the edge of the creek. I met the aging oceanographer in person only a week ago, but I feel oddly protective of him, oddly filial. I watch the trees for bears. Finally he is over to the other side, and we walk together back to the landing on the beach and wait for Larry Calvin to come for us.

The Egg and I

KATIE CAMPBELL

As a college sophomore trying to decide between a journalism or literature major, Katie Campbell thought she had hit on the perfect solution: "Wouldn't it be great, I remember thinking," she says now, "if I could tell journalistic stories with a novelist's voice? I would combine the best of both worlds and come up with a hybrid that could accomplish more than either fiction or journalism alone." (Then she discovered Tom Wolfe's The Right Stuff *and realized others had already had this idea.) This story first appeared in* Etude, *an online journal published by the University of Oregon School of Journalism and Communication.*

Two five-inch syringes with bright orange caps have been placed atop the white linen of the grand banquet table, like little sterile centerpieces. The table sits in an elegant meeting room—arched floor-to-ceiling windows, rich floral carpet—on the second floor of a posh downtown Portland, Oregon, hotel.

Although I pretend not to notice, I can't stop staring at the needles, and neither can the three women seated to my left. The four of us have never met, but I know we have more in common than aichmophobia. We're all height-and-weight proportionate, cancer-free, nonsmoking, college-educated twenty-somethings.

And we're considering donating our eggs.

"It could take months before a couple chooses you, but once you accept, the donation process takes as little as six weeks," says Catherine, the donor agency representative, a woman who looks as though she could be a plus-size model, hefty but curvy with intense dark eyes and a flashy smile.

She invites us to open to the sample calendar inside the information packets, which have been set before us as though they were the main course.

Week One: donor matched with couple.
Week Two: psychological evaluation and legal consultation.
Week Three: physical assessment and genetic testing.
Weeks Four and Five: fifteen days of hormone injections.
Week Six: egg retrieval and $6,000 payment.

As we listen to the details, nobody squirms at the mention of the physical concerns: cramping, weight gain, and mood swings associated with the hormones; the risk of ovarian hyperstimulation, which can require hospitalization and has in rare cases lead to death. Nor do we react to the news that we could face a lawsuit if we back out midprocess. We don't even flinch when Catherine assures us, with a practiced smoothness, "There's nothing that links egg donation to infertility."

Only the syringes make us shudder. Our decades of experience with needles—all those vaccines and tetanus shots as kids—have told us how to feel about them: scared. But egg harvesting? None of us has been through that before, so we're not sure how to act.

While explaining the twice-daily injection regime, Catherine passes around the syringes. I uncap one and inspect it; it looks as thin and fragile as mechanical pencil lead. But the second one, the intramuscular, reminds me of a fat sewing machine needle that can plunge through denim. My hands sweat.

"Don't worry, the big one is used only once. It's the final shot, the 'trigger shot,' which prepares the ovaries for retrieval," Catherine says. "By then you're used to giving yourself the injections. Donors tell me it's no big deal."

I want to believe her. The entire process doesn't sound dreadful; it actually seems simple and straightforward. But a refrain keeps playing in the back of my mind, asking, "Could it be that easy? Can I actually do this?"

As I muse, I realize I'm staring at a sleeping baby—bald, button-nosed and eyebrow-less—resting in glossy Technicolor on the cover of the donor information packet. The coral-colored infant has a generic look, like it could be a photo of me as a newborn.

When I was born twenty-seven years ago, the option to become pregnant through another woman's eggs didn't exist. The first pregnancy accomplished with a donated egg occurred in 1984 in Australia and was considered at the time to be a breakthrough childbearing option for women either born without ovaries or whose ovaries had failed because of early menopause, radiation, or chemotherapy.

In the decades since, egg donation has spurred much controversy as people saw using donor eggs as a way to prevent passing on undesirable traits as serious as genetically transferable diseases and as superficial as male-pattern baldness. But, ethical questions aside, egg donation has become a proven method for prolonging a woman's childbearing years far beyond the norm. A woman at age forty-one has a 17 percent success rate getting pregnant with her own eggs, compared with a 50 percent success rate using eggs donated by a younger woman. (In December a woman in Spain used donated eggs from California to become, at age sixty-seven, the oldest recorded woman to give birth.) In the 1990s the average egg recipient was in her thirties. Now she's forty-two and a half. The use of donor eggs has tripled in the last decade. More than fifteen thousand donor eggs were used in United States in vitro fertilization procedures in 2004, the most recent year of data available.

Today US egg donation is an estimated $38-million-a-year, largely unregulated industry. In many countries, including Canada, Britain, and France, it's illegal to pay donors for eggs. That's the rule here as well, but donors are allowed compensation for personal effort, time and expense. Between five and ten thousand dollars has been deemed ethically appropriate by the American Society for Reproductive Medicine. But no limit is enforced. In some cases, infertile couples negotiate directly with young women who have been known to charge upward of twenty thousand dollars for each time they donate.

In most cases, infertile couples find donors through three main routes: by asking relatives or friends who may donate for free, by posting personal advertisements online or in college campus newspapers offering as much as fifty thousand dollars to the right young woman, or by working with an egg donation agency, which acts almost like a dating service, recruiting candidates and posting nameless profiles for couples to peruse, helping them find the right match.

That's how I became interested in donating, through a recruitment advertisement that read, "Women: Help In Medical Infertility/Ovum Donation! Make $5,000–$10,000." I saw it last August as I searched an online job bank for work in Eugene, Oregon. I was starting grad school there in a month and was looking for a way to cover my living expenses while in school. After screens of eight-dollar-an-hour home-health aide ads, the five-figure ad grabbed my attention.

Like me, most who consider donating list the money as what first attracts them. College-age women make up more than 75 percent of US donors, and selling eggs is often seen as a quick way to make substantial cash. One recent survey found donors were most likely to use money to pay for school loans and expenses, followed by savings, credit card debt, and house and car payments.

I didn't call the number in the ad in August, but, after the first few months of school that fall, I ran out of money, couldn't pay my portion of the rent, and was falling behind on my credit card bills. I figured I needed between five and six thousand dollars to get through the year. Hating the idea of being deeper in debt through school loans, I thought donating my eggs might be the answer.

THE FIRST PERSON I mention my idea to is my boyfriend, Michael. We've been together for four years, both of us adventurous spirits drawn to escapades many wouldn't even consider, like skydiving or snorkling with sharks. After a year of long-distance dating, we took a wild leap together. We quit our stable jobs and moved to Central America for two years to teach. Living abroad wasn't the easiest baptism into couplehood, but navigating a foreign land and language together taught us to be a team. Michael is better at that than I am though. My strong-willed independence, an asset in many ways, also makes me less considerate in making joint decisions. So when I bring up egg donation with Michael, it's not so surprising that I'm more interested in hearing my own voice than in listening to his.

Two hours into filling out the application, I read the question, "Is your boyfriend/partner supportive of your decision to be an egg donor?" and suddenly realize that I don't know. I've just assumed.

"Are you okay with this?" I ask, over my shoulder, eyes still fixed on the computer screen.

He chooses his words carefully: "I'm okay with it as long as it doesn't hurt you."

Typing his words into the form, I log that in my head as, "If I decide I really want to do this, I have to persuade him that it's safe." I don't give his concern much heed, though, because in terms of health hazards, he tends to be unduly cautious. If food touches the ground, even for a second, he won't eat it. He often carries emergency hand sanitizer. He would use 85 SPF sunblock if he could. I think his better-safe-than-sorry philosophy is excessive. But most of the time I find a way to appease him. This time it'll require some research.

After four hours, I've logged my medical, family, and sexual histories and answered a list of questions that seem more suited to an Internet survey:

Favorite color? Blue
Glass half-full or half-empty? Half-full
Blood type? O+
High School GPA? 3.85

At the end I look it over and wonder, "Am I egg donor material?"

Fanning out childhood photos on the floor, I choose ten from ages two to twenty-six, as requested on the application, avoiding the awkward pre-teen years of the frizzy perm and tapered, stonewashed jeans. Scanning the pictures, I don't see anything extraordinary. Nothing really stands out, except my lack of height and my expressive blue eyes, the only feature that garners regular compliments. Otherwise I'm common, too common, I've always thought. All my life people have said things like, "You look just like my niece." People stop me on the street regularly because they think they know me.

Being ordinary can be maddening. I spent my teen years to trying make my appearance stand out, wearing yellow overalls or white go-go boots and dying my hair black when everyone else was going blond. But I can't help but think that my natural girl-next-door look might actually help this particular cause.

A couple of weeks after I submit my application, I attend the egg consultation, where I notice that the other young women are all attractive, slender, and of average height. Two are sisters with black hair that shines like patent leather, standing out against their skim-milk skin. The other woman's hair is sepia brown. She's busty with hazel eyes and thick Angelina Jolie lips. They're all good-looking, maybe too good-looking. I wouldn't want their eggs. I'd choose a donor who looks more like me.

"Each couple is looking for something different," Catherine tells us. Usually couples have already spent as much as one hundred thousand dollars on fertility therapy using the mother's eggs. It will cost another thirty thousand dollars at least to try to get pregnant through donor eggs. The investment is significant, and they tend to be choosy. It's not necessarily superior characteristics they're after, she tells us. More often they're looking for something specific that matches the mother. The deal sealer could be hair color, physique, race, artistic abilities, or an affinity for chocolate and classical music. Certain characteristics will bring a higher price though. Right now people are paying more for Asian and Latino eggs. When one of the sisters asks about our chances of getting chosen, Catherine says the agency currently has three hundred donors and three times as many couples looking for eggs.

"It's just a matter of time," she assures.

As the session closes, I'm still processing everything Catherine has told us. Donation, she has explained, is a simple, twenty-minute surgery, in which a thin, hollow, twelve-inch needle takes a shortcut through the vaginal wall to the ovaries where ten to twenty eggs are sucked out, becoming the legal property of the couple. I've never had surgery before, never been sedated, but the thought of being in a twilight fog makes the procedure seem much more palatable.

Catherine hands out forms for us to sign, giving our permission to post the personal profiles online for couples to view. My pen hovers as I scan the fine print, looking for anything that should worry me. I glance up to see the other donor wannabes scrawling their signatures. I hesitate.

"This isn't my final decision," I tell myself. "I'm just joining the pool of candidates." But as I hand Catherine my signed form, I feel as though I've just placed myself on a conveyor belt leading somewhere I am not sure I want to go. I'm standing and staring into space when I notice Catherine's impatient look; it says, "Unless you have a question, you need to leave." Loitering at the entrance is the next round of donors to court.

In the hotel elevator, a mirrored box, my own face startles me. The light layer of foundation I thought I ought to apply this morning looks like dried vanilla cake mix under the harsh lights. Makeup isn't my style. I prefer all-natural everything. I avoid antibiotics. I've sworn off headache medications, antacids, cough medicine, and any other meds that treat the symptoms and not the root cause. I eat organic when I can afford it. I'm not even on birth control.

Could I cope with heavy-duty, ovary-stimulating hormones?

"It would only last for a couple weeks," I tell my reflection. "You're tough. You could handle it."

I hang on to that thought for now, but deeper questions are forcing their way into my consciousness: Could I deal with knowing a genetically related child of mine exists somewhere?

"YOU SHOULD READ this when you get a chance," says Michael, placing a magazine before me, the pages curled back. I ignore the article for a week, hoping to avoid a discussion of the story, which is about a thirty-four-year-old who donated sperm anonymously at age eighteen and was found last year by the product of his donation, a thirteen-year-old boy. The sperm bank hadn't protected his identity well enough for today's Internet age, where almost anyone can be found through online social networking sites.

"What if a child fifteen years from now wants a relationship with you?" Michael asks, when we finally have the discussion.

"Well, he or she will have parents, so it's not like the kid would be looking to me to be a mom. I guess I wouldn't mind meeting with a child to answer medical history questions."

"But what if he or she wants more?"

"I suppose I would decide then and set boundaries if I didn't want a relationship."

"But can we really set boundaries like that?"

He has a point. But I'm more intrigued than concerned by this scenario. I hate to admit it, but I find the drama appealing. As an adolescent, my best friend told me her family secret: Her older sister had birthed a child as a teen and given it up for adoption. As I gasped in shock, imagining this baby out there with some other family, I was silently wishing my family had some kind of parallel mystery. I pondered the possibility of a long-hidden sibling showing up at our door one day, making our lives suddenly interesting.

I can tell that Michael is not keen on our lives suddenly becoming interesting in that way.

A WEEK AFTER the consultation I receive a call. It's Catherine. She tells me a couple in Orange County is interested in me. I'm shocked, excited, and even a little proud. Somebody thinks I'm egg material!

"The couple is even willing to wait until the end of the school year. That way I won't have to be on hormones while we're in school," I tell Michael. He's standing in our kitchen peeling an orange. I'm sitting on the floor looking at the calendar. I haven't noticed that I stopped speaking in the hypothetical, but he has. I've begun replacing my "ifs" with "whens" as I speak of egg donation. When he doesn't respond, I look up to see him avert his eyes.

"You feel strongly about this," I say, disappointed.

"Have you already made a decision?" he asks.

"No."

"Can we talk about this?"

"I haven't done enough research yet. I told them I needed two weeks. Let me do more research, before we talk. Okay?"

While I truthfully hadn't decided, I could tell that he had—and I wasn't ready to hear him out. I wanted to fully consider the decision myself and gather the evidence, if necessary, to defend my position.

Michael agreed to wait.

THE NEXT DAY I consult my gynecologist.

"Well, the procedure itself isn't very invasive," she says. "But we don't know much about the long-term effects."

Data on egg donation, I discover, has only been tracked since 1995 by the Centers for Disease Control and Prevention, but all they do is require the 428 US fertility clinics to disclose the number of donated eggs used in fertility treatments and their success rates. Data related to the long-term physical, psychological, or emotional health effects on donors are scattered, conflicting, or nonexistent.

As I learn this, I remember Catherine's comment from the consultation about nothing linking infertility to egg donation. Technically, she was telling the truth, but it seems dishonest because nobody has been tracking whether egg donation leads to infertility or any other long-term effects.

Only since California voters approved a three-billion-dollar embryonic stem cell research program in 2004 have scientists become interested in understanding the potential dangers of donating. Recruiting donors for stem-cell research has been a challenge because so little is known about the medical and psychological risks. The California Institute for Regenerative Medicine announced last fall it would sponsor the first study on the subject. The findings were published in February, the same week my donor profile posted to the Internet, but I didn't know that then.

LIKE MOST PEOPLE, I'm more aware of sperm donation than of egg donation. It's been around longer and is more accepted. Artificial insemination through donated sperm has been practiced for more than a century but was popularized in the 1970s as a standard way to treat infertility. Today physicians around the world provide artificial insemination services to hundreds of thousands of women. Twelve years ago my aunt tried in vitro fertilization with donated sperm. She always knew she wanted children but couldn't have them naturally. For her and so many infertile couples, in vitro fertilization has the power to make the impossible possible. After three unsuccessful tries, she gave up.

Remembering this has struck something deep in me. Maybe the money isn't at the heart of this. Maybe, for me, it's the chance to give a gift to someone like my aunt.

For the next week I think less and less about the six thousand dollars, even as I think constantly about the impending decision. One moment while driving, a feeling of sureness wells in my gut. Donation feels right. It feels almost like a calling.

But moments later, I'm conflicted. How could I know that the couple receiving my eggs would be as worthy as my aunt? The majority of in vitro fertilization patients are Caucasian women in middle to upper socioeconomic groups. What if these Orange County people are two close-minded, elitist workaholics who think television is a parenting tool? I start to wonder if I'd prefer to meet them before donating. Would that help me decide?

But a few days later, deep in research mode, I encounter the story of a young woman from Alamo, California, who donated eggs to a beloved aunt and uncle when she was nineteen. Now thirty and a mother herself, she says she never fathomed all the emotional problems she would face. When she started thinking about having children herself in her midtwenties, she began having maternal feelings toward the child conceived with her eggs. Egg donation eventually destroyed the relationship she had had with her aunt and uncle.

Now I see why many donors prefer anonymity. Not knowing the details might make it easier to detach emotionally. Maybe I can simply imagine this Orange County couple as I'd like them to be. They could be professors, born educators, natural parents. She teaches something right-brained like physics. He's a poet. Together they'll raise an intellectually balanced, emotionally stable child. That sounds about perfect.

Michael walks in the room, and my reverie shifts gears. In this new daydream, I plant an imaginary toddler in his arms. The child prattles questions while Michael, ever patient, explains the world. It's a sweet scene, a scene for the future. We've talked about having kids, but the day for that is far off still.

I have hundreds of eggs that will go unused, though. Surely I can spare a dozen.

A FEW DAYS later, I ask Catherine if she can arrange a phone conversation with an experienced donor. I want to hear about the procedure firsthand. She sets me up with Monica, a single, twenty-four-year-old college student in California, who went through her first donation cycle at the end of January. Monica decided to donate after her twenty-one-year-old sister did so last summer.

The side effects were minimal, she tells me, just a sore tummy, bloating, and slight bruising around her bikini area because of swelling ovaries (stimulated ovaries expand from the size of walnuts to oranges to accommodate ten to twenty eggs instead of the usual one per month). The worst part, she says, are the daily injections;

she'd never given herself shots before, but by the end of the first week it was easy, even the fattest needle only hurt for a second.

She didn't even have mood swings, she says. "I actually felt happier than normal."

All she remembers from the surgery itself is waking up a little teary-eyed and crampy. She felt emotional, not because she had been so attached to her eggs, but because the process was over so quickly. She'd become attached to the idea of giving her eggs away. And now that it was over, she felt sad.

"I almost would have done it regardless of money," she says, although she admits that before she got the check, she was broke. She says she donated first and foremost to help an infertile couple. She had heard so many stories of couples breaking up over infertility issues. As a child she hated watching her parents get divorced. She couldn't save their marriage, but she's hoping her eggs can save someone else's.

THE RESULTS OF that first-of-its-kind study of the medical and psychological risks of egg donation are actually encouraging. Of the hundreds of thousands of cases they reviewed in which women underwent ovary stimulation and egg extraction for personal use or donation, only a fraction of 1 percent experienced short-term effects that were severe. The report also says nothing in the present data links fertility drugs to a higher risk of infertility or uterine or ovarian cancer.

But I'm discouraged to read the final summation, where one point is glaringly clear: There is no long-term data. No registries track the subsequent health of women who have eggs extracted.

Overall the report makes donation seem reasonable and not as dangerous as I first imagined. It gave better odds than many other things I'm willing to do every day, driving a car, for example. I ask

Michael to take a look at the report, hoping his concerns will be allayed.

"Did you see that somebody died from this?" he asks, referring to the one case of death by ovarian hyperstimulation in the nation.

"Yeah, one person *ever*. One in hundreds of thousands," I say, thinking I better not tell him about the few cases of brain damage I've read about. Why am I protecting this decision I am not admitting that I've made yet?

"Some ... one ... died ... from ... this," he says, emphasizing the words so that they might have enough *oomph* to break through the wall I've raised.

"But thousands of others do it without having any problems. Look, this chick has donated five times and she's going for round six," I say, showing him an online advertisement I've just found. He's not impressed.

"This isn't something trivial," he says. I bristle at the tone; it sounds as though it's coming from someone looking over the top of reading glasses at a child. "Sure, maybe it only happened to one in how many people," he continues, softening. "But it happened. And what if it happened to us? When is the risk small enough to ignore?"

I don't have a good answer for him. So I say nothing and focus on the computer where I see screen after screen of discussion boards full of anecdotal evidence, countless making-dreams-come-true stories from parents and donors. I still see the dangers as minimal.

"It can't be that bad," I say, under my breath.

Sunday morning. I lie in bed and stare at the ceiling. Today is the due date for my final answer. Through these weeks I've steadily crossed concerns off my initial list, but there's one looming. I've been avoiding it, but I can't anymore. It's lying beside me.

"Do you want to talk about this?" Michael asks again. It's the same question he's repeated patiently during these two weeks. I've been shrugging it off, but this morning I hear what he's been trying to say: "Are you ready to listen to how I feel?"

I'm silent for a moment. We're still and quiet, but the tension, which has been building for two weeks, is nearing a crescendo. I don't want to have to persuade him. I don't want to sell him on egg donation. Can't it be enough that donating just feels right to me?

"Okay," I say, unable to hide the reluctance in my voice. "Let's talk." His intense brown eyes look straight into mine.

"I just think this decision is shortsighted. There are too many risks." His words are calm but resolute. "In the big picture of our lives, six thousand dollars is a pittance. It's nothing."

"But . . . I really believe this is a good thing to do . . ."

My frustration is morphing into anger, and I turn on my side away from him, seeking space to understand my feelings. They are my eggs. It's my body. Why can't it be just my decision?

He eases his arm through the gap between my neck and the pillow and slides close. As I let myself lean against him, I suddenly understand that this is not about asserting my independence. This is about deciding to be a couple and make what could be a life-altering decision as we should make all important decisions—together. My eggs don't belong to him, but our futures are intertwined. And ignoring that would be disregarding the partnership we've created.

My tears surprise us both. I didn't realize until that moment how attached I'd become to donating my eggs. I'm filled with a sense of loss, but at the same time, I realize what's at stake here: our relationship, the life we intend to share with one another, our future. I turn to him.

Figurines

EMILY BERNARD

"Writing is my gift to myself, but it is also the best thing I have to give to anybody else," observes Emily Bernard. "The older I get, the more things in the world confuse me. I write because I feel certain that you must feel that way, too." In this previously unpublished essay, Bernard tackles the often confusing and uncomfortable topic of race in America, using the story of a pair of figurines to explore her experiences in a mixed-race (and -class) marriage.

There are two wooden figures on my husband's desk. Figurines. They are meant to resemble humans, black humans. African Americans.

Every time I enter my husband's office at home, which is several times a day, I look for these figurines. Sometimes they are hiding under mail and memos. Today they are exposed. They lie flat on their backs. Their little wooden legs dangle off the edge of a fraying green silk box John has owned since before I knew him. Inside the silk box are two silver balls that chime when he rolls them between his fingers.

"They're Chinese," he says one morning, "to relieve stress." He looks up at me and smiles. I am warmed, as always, by the sight of him in his morning face: open and vulnerable. Defenseless.

The figurines are black *and* black. Meaning, they are black in the racial sense, like me, and black in the literal sense. Their faces and arms are as dark as the middle of the night. The female figurine wears a dull red dress with painted flowers and a kerchief on her head. The male has little tufts of hair around his head. He wears blue overalls with a pocket on the right side. Both of their mouths hang open in circular Os. Their eyes are vacant white dots, no pupils.

The figurines didn't always belong to us. We found them originally in the home of my in-laws. They were sitting above the *Four Freedoms,* the quartet of Norman Rockwell images. First, *Freedom of Speech* (a working man stands up at a town meeting); then, *Freedom of Worship* (heads bent in prayer); then, *Freedom from Want* (a Thanksgiving dinner); and finally, *Freedom from Fear* (a couple putting their children to bed). After nearly ten years of visits to my husband's family, I now think of these images when I think of Norman Rockwell. But I also think of the only Norman Rockwell painting I knew growing up, long before I had in-laws: *The Problem We All Live With.* It features a black girl, Ruby Bridges, being escorted to school by white federal marshals. "Nigger" and "KKK" are scrawled on the wall behind her. John grew up with *Four Freedoms,* and I grew up with Ruby Bridges.

Family (1)

John, my husband, grew up in Lenox, Massachusetts. His parents still live in his childhood home. His parents, my in-laws, are good people. They care about decency, fairness, other people: the right things. They are canny, smart. My father-in-law did not attend school beyond the sixth grade, but from him I have heard the most astute analysis of the Bush Administration that I have heard or read anywhere, from anyone. He has a sly sense of humor; he is a careful observer; he can fell a tree with his bare hands.

"Is it true that Pop can fell a tree with his bare hands?" I ask John.

"Well, he can take down a tree without any mechanical aids," John replies.

My father-in-law and his brothers built the house John grew up in.

My mother-in-law's charms are undeniable. A word people use to describe her is "pip," as in: "Your mother-in-law is quite a pip." A phrase might be "salt of the earth." She is warmhearted. "Heart person" is an expression she uses to describe her kind of people. A heart person, as opposed to a head person. The older I get, the more time I spend in academia, the more I know that heart people are my people, too.

My in-laws might say that being heart people, in their case, has something to do with being Italian. Touching, laughing, and talking, really talking—these are acts of the heart, the emotions. My in-laws are defined by the heart, the body, but not by race. Asked whether she believes that being Italian means having a racial identity, my mother-in-law says, "That's a southern Italian thing."

When I came along, my mother-in-law fretted to John about what might become of our children, should we have any. But then my father-in-law quoted some statistics about the United States becoming more and more multiracial. "They say, in fifty years, most of the world's people will be brown," he said. With that, my mother-in-law put her worries to bed.

Landscapes (1)

I grew up in Nashville, Tennessee. Recently, I attended a party at my sister-in-law's house to celebrate the induction of John's nephew, Michael, into the Eagle Scouts. I got into a conversation with

Michael's troop leader. We talked about Vermont, where she went to college, and where I now live. She asked if I like it there, and I said yes. "I love the landscape," I said, and as the words came out, I realized that they were true. "It must remind you of Tennessee," she said, "those rolling hills." I put them side by side in my mind: Tennessee and Vermont. "No," I said. "I grew up in the suburbs."

"I am not a visual person," I often say to people as a way of explaining why it is so hard for me to remember the simplest directions, like which stairwell leads most directly to my office at school. Every time I go to my office, which is nearly every day, I must repeat aloud the association I have devised to lead me in the right direction.

I am not a visual person, but I recognized the topography of Lenox on the first day that John took me home to meet his family. "This is the famous hill," John said, and pointed. It was the hill where a young woman on a sled crashed into a lamppost and died a death that inspired Edith Wharton's *Ethan Frome.* "Yes," I said, because I remembered it—or rather, I didn't so much remember it as feel it. I felt the hill as it had imprinted itself in my brain, beyond my brain. In my body, into the marrow of my bones, the center of my being. When I was a child, my family made yearly trips to Mississippi to visit my grandmother. Even as a child, I knew those trips were circumscribed by fear. Like most black families who traveled in the South in those years, we were aware of history, of where we were not welcome. I bent my head as rolling hills passed my window, and burrowed deep into *Ethan Frome, The Scarlet Letter,* the poetry of Emily Dickinson. Perhaps, even then, I was plotting my future, planning where I would eventually make my home, or simply discovering the home that had already begun to make me.

Traveling like that, head in a book, I missed some remarkable landscapes. I missed my childhood. When I imagine Nashville, I see only glistening car dealerships, palatial houses barely visible beyond gates with gilded monograms. Horses. I see shopping malls, acres of

parking lots. I see the Ku Klux Klan marching in front of the glistening car dealerships. "Roll up your windows," my mother would say to
my brothers and me. I see these things, and feel nothing.

"Like every black child in the South since Emancipation, I
dreamed of going North," I sometimes say, laughingly. It is true. And
now I am in New England, in the landscape of my fantasies, having
tunneled through some kind of literary underground railroad, and I
can't find my way to my own office without a mnemonic. I am in Vermont, where slavery was abolished nearly one hundred years before
the Civil War, and I miss black people. "You pick your white people,"
I joke, when friends and acquaintances ask how I am faring, all the
way up North, so much a minority. "They are everywhere, I have discovered." And I picked my white person. His name is John.

Family (2)

Over the course of our relationship, names have been important to
John and me. Right before we got engaged, I asked John, "What is
Jim's middle name?" Jim—James—is his brother. "Bernard," he said.
"James Bernard Gennari?" I asked, and John and I regarded each
other with wonder. My older brother's name is Harold James
Bernard. John and I had already established that our mothers also
share the same name: Clara.

Clara and Clara; James Bernard and James Bernard. There is a Yid-
dish expression for this: *Besheirt.* "It means 'meant to be,'" said my
close friend, Davida. The name thing certainly made it feel like destiny. And anyway, Davida is always right. John and I got engaged.

My father, who is from Trinidad, liked the fact of John's Italianness
right away. "Italians and Caribbeans," he said, "we care about food.
We care about family." I knew that what my father liked about John
was his masculinity, his smoothness. My father was impressed by
John, an intellectual who was unafraid of physical labor, who felt as

content in front of a football game as he did inside of a book. Like most fathers, my father may have wanted me to bring home someone who looked a little more like him, but John would do. He was certainly better than the spindly, sun-deprived academics I *could* have brought home. Better for my father, better for me. John would do just fine. He was something my father and I could finally agree upon. I was surprised by how much this pleased me.

My parents attended the same elite black college and went on to earn professional degrees; my father is a physician. The story of our different class backgrounds is a topic of endless fascination for John and me. We tell the story using different metaphors, like diners, how much John likes them, how much I don't. Maybe this says something about the vagaries of race and class, or maybe it only says something about aesthetic preferences and personality quirks.

The truth is I like diners: the ones in which I feel welcome.

Welcome

As I walked into the church where the Eagle Scouts' induction ceremony was being held, I braced myself for the looks. I put on my sweet smile and tried to make my face look open, like John's morning face. I smiled, and thought "open," but my body tensed. And there they were: looks upon looks. Curious, surprised, shy. I sensed people move aside involuntarily. I looked around for other brown people; there were none. I looked around for my in-laws. Suddenly a little girl ran up and flung her arms around my waist. It was Shenna, my niece. "Aunt Emily," she said. And then, out of the curious crowd, emerged my in-laws, one by one. There were more kisses, more hugs. I found Michael, uniformed and nervous, and forced a hug from him. "Come here," I insisted, just as any aunt would do. There was room for me here, and room for me over there. I chose over there, with John, his brother, Jim, and Jim's wife, Geraldine. "That's okay," said my mother-in-law, and gave my arm a squeeze. I thought of something a black female friend once said about Bill Clinton, about why he had so many African American admirers. "He's not *afraid* of black people," she said. "He's not afraid of our bodies."

Smooth

"A 'white Negro.'" This is what a female friend—non-white—called John when I first described her to him. She meant it derisively, and I forgave her. I felt then, and still feel, that her barb was borne of envy. She had recently complained to me that her own partner, who is white, is, woefully, "not smooth." I understood, and felt bad for her. I could forgive her because I knew when she eventually saw John, she would see that he was, undeniably, smooth. What is smooth? A man who takes a woman's coat; who holds the door open; who says, "Let me get that," when the check comes; who drives, in the summer, with one elbow out of the window. When my friend's partner drives, he jerks his foot up and down on the brake, as if it were the pedal of a sewing machine. *Smooth* is masculinity: fluid, assured, and delightful. John would say that it is Italian masculinity, and that it has very much in common with black masculinity. And, in fact, one of the things first pointed out to me by the woman who introduced us, a black woman, was how well John dances.

Marriage

I have picked many white people over the years. Friends, colleagues, and confidantes. Even my closest white friends called race the prob-lem when I complained about John in the early years of our relation-ship, outlining this or that grievance against him. "Well, that's because you are black and he is white," they would say. Each time I would hold the phone away from me, amazed. And then I would feel sad for them—yes, sad—locked, as they were, in the prison of black and white. These were progressive, open-hearted white people. My closest black friends, as well as my mother, however, seemed to get it: it wasn't intimacy with a white person that posed the greatest problem; it was intimacy with a man.

And yet we got married; I married the man. The longer I am married, the less I understand it. Marriage, that is, with a capital M. What does it look like? I don't know what Marriage looks or feels like, but I know what it feels like to be with John. Most of the time, it feels good. "When we are getting along, I feel like I belong on the planet," I told him once. "But when we aren't, I'm the loneliest person alive." He looked at me, considering. "That's beautiful," he said.

I know what some people see when they look at us together. When we first arrived at the University of Vermont, we attended an orientation session for new faculty. Most of the new faculty members were white; a few were not. When his turn came to introduce himself, John talked about his research. "I do work on jazz. I have a new project on the intersections between Italian American and African American culture." There were titters, and then frank laughter. The laughter was not malicious, just surprised, even pleasantly surprised. I knew this, and yet I felt annoyed, and exposed. Our union: an area of research, a new project. It was our first year of marriage. The laughter was not mean, but conspiratorial, like they were in on our grand joke. Maybe it *was* funny, but I did not know those people.

When I was dating, I knew I was supposed to be looking for a black man, of a certain background, with certain ambitions, to marry, but I wasn't. I was not explicitly looking for someone opposite to me to marry either, and my opposite was not what I ended up with. In fact, John and I are more similar than I would like for us to be sometimes. We share the same interests, the same books, even the same job.

We care about race. We *like* racial difference—to experience it and then discuss it. There are interracial relationships in which each party claims not to see race in the other party. I don't understand those couples, and consider their relationships fundamentally humorless.

John was once in one of those relationships. After reading an essay he wrote for a book I edited, *Some of My Best Friends: Writings on Interracial Friendships,* a former flame—non-white—wrote to tell him she felt sorry for me, since John obviously had so many "racial hangups." John printed out her e-mail and read it to me. We laughed together; no words were necessary.

Another former flame—non-white—told him he was "obsessed" with his class background. He told me this, and I laughed. "That's ridiculous," I said. This was early in our relationship. I think my laughter made him understand me a little bit more, made him believe I could eventually understand him.

Landscapes (2)

I am not a visual person, but one day I noticed the figurines in my mother-in-law's kitchen. I don't know how long they were there before I actually saw them. All I know is that, one day, there they were, their feet dangling above the *Four Freedoms*. My mother-in-law doesn't remember how or when they got there either. "I think they were a gift from the boys," she says, meaning John's nephews. "They know I like things to sit on that lip," she says, pointing to the lip of the frame, where figurines of a pig, a Singer sewing machine, and a farmer (white) now rest. "I don't think they meant anything bad by it," she says.

For years into my relationship with John, I did not want to talk about race around his family. When racial topics came up around the table, I felt seized with physical discomfort. My heart would beat hard, my face would heat up, my hands would clench into fists. I didn't want them to notice my difference from them. I didn't think they could understand my difference from them. I didn't think they could understand me.

I was afraid someone would say something that could never be taken back, that someone would take us to a place from which there would be no return. Each and every time, however, the discussion would move easily onto another topic: we were a family discussing current events at Sunday dinner. But look again: we were not a family. A lace tablecloth, a charming centerpiece, the tick of a grandfather clock. That was them, not me. I was visible, yes; so visible as to be completely out of sight. I was like the centerpiece in the middle of the table; I was sitting on the lip of *Four Freedoms*, wooden feet dangling off the edge.

Once I noticed the figurines, I could see them from anywhere. No matter where I was in the house they confronted me, their vacant white dots blaring: "You do not belong."

Home

Norman Rockwell lived in Stockbridge, Massachusetts, about five miles from where John grew up. Stockbridge borders Great Barrington, which was the home of W. E. B. Du Bois, and the site of Five Acres, the country home of James Weldon Johnson, who was killed in a car accident in Great Barrington in 1938.

Du Bois taught at Fisk University, where my parents went to college. When he was born in Great Barrington, his family had been residents of the county for nearly one hundred years. He drew upon his life there in his writing. I have often imagined Du Bois on my walks along the wide streets of Great Barrington. In my fantasies, he strolls along, in short pants as a boy, in his signature three-piece suit as a man. He walks easily. People waves and he nods; he is known. He is home.

John's home is in Lenox, but he was born in Pittsfield, the next town over. Back then, Pittsfield was a thriving community, largely because of General Electric, where his father spent years as a welder.

Pittsfield has a sizable Italian American population. It is a very different town from Lenox, which was once known as the "inland Newport." You don't see many poor people, black or white, in Lenox. You see them in Pittsfield, however. GE left and the town collapsed. These days, Pittsfield is desperately trying to revive itself. John's family recounts stories of its rejuvenation around the kitchen table.

Nashville has its own Pittsfield, called North Nashville, which like Pittsfield is currently undergoing gentrification. "The Titans—it really helps," my father says, explaining the effects of the recent boom in tourism.

When I was growing up in the 1970s, there were no shiny horses or gilded gates in North Nashville, as there are now. Instead there were boarded-up buildings, cars on brick stilts, people sitting on crates. Railroad tracks used to divide North and South Nashville. "When those freight trains would come by, you had to wait for thirty minutes, sometimes, before you could cross over to Charlotte Avenue," my father tells me. That is what it meant to be black in Nashville in those years.

"Did we have to wait on the freight trains?" I ask my father.

"Yes, we did. When we left Fisk, or church, and needed to get back to the other side of town." Much of our world was North Nashville, though we lived in South Nashville. My parents still live there.

"I don't remember that."

"Well, you were young. Why would you remember?"

I don't remember the trains or the waiting. But I remember the books I read, books set in New England. I remember how I wanted to live in the books more than I wanted to live in Nashville. In the books, the landscapes were pristine, even if they were bleak. There were no people sitting on crates, or signs in the front yards saying "Niggers go home." I do not believe it is a coincidence that I fell in love with a man from the pristine landscapes of my fantasies. The topography is in me. I walk along the streets of Great Barrington, Lenox, and Stockbridge and look around. There are humble structures: churches and clapboard houses, mostly white with black trim. There are cemeteries sprouting like fields of wildflowers. There is, always, a Main Street. My memories. I drink them in. I am home.

Memory

It takes years to get rid of the figurines. It takes years because I can't decide. One year, I fret so much that John insists we ask his mother to remove them. I talk him out of it. I don't want to create a rift between me and my mother-in-law. I don't want to call attention to our difference. Another year, I agonize over what impact those figurines will have on our children, the impact they have already had on John's nephews and niece. John agrees, and moves to take them down, but then I talk him out of it. Another year, a friend comes home with us, and I point at them, and she insists we talk to John's mother about them, and I say, "Maybe." John gives me a look, shrugs, and shakes his head.

Finally, one year, John goes home alone and talks to his mother at the kitchen table. I can see her listening, nodding her head. She takes them down, or John takes them down. He pockets them.

Today, I sit at the kitchen table with John and his mother. I ask my mother-in-law, "Do you remember those figurines?" I look up at *Four Freedoms,* and her eyes follow mine.

"Yes," she says. "I threw them out."

"No, you didn't," John says.

"I threw them out," she says.

"I have them," John says.

"What?!" she says.

"I'm going to use them in my Black Popular Culture class," he says.

"Oh," she says, and we move on to something else.

I don't say that I used them in my own class, Black Aesthetics: Race and Representation. We were talking about the figurines as an example of the racist collectibles that are now commercially popular. At the break, one of the students asked where I got the figurines. I said, "They were in the home of some people very dear to me."

"Who is that?" asked Hazel, a student very dear to me.

"My in-laws," I answered. I thought she would find it interesting, but instead, Hazel, and a few other students, looked alarmed and disgusted. I picked up the figurines protectively, embarrassedly. Suddenly, I saw how the little wooden figures looked to them, flat on the institutional white table, outside of my mother-in-law's kitchen. "It's complicated," I said.

It's complicated, and simple, too. Now that the figurines are gone from my in-laws' home, they are gone. Vanished. Their ghosts do not haunt me. On top of the lip, the Singer sewing machine, the pig, and the white farmer leave no room for memories.

The Writers in the Silos

Heidi Julavits

Creative nonfiction is often based on careful research, though that approach is a little tricky when the subject is the future. Nevertheless, in this essay written for a special issue of Creative Nonfiction *devoted to imagining the literary landscape of 2025, Heidi Julavits used current trends and conventional wisdom as her starting point. The scenario she imagines is fantastic and and necessarily speculative, but that doesn't mean it couldn't happen . . .*

It requires neither imagination nor acumen to predict that our current conglomerating, lowest-common-denominator, demographically targeted publishing industry will soon achieve its streamlined apotheosis—a single, worldwide, Exxon Mobil–owned literary empire offering a list of seven books twice per year. The lists for these two seasons—Holiday Gifts and Beach—will each include one of the following: a Dickensianly sprawling Antarctic thriller; a faux-intellectual, faux-experimental novel packaged with enticingly gimmicky swag (such as a French Existentialist pashmina); a World War

II historical novel wherein one or more ex-Nazis, in the flash-forward sections, live as kindly sausage-makers or residually evil schoolteachers; a winningly bitchy PTA tell-all, written by an overeducated mother of multiple-birth ADD children, living in a suburb of ecofriendly prefabs; a spiritual-conversion-after-brush-with-Ebola memoir; an inspiring life-lesson book for the left- or right-leaning (left for Holiday Gifts, right for Beach) written by a long-shot gay pro-life female minority ex-Klan presidential hopeful; and a "quick fire" cookbook for people with intimidatingly professional kitchens and no time, inclination, or skill to cook in them. Books will be compiled by a team of content providers; "the author" will be represented in photos and on tour by actually attractive people. Blurbs will be supplied by eBay sellers with the highest approval ratings.

This, we all know, is the inevitable future.

But while many have doomily predicted the death of literary culture as a byproduct of this future, few have wrestled with the possibility that deaths—actual human fatalities—will result. Indeed, in this not-so-distant and inevitable future, people will begin to sicken, and the weaker among them will perish. Initially, a batch of *E. coli*–tainted produce is fingered as the culprit, but eventually the source of the contagion is determined to emanate from a most innocuous source: books. The sick and the deceased, the investigation will show, each read two or more books published during the Exxon Mobil Holiday Gifts '25 season. A team of crack scientists in Hazmat suits will convene in Houston's Astrodome with box upon box of Exxon Mobil text product. While their tests will prove inconclusive—Was the literary DNA of books so tampered with that a viral mutation was unwittingly released? Have terrorists finally perfected the Text Bioweapon, thereby rendering all acts of reading potentially fatal?—the consumer panic will result in a conclusive cultural shift. (Death of the intellect is one thing, but actual death is quite another.) Exxon Mobil's book sales will drop to nearly nothing. In a public-relations recovery attempt, Exxon Mobil will assemble the hundreds of content providers who constitute its "authors" for an Inquisition-style trial. But since all work is e-mailed from afar and hybridized in a central editing location, it will prove impossible to track the source of the contagion, and the content providers will be released without even so much as an innocent scapegoat to justify their travel costs.

Suddenly, there will be no new books. Shockingly, this will sadden people and make them yearn for a golden literary era none of them actually experienced. The actual writers, those few who are still kicking around, will emerge from their surprisingly swank hovels (not writing will have served them well). At first, these writers—mostly buffed, androgynous sorts—will be spotted at farmer's market stalls, selling clipped sheaves of laser printouts beside the cider-donut lady. They will shake your hand, these writers. They will promise that their literary wares are the product of a single, careful mind, unmutated by mass production and untainted by viral collaboration, and since these writers are plain-looking people, even downright unattractive and badly dressed, they will seem instantly more believable and less possibly evil than the glossy actor-authors of recent yore. Soon a slogan will attach itself to this phenomenon—"Read Locally"—and the new AgriCultural movement will emerge. Writers will begin to form allegiances with small farmers, and soon every small farm will have a writer. The farmer and the writer will decide that mutual dependency and market diversification are the keys to survival: When the writer produces a less-than-stellar product, he will be buttressed by egg sales; when the farmer has a poor strawberry yield, he will be buttressed by the writer's pure and homey creative output.

Of course, the success of this system will mean that farms will begin to merge, and writers will begin to work in greater numbers on larger farms, and eventually people from afar will want to read the works of writers whose hands they cannot personally shake, and so the inevitable human impulse to slake all desires and improve efficiency (and thus profit) will mean that by the dawn of the next millennium, we'll be right back where we are today. But for a few decades at least, just before the seas rise above the writers' silos and drown us—oh, what a golden age of literature there will be.

My First Fairy Tale

VIJAY SESHADRI

*"The earliest memories I have are fugitive images and intense—
and more or less incomprehensible—feelings, so the literary problem of rendering them became one of context rather than text,"
says Vijay Seshadri. "The context I chose—a rumination on stories and storytelling—gave me a way to impart function and purpose to those memories . . . which up until the time I wrote the
piece had just been gathering dust in my inner attics." The result-
ing essay, which appeared in* Open City, *illustrates the staying
power of early memories, as well as the extent to which they are
often accessible, once a writer starts to focus on and try to make
meaning from them.*

1.

My first exposure, or the first exposure I can remember, to the
pleasures of narrative happened when I was a little over two
years old, in Bangalore, in the second half of the nineteen-fifties. My

father was in America, studying. My mother and I were living with my grandfather and his family in a house in the neighborhood known as Malleswaram. My grandmother had just died; the second- or third-earliest memory I have (the sequence of events is lost to me) is of making my way through a forest of adult legs to look into the room where she had been laid out on the floor, according to Indian custom, and was surrounded by her children, who sat in a semicircle and wailed and wept. My mother insists that I can't remember this, that I was too young, but I do, and remember many other things, too; the trauma of those weeks must have induced the birth of my consciousness. I remember the house was large, with mango and pomegranate trees and coconut palms in the garden and flowering bushes—hibiscus, I would guess—dotting the borders; with verandas, broad teak doors (I didn't, of course, know then that they were teak), broad windows open to the subtropical breezes, and cool marble floors, which left a smooth sensation of stone on the soles of my bare feet. It had a long driveway leading from the imposing iron gates in the wall that separated us from the street to the porte cochere at the main entrance. Sometimes a car, probably a Citroën but maybe an Indian-made Ambassador, would be parked there, its driver idling near it.

My grandfather was entitled to the car and driver because of his position in the administration of the state of Mysore, of which Bangalore was the largest and most important city. He was the chief engineer of the state and had reached a position eminent enough that it made the subsequent and rapid decline of his fortunes in the next decade even more unaccountable and shocking. His narrative is the one that dominates my mother's side of the family, and it has a tragic arc, given shape by the elements that often define tragedy—hubris (he was caste-proud, proud of his intellect, and indifferent, or seemed indifferent, to the vulnerabilities of others), fate (which took form in my grandmother's untimely death; in his diabetes, which he was too self-indulgent to control properly; and in the terrible, self-destructive rebellion of some of his children), and a series of incalculable, unforeseeable, and disastrous coincidences. It was anything but a fairy tale, and not just because it didn't have a happy ending. Unlike a fairy tale, it had no conclusion. Its morals were forever withheld; its meaning could never be resolved; nothing came full circle but, instead, trailed off into the enigmatic and incomprehensible. I sometimes think nothing is more important to my mother than finding a way of telling her father's story that will force it to resolve. She tells it over and over again, to herself, to us, to whoever will listen, re-creating in helpless, frustrated, Balzacian detail, in order to find an escape hatch of narrative conclusiveness and thereby free herself, the early triumphs, the pride they engendered, the recklessness of this self-love, and the horrifying fall, which she avoided witnessing by moving to North America with my father after he received his degree and won a postdoctoral fellowship in Canada. About that fall, for no reason I can see—since she was blameless and couldn't have imagined what would come—she feels unassuagable guilt.

Indians have a talent for grief. I remember a lot of crying going on in that house after my grandmother's death, weeks and weeks of it. Her many children would get together in little groups and talk and weep and weep again, or go off singly to weep in corners, on staircases, near the well in the garden. My babysitters were my teenage aunts, but because of their grief they were lax in watching over me. The house had a large interior courtyard, along one side of which, near the entryway to the kitchen, was a brazier of coals, over which, among other things, coffee beans were roasted in a round-bottomed pan. I must have been left to myself one day, and I decided it would be fun to run and jump back and forth over the brazier, which had been left burning and unattended. On one jump, I tripped and the coals scattered over my bare legs, giving me extensive third-degree burns. (I had the scars for a long time and I assumed that the discoloration of the skin on my legs was permanent, but looking just now, while writing this, at my legs, I find that, finally, no trace of the scars remains and the discoloration is entirely gone.)

I don't remember pain—the human body supposedly suppresses the memory of pain—but I do remember that I suddenly became the center of attention. I was carried up by the ubiquitous grief, as both an object on which it could focus and a distraction from it, and put in the bed my grandmother and grandfather once occupied (my grandfather wouldn't sleep in it anymore), a big four-poster in the biggest bedroom of the house. The doctor came, dressed my burns, and confined me to the bed for weeks. It was there, in a blistering South Indian April, while recuperating under the mosquito netting, that I first heard the story of the birth of Rama, incarnation of the divine principle, embodiment of kingly and husbandly virtue, slayer of the demon Ravana. The three wives of Darsaratha, King of Ayodhya, are barren. The king performs a sacrifice to petition the gods for an heir to his throne. Out of the sacrificial fire a divine messenger appears with a silver chalice full of *paisa,* an ambrosial liquid pudding, which Indians consume to this day, and which is made, in our household, of milk, sugar, cardamom, saffron, and either vermicelli, poppy seed, or tapioca. The king gives half the paisa to his first wife, Kausalya. She will be the mother of Rama, avatar of Vishnu. To his second wife, Sumitra, he gives half of what is left of the paisa. To his third wife, Kaikeyi, who will give birth to Rama's brother Bharata, he gives half of what remains (notice here the delicate hierarchical arithmetic at the heart of the domestic order of Indian kings). He bestows what little is left over on Sumitra, who because of this extra portion will give birth to twins—Lakshmana, Rama's shadow, and Shatrunga, bane of Rama's enemies.

2.

Do children like fairy tales? And, if children do like fairy tales, why do they like them? The answer to the first question has been deemed obvious by modern and contemporary culture (even though it doesn't follow that because fairy tales often have children as main characters they were told and subsequently written down for children). Yes, children like fairy tales (though I have known at least one child who couldn't stand fairy tales; his favorite bedtime story was about Hans and Peter, two boys in socialist Denmark who build a clubhouse out of odds and ends and invite their parents over for tea). And, moreover, as Bruno Bettelheim has told us, fairy tales have an important cultural function. They're therapeutic; they allow children to process the dark materials of experience. Fairy tales are useful, for both children and society, a notion which contains the answer to the second question. Children like fairy tales because they are an aid to cognition; they help them order the world around them. But is this actually the case? These assertions and explanations aren't self-evident, and seen a certain way they look suspiciously reductive. Could we possibly know what a child likes and why, or what the intensity of his or her approval is? How, for example, would I have responded at the age of two to a Nathalie Sarraute novel? Or what sort of stories was I telling myself? It's hard to say.

But I know that I liked the story of Rama's birth not because of its fairy-tale qualities—the magical potion, the number three, and so forth—or because it was an illumination of, or an antidote to, the grief floating around me, but because of the paisa. I've been told that the entire Ramayana was recited to me while I was recuperating under the mosquito netting in the house in Malleswaram, but the paisa episode is the only one I can remember from that time, and it is still the only one in that vast and various epic which has resonance for me, and that was because of the paisa itself. Paisa was a dessert I loved throughout my childhood, and food is something a two-year-old understands. I can make a case, in fact, at least to myself, that all the fairy tales I liked—the ones I encountered in the English-language school run by Anglican nuns, where I was enrolled at three;

in the elementary school in Ottawa, to which I was translated at the age of five; in the grade school I went to in Ohio—had something to do with eating. The wolf eats or gets eaten; the idiot girl (hasn't she figured it out yet?) eats the apple poisoned on one side; the birds eat the bread-crumb trail; the abandoned boy and girl eat the ginger-bread house and will soon, if they don't watch out, be nicely cooked themselves; Goldilocks eats the porridge (a delicious word that made my mouth water when I was a kid). I dislike Hans Christian Andersen's stories almost as much for the fact that his characters rarely eat in them, and certainly never with gusto, as I do for the punitive and hideous Calvinism that secretly infects each sentence.

I was a good eater as a child, and had a capacity for taking things as they came. I didn't have a trace of sentimentality about my grandmother's death (older and more vulnerable to human beings, I did grieve for my grandfather twelve years later, though I had hardly known him). I was puzzled at my mother's behavior, but not overly. Big things were happening around me in those weeks of death, grief, and burns, and I had snapped to attention. It would be years before events made as vivid impressions on me as the events of those weeks did. Also, and this has stayed with me, I developed, out of the different elements of which I was suddenly aware, an excessively precocious maturity about narrative, about stories and storytelling. I've read my share of fantasy fiction, but I have always taken greater pleasure in realism. I read Balzac all the time, and it would be nice to think that such a taste was vouchsafed to me in Bangalore when I was two. I enjoyed the story of Rama's birth. But I like to think that even then I knew it was just a story, while all the other things happening around and to me were anything but.

A Sudden Pull behind the Heart

Notes on an Epiphany One Afternoon in a Silver City on a Silver River

Patrick Madden

Years ago, Patrick Madden says, he realized "that what I loved to do most was think, without constraint, without pressure, without system. I wanted to be free (from the grind, from the workaday, from the hubbub), an idle speculator, engaging curiosities, examining the quotidian. Essaying is a way of sustaining thought, of finding and exploring and creating connections, and of making sense of life. It's a delicious pursuit, never dull, ever available and abundant." This attempt to tease meaning out of a brief experience first appeared in Portland Magazine.

This essay is about three words I can barely make out in Latin on the cupola of the Catedral Metropolitana on the Plaza de Mayo in Buenos Aires. It's about a flailing attempt, in words, to re-create some bit of epiphany. It is about the fact that every Thursday afternoon the grandmothers of disappeared children (they were mothers of the disappeared, too, once, but they have given up that hope) march in circles around the Plaza de Mayo, in front of the Catedral

Metropolitana, in front of the Casa Rosada, the seat of government, from whose balconies Evita Peron once rallied the *descamisados*, the shirtless, before her death at age thirty-three.

The grandmothers shuffle in their white shawls, in silent protest to the government that knows, to leaders and dealers left over from nearly a decade of "dirty war": military rule, mid-night raids, tortures and assassinations, and the trade in infants across the borders with Uruguay and Chile.

Among so many who lost children and grandchildren: Juan Gelman, a poet, who was not home when they came for him, whose son and daughter-in-law were taken in his stead; Juan Gelman, whose son ended up in a barrel in the river Luján, a bullet in the back of his head; Juan Gelman, whose pregnant *nuera*, his daughter-in-law, was taken to the Hospital Militar in Montevideo, where she gave birth and then was murdered; Juan Gelman, whose new granddaughter was then given to a policeman whose wife was barren. So many pregnant women taken, raped, tortured, executed, their babies kidnapped. This story from Argentina. This story from Uruguay. This story from Chile. Military men who went to church on Sundays, to the machine on Mondays, to beat and prod and submerge and shock and threaten.

Juan Gelman, a poet, self-exiled to Mexico, whose granddaughter was eventually found by the Grandmothers of the Plaza de Mayo, those women whose work the six other days of the week when they are not marching in the square is re-membering, re-constituting families, pestering government officials, pressuring the press, searching in archives and unmarked graves, and they did find Macarena, as they had found more than seventy children before her, and Juan Gelman was returned to his granddaughter in March 2000. She was twenty-three years old, living in Montevideo, Uruguay. Her mother's body has not yet been found.

On a Monday in early April, the feast day of St. Epiphanius, as my own country staged its invasion of Iraq, the grandmothers were not walking. As I walked about the Plaza de Mayo, I kept my eyes fixed; I sidestepped the dirty women languishing under the columns in front of the cathedral doors; I turned briskly to loose my garment from the grip of one who said "Please, anything you have, God bless you"; I eluded another who moved into my path. I half-saw signs scrawled with statistics and sad stories. My downcast eyes scanned the frayed flannel edges of blankets, then returned to tracing the grout between the stones.

I entered the cathedral to escape the rabble. In my head swirled the story of this silver land on its silver river: this unbelievable, this brutal, methodical, mechanical, cold, unfeeling, this rage for order, this Process of National Reorganization, this maniacal torture of misidentity: children the age of my children kidnapped, scattered, unknowing. It was a story I barely knew, knew only in broken ideas and images, my own imagination's impositions on a history that had been hidden, ignored, nevertalkedof. I wondered if the disappeared children like Macarena Gelman might carry in their very DNA some inkling of who they were, if they might have natural genetic tendencies to seek justice for the downtrodden. I wondered if they naturally boiled over into heated arguments with their "parents" whose ideologies must have been at polar odds with their real parents, at least.

Inside the cathedral it was almost silent. I saw the ornate arches, the wrought iron railings, the velvet chairs, the silver-plated altar, the faded frescoes, the gilded window-work, the guarded tomb of José de San Martín, liberator of Argentina, Chile, and Peru, born in rural Yapeyú, Argentina, of stately parents, educated in Europe, returned to set his people free. In a moment of calm, I cast my eyes upward forty meters to the cupola. There engraved, in Roman characters, I read three words: EGO VICI MUNDUM. It was all I could see within the rim.

Even before I could puzzle out its meaning, translate those words (think Freud, Caesar, French newspaper), I understood what it meant, and not only what it meant, but where it came from, who had said it, about what, and why. Jerome's Vulgate translation of John 16:33 reads, more completely: *In mundo pressuram habebitis: sed confidite, ego vici mundum,* which is to say "In the world ye shall have tribulation; but be of good cheer. I have overcome the world."

This was not the solution, a revelation for the revolution; this was not justice delayed and eternal rewards; it was no opiate. It was a sudden pull behind the heart, some opening to compassion, some inscrutable calm regardless, despite it all.

I left the cathedral then. Buoyed in spirit, introspective in mind, I walked out the cathedral doors, past the flyers in the foyers, beside the benedicted mendicants, among the twelve Corinthian columns that grow from south to north as the earth drops away to the river-sea, close to the crest calling out SALVUM FAC POPULUM TUUM, into the good airs. I did not notice then the carved bas-relief watching over me in the pediment above, but I have since studied it, and I tell you that in that stone on the cathedral in Buenos Aires there are sheep and cattle and calm camels in the corners above the cornices, in a reunion scene: ten repentant brothers and the brother they had disappeared, who was lost and then found, dead and then alive, sold by his siblings to be a slave and then turned their savior in time of famine. There is Jacob returned to his son Joseph; Israel's son is revealed, the ten are relieved, Benjamin is released. In this everlasting embrace the father and the son keep watch over the plaza: the speeches and protests, marchers and merchants, the weekly silent procession of old women in kerchiefs keeping vigil, searching, remembering, so we may not forget.

The ~~Suicide~~ Murder? of Joseph Kupchik

JAMES RENNER

In the process of writing, says James Renner, "I've discovered that nonfiction is usually more fantastic than anything I could imagine on my own. . . . I think creative nonfiction allows us to better appreciate the mysteries that surround us in the real world." Indeed, this story, which first appeared in the Cleveland Free Times, *is a kind of whodunit about a young man's death—was it suicide, or murder?*

In dreams, Joseph Kupchik never remembers that he's dead. Seems unaware that he plunged to his death off a parking deck in downtown Cleveland almost a year ago. It's always up to his twin brother, Johnathan, to give him the bad news.

The dreams started shortly after Joe died and haven't let up since. Sometimes the two of them are at home, playing video games. In this one, they're shooting hoops. Joe bounces the basketball against the backboard, into the net, then returns it to his brother.

Joe, you're dead, says John. *You died.*

But Joe only stares at him, uncomprehending.

He's confused, John thinks. *Or maybe I'm the one who's confused. Maybe this is real.*

It's not, of course.

Joe is dead in the Real World.

The cops think he committed suicide. But if it was suicide, he found an unusual way to do it. A growing number of friends and family believe Joe was murdered.

Either way, when John wakes up, he'll have to leave Joe behind. So let's give them a moment alone. They've got a game to finish just now.

JOE AND JOHN Kupchick were hard to tell apart. Both inherited their mother's deep, dark eyes and their father's coarse, burgundy-brown hair. The same smile and gently sloping shoulders. Joe was slightly taller and had a larger nose, and tilted his head when he met someone, almost bashfully. But they looked enough alike that John is reminded of Joe every time he looks in the mirror. He misses his twin and sometimes feels him, like an amputated limb. Their connection, that odd closeness that their sister Kate calls "the creepy twin thing," is still being severed.

The Kupchiks live in a modest two-story home inside a nondescript subdivision in Strongsville, domiciles of the shrinking middle class. Joe—"Kuppy" to friends—graduated from Strongsville High School in 2004. He wasn't much of an athlete; couldn't make a layup to save his life, friends say. But he played games of pick-up football in the neighborhood and loved watching the NFL on weekends, Green Bay in particular. He often wore a giant cheese head in the living room, though it's long been suspected he chose the team for its colors. Sometimes he made minor bets—a dollar or two—with John or his older brother, Michael.

In the fall of 2004, then-eighteen-year-old Joe and John decided it was time to discover their own destinies. John set off for the University of Dayton. Joe stayed home and enrolled at Cuyahoga Community College, taking accounting classes at the main branch in Parma.

During this time, Joe met many of his closest friends while working at Wendy's on Pearl Road. Joe was a crew leader and opened the store on Saturday and Sunday mornings. Megan Rachow, who still works at Wendy's, remembers Joe's knack for making endless shifts a little more entertaining. During lulls they played tic-tac-toe on the parking lot with chalk. Sometimes Joe put sandwich buns in the fryer. In retaliation for some prank she can no longer remember, Megan once put a ladle of cheese sauce in Joe's hat, but he noticed before putting it on. Out back one day, she offered him his first cigarette, the single puff coming out in loud coughs a moment later as he laughed and laughed.

That first year at Tri-C, Joe pulled a C average. He figured his shifts at Wendy's were impacting his studies, so he quit in the fall of 2005. His transcripts show an immediate improvement. That semester, Joe took a full course load and earned two A's and three B's. He also became treasurer of the Tri-C Philosophy Club. Around this same time, he discovered online gambling.

The bets were small at first. He and John anted up thirty-five dollars apiece to start an account at BoDog.com to bet on NFL games. They schemed over the phone and usually picked at least four winners in seven games. By Christmas, their initial investment of seventy dollars had ballooned to nearly sixteen hundred.

Then Joe began betting on college basketball on their account, laying down more money and losing more often than not. When John complained, Joe gave him half their winnings—about eight hundred dollars—and changed the password.

During the long winter break from school, Joe also started a new job at Steak n Shake in nearby Brunswick. He worked the grill at first and then began to wait tables. A co-worker recalls that Joe charmed many of his regular customers, but had a hard time fitting in with other employees. They picked on him for bobbing his head when he talked, a nervous habit. And for talking too smart. Joe complained to a close friend that co-workers would often change his schedule, giving him less profitable shifts. (According to a former manager of the Brunswick Steak n Shake, employees were allowed to change the schedule as long as someone showed up.) All Joe's parents knew was that before leaving for work, he always left a note with his hours on the kitchen counter.

The morning of February 11, a Saturday, Joe's father, George, gathered receipts and W-2s for the family's tax filings. He also planned to fill out student loan paperwork, so that Joe could transfer to the University of Cincinnati later that year. As Joe dressed for work—black pants and white button-up shirt—George stuck his head inside Joe's room.

"How much money do you have in your bank account?" George asked.

"Seven thousand dollars," Joe replied.

Before he left for work, Joe jotted down his work schedule for the day: noon to ten P.M. George heard Joe shut the door of his Honda Civic. The sound echoes in George's mind still; the last noise he ever heard his son make. It was a little after eleven in the morning.

Only later would George learn that Joe had lied about his savings account. Some of the money had been loaned out to family and friends, but a lot had gone toward online bets. That morning, Joe's balance was $4.46.

ADAM WORNER, age twenty-two, left the Blind Pig on West 6th that Saturday night around 1 A.M. and began the long walk back to his apartment on the east side of downtown Cleveland. His path led him down Ontario Street. As he passed Fat Fish Blue, he came upon the body of a young man lying on the cement, just inside a thin alley, below a nine-story parking deck. He wasn't the first one there. Later, he would say that he saw a black man, about his age, dressed in jeans and a nice jacket, standing over the body.

"I don't want to get into the blood and guts and gore of it," Worner tells the *Free Times*. He'll say only that the body belonged to a young man. That he was a bloodied wreck and unconscious, but not dead. That he was not wearing shoes. Worner used his cell phone to dial 911.

Sometime during the frenzy of activity as the EMS crew arrived and loaded the body into the ambulance, the black man quietly walked away. Worner is not sure he could recognize him if he saw him again on the street.

Officer James Foley arrived at the scene first and searched the garage. On the top floor, he found a Honda Civic with its driver's side door open, the keys dangling from the ignition, the engine turned off. The driver's seat was bloody, and a rolled-up white shirt covered in blood lay between the seat and the door, beside a bloody leather jacket. A pair of shoes rested on the floor under the steering wheel. A trail of blood snaked from the door to the railing. A six-inch fillet knife lay on the snowy cement a few feet from the car. Written on a piece of paper on the dash was Joseph Kupchik's name and home address. George later recognized the handwriting as his son's.

At 1:47 A.M., Joe arrived at MetroHealth Medical Center. EMS had placed him in a backboard and neck brace and had him hooked up to a ventilator. ER doctors discovered myriad injuries: broken ankles, a shattered pelvis, internal bleeding, and a punctured lung, the result of a stab wound in the left side of the chest, just below the collarbone. They tried to save him, but the damage was too extensive. Joe was pronounced dead at 3:08 A.M.

About seven hours passed before the Kupchiks learned any of this.

As they arrived home from church at 10:30 A.M., police and media showed up simultaneously. Within minutes of the parents' learning that their son was dead, Channel 5 was at the door seeking an interview. The family shut the reporters out to grieve alone, but the media smelled a mystery and weren't about to forget it.

DR. FRANK MILLER III performed the autopsy on Joe's body. There were some strange details, for sure. Take that stab wound below Joe's left collarbone. Dr. Miller discovered the wound was quite deep, and that the knife had traveled front to back, downward and left to right. That's Joe's left and right. So it didn't come in straight, but at an angle, pointing down and toward Joe's right side.

The other serious injuries were confined to Joe's lower body. His skull was not busted nor his teeth broken, even though he is presumed to have fallen nine stories—Dr. Miller maintains his injuries were consistent with a fall from that height. It appeared that Joe had landed feet first—both ankles, both legs, and four ribs were fractured. Miller also noted marks on Joe's stomach that looked like small cuts. There was no food in Joe's stomach, just a small amount of a red-brown liquid. Most likely it had been several hours since he'd eaten. The red-brown liquid was never identified.

Joe's clothes were examined, too. His socks were clean, but his pants were caked with a white substance that turned out to be calcium sulfate, a compound found in de-icing material. His T-shirt, once white, was now mostly red and stiff with dried blood. It had been cut off during surgery and mended temporarily, like Joe, so that it could be photographed.

Cleveland detectives Ignatius Sowa and James Gajowski were assigned to the case. They declined to be interviewed for this article, but the *Free Times* obtained a copy of their notes.

The detectives returned to the parking garage and pulled the video for the security camera that faces the entrance. Although they could not make out who was driving Joe's Honda when it pulled into the garage, the time on the video matched the time-stamped ticket discovered inside Joe's car: 1:04 in the afternoon. So the car was in the garage for more than twelve hours before Joe's body was found on the street below. (The only thing they know about his travels between leaving home and entering the garage is that he stopped at the Wendy's on Pearl Road where he'd once worked, ordering a chicken nugget meal at the drive-through.)

Near the space where the car was parked in the garage the detectives found a pack of Newport cigarettes, two pens, and a beer bottle. On the street they recovered Joe's belt buckle, which apparently had snapped off upon impact.

Sowa also noted that Joe had a roll of money tucked in his pocket: $103 (a ten, five fives, and sixty-eight singles). On the passenger seat they found Joe's book bag. Inside were two printed magazine articles, "Decisions about Death" and "The Harm That Religion Does." On the floor below was a textbook titled *Deviant Behavior.*

The detectives wondered what a preppy kid from Strongsville had been doing in a downtown parking garage for twelve hours. They wondered if it had something to do with the Ontario Café, a small bar next to Fat Fish Blue that turns queer after dark on weekends. They spoke to a regular twist known to frequent the club, but the man didn't know Joe.

Sowa and Gajowski interviewed co-workers at Steak n Shake. The schedule for the week of February 11 showed that Joe was supposed to come in at five P.M. They spoke to the managers on duty at that time, Amber Cooper and Matt Magale, who told them that because it wasn't a busy night, they decided not to call Joe's house when he didn't show up for work. One employee said Joe had appeared agitated during his Friday-night shift and had forgotten to clock out.

Then the detectives learned of the extent of Joe's gambling habit. In a two-day period in January, Joe had lost eighteen hundred dollars. It appeared he'd withdrawn money from Charter One after a significant loss to his BoDog account. The night before he died, Joe placed a $450 wager on college basketball.

They also reviewed the contents of the computer disks found in Joe's bag. Shortly before he died, Joe had written this passage: *Expectations can either be positive or negative, but rarely am I ever right. Whenever I anticipate an event probably to make my dreams come true, something usually happens where the situation turns into a nightmare.*

Adding this up with the gambling, the somber reading material, and the helpful note with name and address left in the car, the detectives informed the coroner's office of their conclusion: The kid had sat in his car for hours, stabbed himself, then jumped from the building. Suicide.

Dr. Miller had seen cases in which people utilized multiple methods of suicide. There was the man who roped a noose around his neck before putting a shotgun in his mouth, for example. So he accepted the detectives' theory. Dr. Miller postulated that the scratches on Joe's stomach were probably "tick marks" where he'd tried to stab himself before finally getting the nerve to really push. He wrote up his own report for the county coroner, Dr. Elizabeth Balraj.

Again, the media knew before the Kupchiks.

GEORGE KUPCHIK, Joe's father, is director of operations for a company that manufactures silicone sealants and greases. The job is as exciting as it sounds, but after years of analyzing data George's mind has become a finely tuned machine. When something isn't working at the factory, it's his job to find out why. He has learned from experience not to make rash decisions until he has reviewed all the evidence.

George was watching television on May 22, when a local reporter for 19 Action News announced that his son's death would most likely be ruled a suicide. The ruling wasn't official yet, but the news had leaked out of the coroner's office as easily as blood from a hemophiliac's paper cut.

George demanded a series of meetings with Dr. Balraj and her staff to convince them that his son was murdered before the ruling was made official. George presented Balraj and Miller his own report on Joe's death, which he'd worked on during the Cleveland police investigation. He titled it: "Questions and Facts about Joseph Kupchik."

There were many more questions than facts.

- Where is Joe's cell phone? (It should have been on him or in the car, but to this day has not been found.)
- Why did Joe not call off from work if he didn't want to arouse suspicion?
- Where is the other man who found Joe's body, and why didn't he stay to talk to police?
- With all the blood in the car (which George had to clean himself), would Joe have had enough strength to walk to the railing and climb over?
- If Joe was covered in blood, why was there no blood on the railing where he would have boosted himself up?
- Why was there no blood on his book bag if it was on the front passenger seat?
- Why would the police assume Joe was despondent at least in part over money, when relatives and friends owed him a combined $7,300, and he owned stocks worth $4,000?
- If he was contemplating suicide, why did Joe place an online bet the night before—$450 on Georgetown to win the NCAA Tournament, which wasn't until March?

- Where did the knife come from? It didn't match any at home or from Steak n Shake.
- Could the right-handed Joe have inflicted that odd stab wound on himself? And speaking of wounds, couldn't those minor abrasions on his stomach have occurred when his belt snapped off?

George went on to note that Joe had been planning for his future. His grades at Tri-C were improving, and he'd just sent transcripts to the University of Cincinnati. He also explained that the *Deviant Behavior* textbook was required reading for a psychology class he was taking, and the articles found in his book bag and on the computer disk were for a philosophy class.

Dr. Balraj agreed there were enough unanswered questions to merit further investigation. She assigned two investigators from her own office, Alan Clark and Charles Teel. George knew that if the investigators could not prove reasonable doubt in Balraj's mind, his son's death would be forever labeled a suicide.

At the end of June, the Kupchiks were asked to return to the office of the county coroner. Dr. Balraj had settled on a ruling. The stakes were high not only for the Kupchiks, but also Dr. Miller, whose reputation hinged on his own interpretation of the evidence.

Dr. Balraj informed George and Karen and Kate that Joe's death would be ruled "undetermined."

The Kupchiks were handed pictures of the crime scene, taken by detectives.

Although the coroner was not ruling "suicide," she still believed the evidence supported the likelihood that Joe had taken his own life. The pictures were supposed to illustrate her point. Instead, they only confused the problem. One picture showed drops of blood inside the stairwell near where Joe's car had been parked.

"It was like, what the hell is this?" Kate says, remembering the moment. She asked: "Is this Joe's blood? Has this been tested?"

The answer was no. According to Kate, Dr. Balraj took the photo and placed it next to her and exchanged a look with her protégé.

"I think she realized something hadn't been done," said Kate. "It was like, uh, yeah, you better test that."

Additionally, they learned that fresh vomit had been found on the stairwell, near the second floor.

Subsequent testing showed that the blood in the stairwell was from an unknown female. The vomit was not Joe's, either.

But the *Plain Dealer* seemed strangely reluctant to accept the new verdict.

"Apparent Suicide Can't Be Ruled as One" was the title of the article the next day. The first paragraph read: "Joseph Kupchik killed himself but the coroner won't call it a suicide."

It was another blow to the Kupchiks, who were now convinced that Joe had been murdered. It wouldn't be enough for them to prove that Joe hadn't killed himself. Now, they had to find who did.

JOE DIDN'T WORK at Steak n̄ Shake long, but it was long enough to charm Fran Nagle. Fran is a loud-mouthed Italian with a Pittsburgh accent and a friendly spirit. She's hard to forget, and Joe would ask jokingly, "Would you like your usual table?"

When Joe died, she thought about contacting the family. But when the June article appeared in the *Plain Dealer,* she decided to do more than that. She decided to get involved.

Fran met with Joe's mother, Karen, and the two formed a quick friendship. Fran knew how to work public records requests from the classes she took to earn a private investigator's license, which she intends to apply for this year. She helped the Kupchiks gather evidence they would need to force the Cleveland police to take another look at the case.

One weekend she and Karen drove out to the parking garage on Ontario to see what they could find. The two middle-aged women ascended the stairwell to the ninth floor, but stopped short of opening the door. They heard a large group of people talking and music playing. "That place is party central on Saturday nights," says Fran.

They also noticed a large wooden container that garage employees use to store bags of salt to thaw ice and snow. The container was plenty big enough for a body and had a clasp that could be locked from the outside with something as simple as a pen. The inside walls of the container were caked with white residue from bags of de-icing material. Fran wonders if it's the same residue that was caked on Joe's pants when they found him.

Later, Fran visited Steak n Shake and discovered something detectives had missed: Joe's schedule for February 11 had been altered. He'd been scheduled to work noon to ten p.m., like he told his parents, but someone had changed it, and no one could tell her by whom or when. The detectives had spoken to evening managers, who would not have known about the change.

She also spoke to a Steak n Shake employee who had befriended Joe in the few weeks he worked there. Her name was Sarah Esper, a sprite of a girl with amber hair and a mischievous smile. She told Fran that Joe had talked to her about asking a girl from Tri-C out on a date for Valentine's Day, which would have been three days after his death.

WHEN SARAH SPOKE to the *Free Times* last week, she remembered a little more. "Joe told me this girl had a boyfriend and that he didn't want the boyfriend to find out about their date," she says. "When he said that, he said it slyly."

Examining Joe's cell phone records, Fran noticed that in the days leading up to his death, Joe had called a friend named Tim Adams several times a day. Tim had called Joe's cell phone, too. It seemed like a day didn't go by without one calling the other. But on February 11, Joe didn't call Tim. And Tim never called Joe. It wasn't much, but it seemed odd.

She spoke to investigator Alan Clark about it, and according to Fran, Clark told her that he'd interviewed Tim, who'd claimed that his younger sister had told him a rumor about Joe: Someone named J.C. supposedly knows what happened because he took Joe up to Cleveland, roughed him up, left his body some place and then came back later, stabbed him, and threw him off the building.

Tim told Clark that he didn't know who J.C. was, but the sister claimed it was a friend of hers from Strongsville High School, and that it was just a joke he had made in poor taste. Fran later learned something the girl apparently hadn't told investigators, that J.C. has a brother whose first name also begins with J.

When George heard this, he was stunned. He had called every number on Joe's last cell phone bill. One number he hadn't recognized rang into the voice mail of a man who called himself J.C. (*Free Times* is not naming the brothers because they may be minors.)

Tim Adams, a bright-eyed kid with spiky red hair, says in an interview that he started getting together with Joe after Tim's longtime girlfriend broke up with him. They would go skiing or see movies, mostly. Two days before Joe died, Tim says he lent Joe five hundred dollars to place an early bet for March Madness. George repaid Tim at the wake, after Tim asked about it.

"I don't think Joe committed suicide," says Tim. "I think someone had to draw him down there. I don't know if there was a basketball game that night, but if there was, maybe they lured him down for the game."

There was a Cavs game that night.

AFTER SPEAKING TO the Kupchiks and Fran Nagle, the *Free Times* attempted to get more information from Joe's co-workers at the Brunswick Steak n Shake. Employees, however, had been instructed by managers on the day Joe's body was found not to speak to anyone about it, especially reporters.

Amber Cooper, who managed Steak n Shake the afternoon Joe disappeared, no longer works for the company. She claims that the managers who would have seen Joe come in, if he did, were Tonya Walters or Brian Weaver.

When contacted, Walters said that "there's information that should be known" and promised to call back, but never did. When reached again, she said that if she spoke to the *Free Times* she would lose her job.

Brian Weaver, who now works at the Garfield Steak n Shake, was even less helpful. "You put my name in that paper and I'll call the *Plain Dealer,* the Steak n Shake legal department, and my lawyer!" he shouted into the phone. "Stop asking about it. You're an asshole!" Later that day, the *Free Times* was contacted by Steak n Shake's lawyer, who said that employees would not talk to the media.

There was one more thing Cooper said. She claims a Steak n Shake employee named Bryan Trimmer was hanging out with Joe a lot right before his death.

Trimmer moved from Brunswick to Coupeville, Washington, last year. A Steak n Shake employee passed along a message from the *Free Times* to Trimmer and he called one night a little after one A.M. Trimmer confirmed that he and Joe had spent time together; they went to Applebee's once, and sometimes drove around Medina in Joe's car. Sometimes Joe would give him a ride to work or home afterward. Trimmer also said he worked from 3 P.M. to midnight on February 11.

When asked if Joe came in that day only to be sent home, Trimmer says, "He didn't come in, he called. He wanted to change his schedule. Said it had something to do with school."

Joe's cell phone records show no evidence of this.

When asked why Joe would go downtown, Trimmer said, "What's the big deal? I go downtown all the time."

When asked if managers and other employees would confirm that he was, in fact, working when Joe was missing, Trimmer hedges. "I'm not 100 percent sure if I was working that day. But I can't remember what I had for breakfast yesterday."

Brunswick police currently have a warrant out for Trimmer's arrest for failing to appear in court on a misdemeanor charge of underage possession of alcohol.

KATE KUPCHICK SITS at a table inside Caribou Coffee in Akron, sipping her drink and expounding on what may have happened to her brother nearly a year ago. She looks more like her mother than her other siblings, but has darker hair. There's a little bit of Joe in her, too, in the contours of her cheeks. And she has her father's analytical mind; she currently works as an accountant.

"I don't think anybody intended to kill Joe," she says. "I see it like this: They held a knife to him as a scare tactic and someone moved. Someone panicked. He was knocked unconscious. He was stored somewhere. They left and came back and then threw him off. Then said, 'Let's change his schedule to five so that we're gone by then and we'll be off the clock and off the hook.' Maybe they said, 'Here's a thousand dollars to change the schedule, just shut up about it.' Unfortunately, there's people out there that would take the money. I think everyone involved is young, which is a good thing. Maybe they had a girlfriend or boyfriend then who they told. Maybe now, they're broken up. And now, this ex will come forward and say, 'I know what happened.'"

———

ON FEBRUARY 11, as the day faded into evening and a nearly full moon hung in the winter sky, John Kupchik attended a party at a friend's house near the University of Dayton. But he didn't feel right. In fact, he felt distraught for no apparent reason. He wondered if he was getting sick. He left early and went back to his dorm to lie down.

He had no idea that at that moment, his twin brother was dying.

Their connection persists, through dreams. Maybe one day Joe can rest in peace and John can rest through the night.

My Glove

A Biography

STEFAN FATSIS

Participatory journalism is familiar ground for sportswriter Stefan Fatsis, who has often found himself participating in the sports he covers, whether becoming an expert-level tournament Scrabble player or spending training camp as a kicker with an NFL team. In this essay, originally written for a Creative Nonfiction *collection about baseball, Fatsis delves into the history of his glove, chronicling not only his personal experiences but the history of the model itself. His unabashed love for his glove, which might compromise a journalist in search of a traditional story, brings an added dimension to the endeavor.*

"I'll tell you what. It's sure broken in perfect."

In my forty-three years on Earth, this ranks among the highest compliments I have received. Right up there, definitely top five, maybe number one. So tell me more, Bob Clevenhagen, you curmudgeonly craftsman extraordinaire, you seen-it-all, stitched-'em-all Boswell of the baseball glove, you national archive of five-fingered-leather historical facts and figures, you Ravel of Rawlings Sporting Goods.

"It's broken in as well as any I ever get," Bob says. On the other end of the telephone line, I smile so hard that blood vessels threaten to pop in my cheeks. After all, Bob has been making and repairing gloves for current and future Hall of Famers for three decades. "The target for you is the base of your index finger, not the web. That's the way the pro player would do it. Not the retail market. Not a softball player."

Hell, no! Not the retail market! Not a softball player!

"This looks like a major-league gamer."

I move from happiness to rapture. In fact, I might just cry.

"That's high praise," I manage to say, filling dead air when what I really want to do is drop the phone and dance.

"Yes, it is," Bob replies, curt, gruff, no nonsense, Midwestern. He's just the third person in the one-hundred-nineteen-year history of Rawlings to hold the exalted title of Glove Designer, not a man given to bromides and bon mots, which of course makes his words all the sweeter. "Yours looks like—well, look in the Hall of Fame."

I may spontaneously combust.

"Those gloves probably look just like yours. Same color, same shape, same faded-out look," he says. "It's just a nice-looking glove."

MY GLOVE ISN'T just broken in perfect, to quote Bob. I believe it is stunningly perfect, consummately perfect, why-would-anyone-use-anything-else? perfect. To play baseball well, you have to consider your glove an ideal; if not, it will let you down. A glove has to feel like an extension of your hand, something over which you have the motor control of a surgeon repairing a capillary. But my glove is more than just a piece of equipment that works for me. I really think it is empirically flawless.

Let's start with its shape: parabolic from the top of the thumb to
the tip of the pinkie. This is the result of years of pushing those two
fingers toward the middle; there's a slight break about three inches
from the end of each digit. No ball is leaving my glove because it bent
back one of the outermost fingers.

When I put the glove on, the first thing I inevitably do is press
down the index finger. This transforms the parabola into a circle.
Open your palm and spread your fingers wide. Now curl your fingertips forward. That's what my stationary glove looks like.

My glove is soft. It collapses of its own accord when set down. But,
thanks to its aforementioned shape, it never falls completely flat, full
thumb atop full pinkie. Instead, the tip of the thumb and the tip of
the pinkie touch delicately, like God reaching out to Adam on the
ceiling of the Sistine Chapel. I've never understood gloves that open
to a V and shut like a book. The idea is to catch a round ball, not a triangular block. Roundness is essential. Softness is, too. The trick is to
create a glove pliable enough to respond to your slightest movement.
To bend to a player's will, a glove needs to bend. Mine does.

The index finger of my left hand—I throw right-handed—lies on
the exterior of the glove's back, the only digit not tucked inside. This
technique provides bonus protection when catching hard-hit or fast-
thrown balls. I believe it also helps me better control the glove's
behavior. And it looks cool.

Each finger curves gently, like a suburban cul-de-sac. The
adjustable loops surrounding the pinkie and thumb aren't tied too
tightly, but their existence is palpable. The web isn't soft and deep,
so that a ball might get lost, but rather follows the natural curva-
ture from the top of the index finger to the top of the thumb. The
heel of my glove aligns with the heel of my palm. The shearling
beneath the wrist strap is matted but still recognizable. There are
no garish personal adornments, just my first initial and last name
written meticulously in black ink letters three-eighths of an inch

tall just above the seam along the thumb. It looks as if I used a ruler to line the letters up.

Then there's the smell: leather, dirt, grass, saliva, sun, spring, childhood, summer, hope, skill, anticipation, achievement, fulfillment, memory, love, joy.

I BOUGHT MY glove in the spring of 1977. I was about to turn fourteen, out of Little League and over my head in the ninety-feet-to-first-base Senior League in the inner suburb of Pelham, New York. A wall of leather graced the sporting goods store in a nearby town, soft porn in my baseball-centric world. I had to have a Rawlings—it would be my third or fourth Rawlings, one of them royal blue—because that's what major leaguers wore. And it had to be a good one because, while every other kid pined for his turn at bat, I happily chased grounders until dark. Five feet tall and under a hundred pounds, I was a typical prepubescent second baseman: all field, no hit. An adult-sized glove would make me feel bigger, and play bigger.

My choice, the XPG6, was expensive. I remember the price as $90, though old Rawlings catalogues tell me it was probably $70 (or we were ripped off). I didn't know it then, but it was fourth-priciest glove in the Rawlings line. Thanks, Mom, for not blinking.

Not insignificantly, the XPG6 reminded me of the glove my eight-years-older brother wore when he was in high school. Virtually all of my decisions at that age were influenced by my brother, who had taught me how to calculate my batting average when I was in the second grade. (At age nine, clearly my athletic prime, I hit .750, aided, no doubt, by some generous scoring.) He played shortstop and, like me, was a competent but unexceptional player. But his glove was just right: round and bendable. I didn't want his, just one like it.

So the XPG6 it was. It bore Rawlings's famous trademarks: HEART OF THE HIDE written inside a snorting steer stamped in the "DEEP

WELL" POCKET. The TRIPLE ACTION web with a *Spiral Top* (in grade-school cursive). Along the thumb, Rawlings's familiar bright-red Circle R. Next to it, another classic, the EDGE-U-CATED HEEL. Below that, the patent number, 2,995,757. (And below that, my first initial and last name. And a single, mysterious, black dot.) Along the glove's heel, XPG6 stamped just above the handsome Rawlings script, with a long, swooping tail on the R, itself resting atop the letters U.S.A. Only the U and the top of the S are discernible today.

Two other marks cemented my love. Explanation is unnecessary as to why, arcing along the pinkie, FOR THE *Professional* PLAYER was so seductive. The signature's allure was less obvious. My glove was endorsed by Willie Stargell, who (a) threw left-handed, and (b) played one hundred eleven games at first base in 1976. Why his auto-graph—which looked fake, with penmanship-class loops and flour-ishes—was on what I assumed was a middle infielder's glove was incomprehensible, but I loved its cocktail-conversation quality. When you're fourteen, weird sometimes is good.

It's not a stretch to say that I've had a longer (and closer) relation-ship with my baseball glove than anyone or anything, apart, maybe, from my immediate family and a couple of childhood pals. I broke it in in the manner of the times: a couple of baseballs, string, the under-side of my mattress, ceaseless play. It carried me through my last two years of organized ball, on a team sponsored by the local American Legion post.

A black-and-white team photo hangs framed on my office wall now. It's from the end of the 1977 season, and of the eighth grade. I sit smiling in the front row of wooden bleachers along the first-base line at Glover Field with my friends Peter Derby (shortstop), John McNa-mara (left field), and Chuck Heaphy (right field, coach's son), and a younger kid whose name I can't remember. My wavy hair wings out from under the two-tone cap with the too-high crown. Black block felt letters spell LEGION across the chests of our double-knit uniforms. We wear what are essentially Detroit Tigers period road grays: black, orange, and white piping along the neck and sleeves of the buttonless jerseys, black stirrups with orange and white stripes stretched as high as possible to reveal as much of our white sanitary socks as possible. The '70s rocked.

The XPG6 rests on my left knee. My index finger pokes out, pointing directly at the camera lens. The leather is dark and rich. I am young and small. The twelve-inch XPG6 is new and large—much too large for me, a glove worn, I have since learned, by big-league outfielders and third basemen. Joe Morgan used a ten-inch glove at second base at the time. But what did I know? (More relevant: what did the salesman know?) All that matters is that, in that photograph, the XPG6 and I look like we're starting life, which, of course, we are.

How did it do for me? Records of my glove's rookie year are lost to history. But my 1978 Legion season is preserved on a single piece of lined white loose-leaf paper, folded inside a schedule, stored with other keepsakes in the basement. It reveals that I played in thirteen games—with nine appearances at second base, four at shortstop, and a few innings at third base and in right field—and committed five errors, two of them in our 9–4 championship-game loss to Cornell Carpet. (The stat sheet also shows that I totaled just four hits in twenty-three at-bats, an average of, ouch, .175. But that I walked sixteen times and had a robust on-base percentage of .404. Billy Beane would have given me a chance.)

I can still see and feel the ball rolling under the XPG6, and through my legs, during tryouts for the junior varsity the next spring, ending my competitive hardball career. But my glove's best years were yet to come. In college, on fast but honest artificial turf at the University of Pennsylvania's historic Franklin Field, my glove snared line drives, grabbed one-hoppers to the shortstop side, shielded me from screaming bullets, and started more 1-6-3 double plays than you'd expect. My team won back-to-back intramural softball championships, and my glove was one of the stars. Later, it performed well on the pitcher's mound again in New York City softball leagues. It shagged hundreds of baseball fungoes lofted heavenward on lazy afternoons by my best friend Jon.

As I aged—knee surgeries, work, a wife and daughter—my glove lay dormant most springs and summers, its color fading and leather peeling: wan, weathered, cracked. But it's always remained in sight, not stashed in a closet or buried in a box of mouldering sports equipment. Single, on a couch, in Brooklyn, the Yankees on TV—married, in Washington, in the attic, at a desk—I put on the XPG6 and whip a ball into its still-perfect pocket. My glove is a comfort.

MY GLOVE WAS manufactured in 1976 in Willow Springs, Missouri. It is made of tanned steer hide, specifically Code 5 Horween-X Catcher's Mitt Glove Leather from the Horween Leather Company in Chicago, founded 1905. The exterior leather is 0.075 inch thick and cut from a durable two-foot stretch along the steer's backbone, the heart of the hide. The separate interior, a glove within the glove known as the lining, is 0.050 inch thick and hails from the softer belly. The web comes from the butt, the toughest part of the hide. Rawlings doesn't have a slogan for that.

I know all of this because Bob Clevenhagen tells me. To establish my glove's birth year, for instance, Bob has me look on the outside of the thumb, below the patent number. How many dots?

"One dot," I say.

"One dot. That's exactly right. Made in 1976. But it wouldn't have gone out in the marketplace until the first of 1977."

I'd noticed the one-sixteenth-inch dot years ago but had no idea what it meant. I thought it was an accidental factory mark. Bob explains that Rawlings used dots to establish the year of manufacture for warranty purposes. One dot meant a glove was made in a year ending in 1 or 6, two dots was a year ending in 2 or 7, and so on. That way, if someone returned a glove for repair or replacement, Rawlings would know whether it was still under warranty (and the owner would have no idea how the company could tell).

After working at shoe factories in Missouri and Massachusetts, Bob joined Rawlings as foreman of glove operations in Willow Springs in 1977. ("Leather was my life after I got out of the service," he says.) A workforce of two hundred made about one hundred seventy thousand gloves there that year, including fifteen thousand or so XPG6s. As Rawlings and other glove makers began shifting production to Asia, the Willow Springs factory was closed in 1982. Today, Bob runs a four-person operation at Rawlings's main distribution center in Washington, Missouri, making gloves for a couple dozen major leaguers and for a custom catalogue.

The XPG6 and its progenitors were Rawlings's first fully functional modern gloves, created in response to Wilson's A2000, which revolutionized baseball when it appeared in 1957. The A2000 had a larger web, broader pocket, hinged heel, and flatter fingers, thumb, and heel than the standard puffy models of the time. In his artful book *Glove Affairs: The Romance, History, and Tradition of the Baseball Glove*, Noah Liberman explains that the A2000 dispelled a century-old belief: that the glove should look like the hand. "The evolution of the glove is, in large part," he writes, "the slow realization that a glove must reflect how a hand moves to catch a ball, not how it looks when you stare at it." (Liberman and I, it turns out, have something in common, glove-wise. "The XPG6? That was my glove!" he exclaims when I call. "That was my glove in high school!" Liberman swapped his with the shortstop of a women's pro baseball team for a jersey. She never sent him the shirt.)

Rawlings began making XPG prototypes—the initials stood for "experimental glove"—for big-league players in 1958. The first retail model, the XPG3, endorsed by pitcher Herb Score, appeared in the company's 1960 catalogue. The quarter-inch shorter but otherwise identical XPG6 debuted in 1962 and quickly became one of Rawlings's most popular gloves. The autograph inside helped: Mickey Mantle. According to glove historian Dennis Esken—who owns the glove Mantle used to make a one-handed catch in left center field that helped preserve Don Larsen's perfect game in the 1956 World Series—the model name bore a "6" because it originally was intended for Stan Musial, who wore that number. For Mantle, Rawlings designed an XPG7, but, Esken tells me, the famous No. 7 didn't like it. It had a newfangled Trap-Eze web with a vertical strip of leather connected to each side with laces; the Mick wanted a solid web. Since Musial was nearing the end of his career anyway, Rawlings put Mantle's name in the XPG6.

The original XPG6 was a "Personal Model," meaning the pattern of the glove, if not every detail of the glove itself, was the same as what the signer wore on the field. (Mantle wound up using an I-shaped web, as opposed to the two-piece Triple Action web in the retail version.) Mantle retired in 1968, but his name remained in the XPG6 until 1972. Bobby Tolan, a left-handed outfielder on Cincinnati's Big Red Machine, endorsed the XPG6 in 1973 and 1974. (Lefty signatures on righty gloves aren't unusual; glove makers don't sell enough lefties to segregate endorsers by throwing arm.) Then came Stargell. The future Hall of Famer had played in the outfield his entire career, but in 1975, the first year he signed the XPG6, he moved to first base. My glove was stitched in 1976, Stargell's name was shifted to a first-baseman's glove (the FJ9) in 1977, and the XPG6 name was retired.

I tell Bob I think it's the ideal design.

"From a baseball standpoint, I agree with you," he says, quickly noting that he didn't design it. Credit for that goes to the late Rollie Latina, who in 1961 inherited the title of Glove Designer from his father, Harry, better known as Doc, as in the Glove Doctor, who joined Rawlings in 1922. The Latinas were the revered creators of most of the company's trademarked glove innovations and slogans. Bob became Glove Designer after Rollie retired in 1984. The shape of the pattern and the shape of the padding, Bob says, predisposed the XPG6 to excellence. "It's the perfect shape to play it anywhere you want to play it. Bill Madlock wore it at third base. Dwight Evans wore it for fourteen years in the outfield. That glove's been everywhere."

Tom Seaver, Hank Aaron, Mike Schmidt, Billy Williams, Doug DeCinces—I shared a glove with them, too, I learn. "It was the first, most-streamlined model with that U-shaped heel and that nice pocket in it and a little less padding in it. It's more like what we use today," Bob says. "That same glove is still around. The truth is that it's the very same basic pattern. A-Rod's wearing it today," he says, referring to Yankees' third baseman Alex Rodriguez. There are some differences, Bob notes. A-Rod's glove has a single-piece "Fastback" backside with a "Holdster" for the index finger. "The palm area. That's where it's the same as A-Rod, Dwight Evans, right back to Mickey Mantle."

Esken, the historian and collector, puts it to me this way. "Fifty freakin' years. That pattern glove has been synonymous with baseball for fifty years. It's still functional to this date. The A2000 from 1957 is not a functional glove today."

BOB HAS MADE gloves for presidents Carter, Ford, and both Bushes. He has made gloves for movies—Kevin Costner's *For Love of the Game*; *The Slugger's Wife*, written by Neil Simon; Billy Crystal's *61**. After the comedian paid $239,000 at a Sotheby's auction for a glove supposedly worn by Mantle circa 1960, he asked Bob to check it out. Based on the style of Mantle's signature, Bob could tell it was a 1965 model (an XPG3). "I could have saved him a lot of money in ten seconds," he says.

At sixty-two years old, Bob is one of Rawlings's longest-serving employees, and its de facto glove historian, fielding questions from reporters, fans, even investigators. The FBI once called about a 1936 Joe DiMaggio rookie gamer sold by a prominent auction house. It actually had been made two decades later, after DiMaggio had retired. "Some of the experts who write letters, they don't know shit," Bob tells me. "But it doesn't take a brain surgeon to know a '36 glove from a '54 glove." One day when I call, Bob is making a glove for a boy missing some fingers whose parents wrote requesting help. (He made gloves for one-handed big-league pitcher Jim Abbott.) "I get four or five of those a year," he says. "We don't advertise or charge for it. I just do it for a nice letter from the kid. I've got a nice little file of those."

Most big-leaguers, Bob says, don't know much about their gloves. "They don't even know what the hell they're getting. They get oil-tanned leather. It's going to be darker from day one. Probably the last person who knows how to make a glove is a pro ballplayer. . . . They've got a lot of bad habits. They spit in 'em. That just rots the leather. Makes it feel sticky. It just ruins the glove." (I don't confess that I regularly spit in the XPG6, but only because those big-leaguers did.) "They don't care today. It doesn't take another year to break another one in."

Today's pros, Bob says, want supple leather right out of the box. They don't want to have to work it in. Players like Dwight Evans who wear the same glove for an entire career are as rare as perfect games. Modern players burn through multiple gloves in a season; Bob pounds and shapes gloves for Alex Rodriguez six at a time. Of course he does. It's good for business.

"Who wouldn't want A-Rod wearing their glove on TV?" Bob says. "What's a lousy dozen gloves?" Compare that to the old days. "We wouldn't even give Stan Musial an extra glove in the '50s. If he wanted another one he'd have to buy it."

Bob goes on. "These players are much different from your era." The "your era" is simultaneously flattering (I lived in the old days?

And there was something good about them?) and horrifying (It wasn't that long ago, was it?). "They don't care about durability."

They do care about the endorsement money—one hundred thousand dollars or so a year for an A-Rod or Derek Jeter—but they don't need it the way players did back in the day. Bob estimates Willie Stargell probably received "five thousand dollars and a set of golf clubs" to sign with Rawlings, plus royalties on sales above five thousand dollars. "It mattered back then," Bob says. "I know Reggie Jackson made as much off us as he did playing ball. The Mantles of the world had to have a winter job to eat. I'm pretty sure A-Rod doesn't have to check in at Hardee's after the season's over."

ON A BRIGHT afternoon two months into the 2006 season, my glove and I drive to Robert F. Kennedy Stadium—one year older than the XPG6—where the Washington Nationals are hosting the Houston Astros.

I collect my press pass and fast-walk to the home dugout. It stinks of sewage, thanks to some faulty piping manager Frank Robinson hopes the team's just-named owners will see fit to repair. As his players take batting practice, Robinson holds court with a clutch of reporters. He complains about how players won't accept instruction. He says they arrive in the big leagues sure they know everything. He outs slackers on his team by name. Of course, he does all of this off the record. Praise is on the record, though, because Frank Robinson loves and respects the game and loves and respects those who do, too.

When the beat guys finish their questions, I extract the XPG6 from my messenger bag. Everyone eyes me a bit warily—I'm not a regular, and I'm breaking the sportswriters' code of conduct by behaving weirdly in front of the people wearing uniforms. When he sees the glove, Robinson's expression falls somewhere between shame and disgust.

"You should be brought up on abuse charges," he says. "You ever oil that thing?" Well, no, but I did have it restrung about ten years earlier, when the X-shaped lacing between the middle and index fingers broke.

"You don't even want to touch it," I say.

"No."

The manager asks who signed it, and I launch into an exegesis on the XPG6's family tree.

"Why would they change the Mickey Mantle model?" he asks.

"Because he was retired," I say.

"So what?" Robinson says. "I'll tell you what. If they would have kept Mickey Mantle's name on that they would have sold more gloves than they would have with Bobby Tolan's name."

Ice broken, the other reporters join in. One asks Robinson, who won a Gold Glove in 1958, about his glove preferences. He tells us he used only a few in his twenty-one-season career. "Gloves are like shoes with me," he says. "I find a pair of shoes I like, I wear 'em. You just had a glove that felt good on your hand, you didn't quit playing with it."

Bill Mazeroski's glove was tattered, Robinson recalls. Willie Mays's glove was "beyond limit," he says. "It looked like of those things they play jai alai with." Players couldn't be picky. "There were no specifications. They showed you models of gloves and you chose one that you liked." Robinson says he first signed with MacGregor, but didn't like their gloves, so he switched to Rawlings and wore a Spalding occasionally.

Talk returns to my XPG6.

"That's the kind of glove you'd see guys playing with," he says. "Restrung, redone, whatever."

I take this as a compliment, but seek a higher order of validation. "Do you like the shape at least?" I ask Robinson. "Say something nice about my glove. You're killing me."

"It's on your hand. It's not bad. How long have you had it?"

"Thirty years."

"It's not bad. It's not too bad. It's got a nice kind of shape for an infielder's glove."

But Frank Robinson thinks I need to move on.

"Get a softball glove," he says. "Retire that one."

"I can't retire it."

"Why not?"

"Because I love it."

"Sleep with it. But you don't have to abuse it. I love my wife but I leave her to come to work."

"I've had a longer relationship with my glove than I have with my wife."

"That's you. The way you're going with that glove, you're not going to know your wife much longer."

Across the infield, I wait for the Astros to finish batting practice. As the pitchers jog in from the outfield, where they've been shagging balls, I look for No. 36, Russ Springer.

Springer, Rawlings has informed me, is the only player in the major leagues using the XPG6, albeit under a different name, the Pro 6XBC. That model was also discontinued years ago, but the company makes him a couple every year. When Springer arrives at the dugout railing, I introduce myself. I tell him what we have in common, and he says he likes our glove because he played infield in high school and so prefers a smaller model (smaller for him, that is; he's six-feet-four). In his native Louisiana twang, Springer says the glove he's holding isn't his gamer, which is stashed in his locker. "It don't come out unless it's game time," he says.

Springer has used the same glove in games since 1993, his second year in the majors. "It's starting to show a lot of wear and tear," he says. "Sun-bleached on the outside. It's starting to get a couple of tears on it. The only thing I've ever had done is have the top laces replaced, all through the fingers. Just to show you how old it is, and yours is too, they don't make 'em with metal rivets anymore. And mine's still got the metal rivets. You'll see mine. It's a lot like that."

He gives my glove a once over, examining the pocket.

"Mine actually looks worse in here than yours does."

"Can we go compare?" I ask.

"Yeah."

"Let's go."

We walk into the visitors' clubhouse and over to Springer's locker. A few days earlier, the right-handed reliever had been suspended for four games for throwing at Barry Bonds, possibly because Bonds had 713 home runs at the time and Springer didn't want to give up No. 714, possibly to let Bonds know how he felt about alleged steroids-using sluggers. (After throwing one pitch behind Bonds's back and three more inside, Springer plunked Bonds on the right shoulder and was ejected from the game. As he exited the field, Springer received a standing ovation from the home crowd.) I tell Springer our glove originally was worn by Mickey Mantle, which elicits no response. Not a historian, I guess. He pulls his gamer from the locker.

His Pro 6XBC has the cross-hatched (and trademarked) Basket Web. Instead of "DEEP WELL" POCKET, Springer's glove is stamped with GOLD GLOVE. His also doesn't have an EDGE-U-CATED HEEL. His red rectangular Rawlings label on the wrist strap says "Made in U.S.A."; mine says "Est. 1887." Springer's glove is broken in a bit flatter than mine. Otherwise, they are identical: same shape, same stitch patterns, same lace holes, same curves, same feel.

"So when you look at something like this"—I hold up the XPG6—"you don't think: old piece of leather?"

"Heck no," he says. "That's personality."

Springer says he's a creature of habit. He wears the same spikes all season. His black batting practice T-shirt (featuring his once-and-future teammate Roger Clemens) has a giant hole around the underarm. "I just don't like new stuff," he says.

When it comes to our glove, I tell him, I'm the same way. "I was a kid when I got it," I say. "I played softball with it for twenty years, so it's a little bit fatter and wider. But you could play with this? You wouldn't have a problem putting this on?"

"No, that's got personality," he says. "It's better than a new one."

"You need a little TLC on it," Craig Biggio says.

We're sitting on metal folding chairs on the other side of the Astros' locker room. The second baseman holds my glove gently, his thick fingers resting just beneath the wrist strap, but not inserted into the slots. "Never put your hand totally into someone else's glove," he says. Indeed, I always avoided lending my glove. The borrower inevitably would, to my horror, stick his index finger *inside* it. A few months earlier, I'd shown my glove to Cal Ripken Jr., who, as if testing me, inserted his hand and *then* admonished that I "should have been more territorial with it." Ripken said the only person he had ever allowed to use his gamer was Ronald Reagan, when the president threw out a first pitch in 1984. (Of the XPG6, the future Hall of Fame shortstop/third baseman said, and I proudly quote, "You break yours in similar to me.")

Bob Clevenhagen had recommended talking to Biggio, who won four consecutive Gold Gloves in the 1990s and, more important, appreciates the art of the glove. "It's what you make your money with," Biggio says. "A lawyer goes to work with a nice suit on every day. We've got to put a glove on our hands. If you don't know how to use it, you're not going to have a job very long. It is personal. And everybody's different."

Biggio uses one glove per season. He's a throwback, preferring firmer leather that requires attention and work on the part of the owner. But he says he's not an extremist. Steve Buechele, a third baseman for Texas, Pittsburgh, and the Cubs, used one glove his entire career, Biggio tells me, as did journeyman shortstop Jay Bell. Oakland shortstop Walt Weiss's glove was so ravaged it had a nickname: The Creature. Biggio says the great Cardinals shortstop Ozzie Smith took the opposite approach. He could remove a new glove from its box and play with it the same day. "But he had some of the best hands ever," Biggio says.

Biggio does more work on his gloves than Smith did, but not much more. Bob sends the nineteen-year veteran a few gloves before spring training. Biggio picks a future gamer and plays catch with it. He puts a little pine tar in the pocket for "tackiness," which he says helps in cold weather when the ball is slicker. By the start of the regular season, the glove is ready. By the end, the fingers have stretched just enough to force its retirement. Biggio gives the old ones to his two sons. "They can't wait to get this one," he says, showing me his Pro CB (his initials), which is similar to the XPG6 but smaller. "It seems like a good one right now."

Like a diamond-cutter appraising a stone, Biggio studies my glove. I ask what he sees.

"It's got a story to it," Biggio says. "Classic, old, beat up. This is a classic glove of somebody who would use it every day, who wouldn't change it at all. It's got a lot of character."

"Thank you," I say. Craig Biggio understands.

"For me, the pocket's a little deep," he continues, "so it's more like a third baseman's glove. But actually, it's not all that bad. If [the ball] goes in it, I *know* it's not coming out. I'd have the whole thing restrung." His glove has extra laces connecting the sides of the fingers to minimize separation between them. "The leather's a little dry." He points to the pocket and fingers. "That can be padded. They can patch it up."

Biggio tells me to send my glove to Bob.

"He'll fix it up for you."

BOB TELLS ME what he'd do to restore my glove. "It needs new insides and new leather trim all the way around on the inside. And new laces, of course."

The trim curves around the wrist and fingers, holding together the pieces of my glove. Bob says he'll replace the interior lining—the glove within the glove, against which my palm and fingers, back and front, have rested since I was fourteen—with the same durable Horween leather as in the original, not the softer stuff pros and amateurs expect today. ("It took a man to break it in," he says of the glove of yore.) The challenge will be making the new lining fit snugly inside the old exterior; since leather stretches with use, the original pattern for the innards of the XPG6, which Bob has, probably won't match the current size of my glove.

In short, Bob says he will rebuild my glove from the inside, "everything underneath that you can't see." On the undersides of the three middle fingers, he'll install fresh wool-blend padding (minus the asbestos fibers it contained thirty years ago). Beneath the wrist strap, a synthetic wool will take over for the old shearling. The two frayed red Rawlings labels—the rectangular script Rawlings and the Circle R—will be replaced with modern likenesses. "I don't have any more of these antique ones," he says. *Antique!* The exterior will remain unchanged; if he replaced that, Bob says he'd just be making a new glove.

Letting the XPG6 out of my possession had been traumatic. I first packed it at the post office, but decided I didn't trust the government, unpacked it, and shipped it FedEx. I called Bob to make sure it arrived. I had wanted Bob's expert opinion, assuming that perhaps he would offer to string some new lacing or perform some trick to revive the worn leather. I hadn't considered a total makeover. But now, listening to him explain the restoration process like an archaeologist entrusted with preserving the Parthenon, I grow excited at the prospect of new life. I tell myself I finally would be treating the XPG6 right. I finally would be making amends for years of what Frank Robinson called abuse. Spontaneously, unhesitatingly, I give Bob the go-ahead.

"I don't think you'll be upset with the way it looks," he says.

A few weeks later, a brown box arrives. I pull out the XPG6 and say, aloud: Oh. *No!*

It's my glove, but it isn't. It stays open of its own accord, rather than flopping shut on release, the tip of the thumb kissing the tip of the pinkie. The finger slot no longer lies permanently in the off position, pancaked to the lining. I slide my hand in. The XPG6 is snug and stiff. I can't even close it enough to obscure Stargell's too-neat signature.

The insides are burnt sienna, rich with the aroma of new leather. The laces and trim Bob had promised are bright and prominent, mod orange racing stripes on a battered Chevrolet. The replacement Rawlings patches shimmer like freshly washed fire engines drying in the summer sun. The spongy synthetic wool rubs prominently against the back of my hand; I can't even recall feeling the old stuff, tamped as it was. New internal padding forms a thick ridge along the index, middle, and ring fingers, functionally useful but interrupting the pocket's old, uniform concavity. There's even a bump in the new leather exactly where the top of my thumb rests. An imperfection! Bob, how could you?

I feel disappointment and then panic: I'll never again hold *my glove,* the one that accompanied me through adolescence and into adulthood, a life partner whose advancing years were undetectable because we had aged together, an anti–Dorian Gray. I didn't want a trophy wife. But now I have one.

For a second time, I feel like I'm going to cry because of my baseball glove. The XPG6 was comforting because it was so familiar. It had earned its cracks and bruises on the field, over time. Holding the remodeled version, I close my eyes and picture my glove, trying to imprint permanently its sensory qualities on my brain. How I could make the upper half flap by snapping my wrist back and forth. How I could wield it like a lobster's claw to snatch a ball off the ground. Its gloriously battered and decomposing personality, in Russ Springer's apt anthropomorphization. Even if my preschool daughter becomes a softball superstar, there's no chance I'll play enough to return the XPG6 to its old form—not enough throws to catch, not enough grounders to field, not enough time. I feel I've committed a horrible betrayal. I set down the imposter and vow not to pick it up until I'm emotionally willing to give it a chance.

THE PAIN BEGINS to lift a month later. What made the XPG6 special was its artistry, I realize, its shape, form, and feel. The essence of those remains unchanged. In fact, the shape and form are truer, the parabola stronger and more confident. Propped upright, resting on its wrist strap, the XPG6 reminds me of the Gold Glove trophy itself. Its new contrast, I realize, is beautiful: I. M. Pei's glass pyramid at the Louvre.

More than I have in years, I bang the pocket with my right fist, flattening the new padding. I grab the pinkie and ring finger in my right hand and open and close the glove to resuscitate its natural hinge. With my left thumb, I push and flatten the bump under my thumb (caused, I guess correctly, by the difference in size between the XPG6's lining pattern and my stretched-out glove) to which I'm sure Bob was referring in the note that accompanied the glove home: "I wish it was a little better! But!! Good Luck, Bob."

Inside the box, Bob deposited the battered core of the XPG6. It looks like something that's been worn since Honus Wagner was play-ing second base. The leather is as weather-beaten as a cowboy's chaps. Waxy remnants of the grease that affixed the lining to the glove's exte-rior form a dark, mottled circle on the palm. Where the fleshy part of my heel rested and sweated, there's a hole the size of a half dollar and the shape of Wisconsin, and a tear next to that. The padding beneath the three middle fingers is shredded. At the point where the nail of my ring finger touched the leather, there's another hole—the result of untold thousands of repetitions of finger sliding into glove, right fist pounding left hand, balls batted and thrown striking that precise spot.

Then, finally, there's the index finger slot, pressed as flat as a stone made for skipping across a lake. I peek underneath. The leather is smooth, dark, unblemished, my glove in 1977. Still with me today, still perfect.

I'm going to use my new glove as much as possible. What's left of my glove—My Glove—I'm having framed.

Teaching the "F" Word

Hauquan Chau

As an English teacher in Japan, Hauquan Chau has noticed that "when given the opportunity to speak, particularly in another language, the inhibitions students may have had in their native language tend to disappear. . . . I am in a fortunate situation to just sit back and let my students tell it all. My conversation class is a gushing spring of fascinating narratives. Later, as a writer, I brood over what it all means and try to convey it in words that readers can sympathize with." Chau tells one such story in this piece, which originally appeared online in In the Fray.

Sachiko must be considered "different" here in Japan. She works in the male-dominated research and development section of a major automobile company. Her interests include English, Hollywood movies, and fast cars. She wears dark, thick-framed glasses that cover most of her round, childlike face. She could easily pass as an elementary school student, but was taking an adult, basic-level English class I was teaching.

One day, she stayed behind to ask me a question. She could hardly put two words together. But no matter. I have taught English for more than ten years in Japan; my teacher instincts fill in those pesky prepositions or pronouns that often make even the more advanced students cringe with fear. It's amazing how ideas can be conveyed without these trimmings. Such bare, stripped-down sentences deliver more impact to what the speaker wants to say.

"Very sorry. I have question. What do you say, 'don't touch me' in English?" she asked, in broken, uncertain English.

I asked what she meant. And she began to tell me a story in a pidgin mix of English and Japanese about what had happened to her.

It was at an art museum, she said. While she was examining a print, a man came up to her and began stroking her on the buttocks. She pleaded with him in Japanese to stop, but he continued to harass her, and then began touching her breasts with impunity.

I asked why she didn't scream out for help or run away, but she only said she didn't want to make trouble, and therefore endured the harassment. Then she told me it was not the first time. Her pleas in Japanese were always ignored.

If her pleas were in English, she said, everything would change. She's seen the movies—the Western women on celluloid who take no shit from anyone. Even if the guys who touched her didn't understand a word, it wouldn't matter. The English would be enough to send them scurrying away.

The language has the potency of a karate chop to the head. The economic and military superpowers of the English-speaking world were to thank for that. And an appreciative nod goes to Hollywood as well for making English the world language. Thank God Johnny Depp was endowed with a native English tongue.

The dialog in our classroom's English textbook always seemed dead to me: a utopia on paper where everyone wants to be your friend, where a "Hi, how are you?" will make you the instant life of the party.

Finally, here arose a lesson that was practical, one a student could use and benefit from, as opposed to the American middle-class values instilled by those textbooks.

After some hesitation, I finally wrote "Get the fuck off me!" on the blackboard, and began teaching her the unsubtle nuances of the word "fuck."

She read the words slowly, deliberately, and in monotone: "Get . . . the . . . fuck . . . off . . . me."

The softness in Sachiko's voice sounded as if she were reciting *Mother Goose* to a group of children. "Fuck" never sounded so sweet.

English, especially "combative English" (for lack of a better term), was all about stress, I emphasized while pointing at the word "fuck" on the blackboard. This, I said—tapping at the word—is where the stress should lie.

Even if the intended listener didn't understand, it wouldn't matter. The strong vocalization of the one word alone would do the job. Even the formation of the sound of the letter F looks intimidating. The raised upper lip reveals the front teeth while the lower lip is tucked underneath. Any such articulation that bares a set of teeth brings us closer to our primal instincts of survival. If that isn't enough to scare off a predator, the hard, menacing sound of the K could be the coup de grace.

Sachiko repeated the phrase on the blackboard with more emphasis, more confident about what she had to do. While most of her classmates talk about learning English to learn about other cultures, to have an advantage in the workplace, and to meet Westerners, Sachiko won't be making new friends with this newly acquired phrase. She said it to herself a few times, and even began to sound a little menacing.

For her, it's just a sound, a magic word. She knows it's swearing, but she's unaware of the hatred, anger, and confrontation that its English speakers intend to express when using the word. You could say *baka yaro* until your face turns blue, but more likely than not, you wouldn't get that same tingling in your stomach as you would from saying "Fucking idiot."

English sells. Or rather, the likeness of English sells. In Japan, the language is hip, even if you don't understand what is being said.

Sachiko thanked me and practiced the phrase over and over again under her breath as she walked out the door. She's finally mastered it. She's armed—with a phrase that will embolden her.

Hi, I'm Panicky.

FINSLIPPY.COM

I've always lacked confidence regarding my ability to move through space. There was the Bike-Learning Failure of '73–'78, the Roller Skating Catastrophe of '79, the Uneven Bars Horror of '83. And then there was driving. I never had the slightest interest in driving, except inasmuch as it could get you places, and I liked places. I had never even sat in a driver's seat, when I found myself in just such a seat, my foot on the pedal, in a driver's ed car, careening down Main Street. I don't remember much from driver's ed, but I do recall a lot of screaming, most of it not coming out of my own mouth. I may have hit a few things. Not surprisingly, I failed. I took driver's ed all over again. I passed, but barely. I failed the driver's test. I figured that this was a sign that I should be chauffeured everywhere, but my parents made me take it again. I passed, but just slightly.

Then I moved away, away from the Land Where Everyone Drove, and that was that for twenty years. For twenty years I haven't had to drive. I think I drove a few times in college, when my a cappella group (don't laugh) went on tour. There was a familiar screaming sound when I did that. My fellow a cappella mates stopped asking me to drive. I moved to the city, where no one had cars. I was all set.

But then I moved *here*. Figuring I would get used to driving, I moved to this place. And I did, mostly. I was a little sweaty-palmed for the first couple of months, but now I can get around town without a problem. Then I tried to drive on the highway.

And I completely freaked out.

Without going into too much detail about it because reliving it makes me want to die, here was how much I was freaking out: My vision tunneled. I was fairly certain that I was going to throw up on myself. I lost all feeling in my arms. My hands were sweating so badly that they were slipping off the steering wheel. My hearing went all funny. Then I started crying, which, in addition to the tunnel vision, made it awfully hard to see. I got off at the nearest exit.

I was probably on the highway for ten or fifteen minutes. That was one year ago.

I know what you're going to say. I can hear you saying it. Highway driving is scary, you're saying. You have to keep on trying! It's a skill! You'll get better! Do you always use all those exclamation points when you're talking?

What we have here is not a lack of confidence—well, okay, it *is* a lack of confidence, but also it is a fear that grips so tightly to me that I can no longer reason. I've tried driving on the highway a couple of times since then. I've tried to work through it. I did some cognitive behavioral therapy; I learned about dealing with panic and breathing the right way, and I tried talking myself through the panic, blar de blar, and I am here to tell you that I *cannot*. I don't want to sound defeatist here, but all the talking to myself and breathing just makes me calm enough that I don't run off the road and run screaming from the car. I can manage it, but I still get the numbness and the tunnel vision and the nausea—and the sweating, don't forget the sweating!—and I feel absolutely dreadful.

I tried going on the Garden State Parkway last week. My panic was so intense that I was nauseated for *days* afterward. It was like I had been poisoned. Why would I put myself through that again? Except, you know, for all the really smart reasons, like I need to get around and do things and be independent and GOD SHUT UP WITH YOUR REASONABLE ATTITUDE.

I'm sorry, baby, I didn't mean it. It's the fear, is all. It's got ahold of me.

All of this is leading up to one question, which is: What do you think of hypnosis?

Anyone? Anyone?

Wednesday, August 23, 2006

MADRIDWS.BLOGSPOT.COM

"Alzheimer's is one of those cataclysms that seems designed
specifically to test the human spirit."

—Sherwin B. Nuland, *How We Die*

—We say look forward to and we say look back. The first suggests desire, "I look forward to seeing you," but the second requires the confirmation of "in anger" or "with nostalgia" or "in time" to give it credence. (It's not adjectives we so dislike in poems, it's the judgment they offer before the crime is solved, as if the noun were presumed guilty of its qualities before they were assigned.)

—Sherwin B. Nuland, whose name compresses hope, describes the end of an Alzheimer's patient's life: He is tied to a bed so he will not wander; he forgets how to eat or drink; before he loses language, he forgets what it means. "The trains are not on time, do something!" comes to mean "tie my shoes." He becomes comatose, he gets infections, and then he dies. The End.

—When is the future not forward, then? Look Forward in Anger.

—That the past is not back is a given. Karen says mom was angry at her for visiting when the cab might arrive to take her to Ohio. If she lives now in the past, in what tense do we write the present or the future, when mere reversals don't work, either?

—Can I say I look forward to my mother's death? I would be assured she does not suffer. Or is there a suffering in that state, which, if not directly felt by her, is commentary on us? If she uses Afghanistan as a word, and I know it as a war zone, can I not still say she suffers for being there—apart from where she is? When is a word only a word? When is a word no longer a word? When does "Ode on a Grecian Urn" become a sound poem? When is Keats Khlebnikov?

—Can I say I look forward to her death without wanting it? Not as desire but as fact. No, I cannot say that yet. It's that word, *yet*, that keeps us, not from despair, but from act, even when that act makes sense. Nuland admits to "breaking the law," easing his patient's pain. "I want to make sure they know not to resuscitate," Karen says, as my mother would not want that. She did not want that when she could still imagine it.

—"Show Radhika your monkey face," I tell Mom. She pushes her lower cheeks out with her tongue. For just a moment she plays.

Cracking Open

PATRICIA BRIESCHKE

"Re-creating my life in narrative is the parachute I use to keep from crashing," says Patricia Brieschke. "Retelling my story allows me to have an active voice on the page when I don't always have one in the world, to find the sympathetic character in my angry hag of a self, and to connect to others in a way that links our tiny, troubled universes." In this piece from PMS poemmemoirstory, *Brieschke depicts the tiny, heart-wrenchingly troubled universe she inhabited in the year following the birth of her son, Ollie.*

Four decades ago, when I was young and stupid and didn't know a baby from a wormy *kapusta,* according to my Polish mother, I gave birth to a tiny damaged boy on my kitchen table. Just out of high school, I was working in a fertilizer factory, going to night school, and writing frantically in my spare time to reshape myself in the image and likeness of George Eliot. But she never had children. Nevertheless, I figured since an infant is small and portable, it wouldn't interfere with my plan for the contemplative literary life. The day I decided to go off the pill, John Lennon and Yoko Ono staged a bed-in for peace in Amsterdam. One thing I knew with missionary clarity: this baby was my olive branch to the universe. Unlike my mother, who produced misfits who could only hobble and crawl, my child would be so loved he would soar. Our bond would heal every rift, every schism, every abuse. My husband, Matthew, an Irish boy who had been dismissed from his religious order at age twenty for chugging brandy in the Christian Brothers winery, was another hobbler and crawler. He wrote me poems, I gave him sex—an elegant but sparse compromise.

I registered at the Chicago Maternity Center for prenatal care: two rooms over a store facing the Maxwell Street Market. Toward the end of the pregnancy, I made weekly bus trips to the Center, where a volunteer palpated my belly to the crooning of Muddy Waters. I prepared my supplies for the time of delivery: a two-foot-high stack of newspapers, a large plastic sheet, a dime for calling the Maternity Center, a strong electric light, and a kettle for boiling water.

Giving birth was like my first accordion lesson. When they put the bellowy instrument in my lap, I didn't know where to put my hands, how to hold it. I had no idea how to have a baby, so I sat on the beat-up couch in our third-floor flat on Ainslie Avenue, crossed my legs and asked Bernie, a pink-faced intern, "Okay, what do I do?"

"Maybe we should have read a book," Matthew said, gathering up empty beer cans from the coffee table.

Bernie took one of Matthew's poems that I had framed from the wall. I read a few lines before he hung a makeshift IV from the nail. *A small bright delighting thing / A dark deep beckoning / Embodied twilight turning day to night.* My baby, a small bright delighting thing, felt huge inside me: a nuclear fission ready to break upon the world. I pressed my thighs together to hold back the dribble of green water that had been leaking for a couple of days. The baby was still head up and had no intention of turning and preparing for descent.

Oxytocin dripped into my veins. Bernie's partner, a small Filipino woman, boiled water, spread my stack of *Chicago Tribunes* over the kitchen table and floor, and swung a hundred-watt bulb from an extension cord above the table. Matthew tamped his pipe, composing a poem in his head. "Change into something comfortable and crawl up on the table," Bernie said, as he unpacked his doctor's bag on the kitchen sink, clanging shiny tools on paper towels. I grabbed an over-sized Beatles T-shirt. The Filipino woman helped me maneuver the IV tubing as I hoisted myself up on the table. Earlier, I had been paying bills there, flipping a penny to decide who would get paid—Con Ed or Ma Bell. Envelopes scattered on the floor. Would Bernie and the Filipino woman ask for money?

Perfect control. Nobody will see me flinch. I lay on newsprint, naked from the waist down. Not a telltale sound or revealing grunt. My belly heaved. Muscles closed around the baby like a slow glacier. I controlled the pain by imagining an advertisement for a Burberry raincoat permanently affixed to my back thigh. Finally, I began to crack open: one centimeter, two centimeters . . . six, seven. After several hours and a few choruses of "don't push, don't push, don't push, okay push," two little legs dangled out of me. "Where's his head?" The kitchen was eerily quiet. I heard the baby cry inside me. He didn't want to be born.

"You must move bowels in twenty-four hours," the Filipino woman said, lecturing me about hemorrhoids and sitz baths. Bernie called for backup to figure out how to get the rest of the baby out.

My son wasn't exactly what I had expected. A blob of protoplasm, shiny and translucent. But he was my first wonder of the world, my Grand Canyon. When Bernie cleaned him off, his skinny legs twisted around themselves like Gumby. He looked more poultry than baby, but the most exquisite chicken I had ever seen. For a moment, I thought there must be something wrong with him. But what did I know. The only baby I remembered clearly was my youngest brother, and I never really looked at him, just plotted how to dispose of him. My baby was perfect, if a bit crooked.

In the days that followed, I became sweet with curiosity about this new little being, in the larger scheme of things nothing but a speck of dust on the earth, but for me, a reason for living. I nuzzled his swollen belly against mine, cooed over his soft crown and doll fingers, drank in the perfume of yellow diapers. *Little caterpillar.* It was now my life's work to protect, honor, and celebrate this delicate creature. *Snail without a shell.* After two weeks, I was in love. We were a team: I gave him life, he gave me breasts.

The name on his birth certificate was Beckett. Matthew rejected my choice, which was Oliver. Reminded him of olives or liver. But it didn't matter what anybody else called him. Ollie and I formed a secret bond. At night in bed when he whimpered, I whispered his name. His fish mouth, heat-seeking and hungry, clamped on to me. My mother called in her blessing: "Now you'll know heartache. May your child do to you what you did to me." *You had only weak tea in your breasts; mine are filled with crème fraîche.* I would do motherhood right and love my Ollie better than all the Polish mothers of the old neighborhood, stuffed into their Goldblatt housedresses.

During our two-week checkup at the Maternity Center, I ran into Debbie, whose prenatal visits had coincided with mine. "He's beautiful," she said.

"You don't think he looks like a chicken?" Ollie and I were so tightly swaddled in my Madonna and Baby Jesus fantasy that I half wanted a reality check.

"All babies look like chickens."

When the doctor held him up, his legs didn't uncurl. "Dislocated hips." *There's nothing wrong with my baby. Maybe he looks a little funny, but Matthew and I aren't exactly centerfolds.* A common mixed-breed girl: Irish milk skin dinged with acne, Germanic chin, and Polish thighs, too lavish for their petite frame. A dreamy Irish boy, bone skinny and delicate. *Ollie's one of us.* "Take him over to the hospital," the doctor said. "They'll snap his hips into place, and he'll be good as new."

I zipped Ollie inside my jacket, snuggling his tiny ear to my heart, as the bus dodged potholes down Lincoln Avenue. My mother cautioned me: "When I was eight, Pa took me for my first streetcar ride. I woke up in Cook County Hospital without my tonsils. My sister Josie was supposed to get the operation, but she run away." A few years out of Poland, they believed they'd be kicked off relief if someone didn't show up. *Does Ollie's doctor need to fill a spot on his docket? Get a grip, you're not an immigrant.* I was clumsy at nurture. He was my practice case, and I might as well have been in a foreign land.

Ollie became a file number: 127164. Snapping his baby hips back into place took more than a flick of the orthopedist's wrist. "Leave him here, come back in a week, maybe two, he'll be fine," the doctor said. Like taking a car in for service. His femurs were deformed, and they put him in traction, hanging a five-pound weight from eight-pound Ollie. *Do it to me, hang me upside down, pack me in concrete, but don't touch my baby.* Only two weeks old, he was so new to the world, my little pot roast, fresh from my kitchen table.

I left the hospital without Ollie, escorted by a burly security guard who smelled like fried carp and who offered me a Lucky Strike. "Don't go gettin' all hot and bothered, honey, visiting hours is over, and you can't stay here no more." But where was I to go? Ollie couldn't live without me. They'd ignore him, starve him, experiment on him. I was his milk, my arms were his skin. It was as if they had taken one of my organs and left it, disconnected and bleeding, to die. "Go get yourself some broasted chicken," the guard said.

I sat with Matthew in the coffee shop across the street from the hospital until it closed at midnight. Do something! Kill the guard, storm the hospital, file a lawsuit, kidnap our baby. Didn't he see that I was coming apart? Why had I married him anyway? He had wooed me with his poems, so light and airy that the groaning breath of the world seemed to stand still. The poems held me tight, and I clung to them the way Matthew clung to me. Before we got married, my father had been calling at three in the morning, dawn, noon. "Whore, I know you're on drugs! No good Catholic girl runs away from home and shacks up with a man. Where you getting them drugs? Give yourself up." He said the narcotics squad had surrounded my apartment and would take me away in a white coat and lock me up. After months of intermittent calls, and the silence of my mother who drew the shades and told everyone I was dead, I said to Matthew, "Let's get married. Maybe it'll stop."

"Sure," he said. I picked out two rings at Woolworth's, ninety-nine cents each, and when it was my turn to say I do, I started to laugh. The Cook County magistrate said stop cackling or leave the courthouse. *But it's not in the plan. I'm not supposed to get married. Not supposed to be my mother.* I tried to think of one thing I liked about Matthew: Even his poems couldn't save me now. Myrtle stamped our marriage certificate: E 7766. The next day, my father called: "Now you're a legitimate whore." My mother broke her silence and took the telephone: "Father Boniface says now you're excommunicated. You didn't get married in the Church." A week later, Matthew received a telegram from his parents: IF YOU MARRY THAT POLISH GIRL WE NEVER WANT TO SEE YOU AGAIN.

During Ollie's second week in the hospital, I rented a breast pump. I couldn't hold him or nurse him because it would interfere with his traction. So he lay in his steel crib at night, under the weight of a Rube Goldberg contraption, while I lay in my bed with rubber suction cups over my nipples, trying to keep the nectar flowing between us. Matthew drank at his desk until the apartment was dark and the only poetry he could get out was a grunt. Mornings, I waited at the hospital with my Styrofoam cooler filled with plastic bottles of breast milk, peering through the glass door, counting minutes on the clock

above the lobby desk until, at ten o'clock, the security guard released
the latches, and a stampede of mothers were let loose to find their
babies. I gave my bottles of milk to the nurse, small offerings to let
Ollie know that I was still the source of good things. But when shifts
changed, the bottles were lost or emptied down the sink.

With Ollie's legs still crooked after ten days in traction, the doctor
attached a heavier weight to loosen his hips. His body slid across the
sheet, jamming against the steel bars of the crib. They strapped him
to a board to hold him in place, but the straps tore his skin. "We have
to get serious, Mother," the doctor said. In the cast room, he drove a
metal pin through Ollie's femur, drilling through bone without anes-
thesia. Matthew and I stood at the window watching Ollie's body
stiffen and turn scarlet as the doctor hammered the pin through his
leg. Ollie gasped, and I pounded on the window. His fists opened and
closed like fish gills sucking in air, and I lunged for the door. He
screamed, I answered, and for the only time since his birth, we were
in complete synchrony: an aria of mother and child wailing. When
the pin was in place, the doctor stopped drilling, wiped beads of
sweat from his brow, and looked quizzical. "What's all the fuss about,
Mother? Babies don't feel pain."

I kept vigil at Ollie's bed. I would leave the apartment in the morning, mostly unwashed, often in the same clothes from the night
before. Circling the hospital, I searched for the window to his room.
From the moment the lobby doors opened until a polite voice on the
loudspeaker informed all visitors to leave, I was at his side, petting the
downy hairs of his head through the metal bars as he lay on his board.
He cried all the time, even in sleep. Matthew sat on the other side of
Ollie's bed, no longer able to write an unslurred word, hiding whatever he found to drink in a brown bag. I circled the hospital again at
night when the security guard forced me from his room. Sometimes I
didn't go home at all but lived on the street, watching for light in his
window. Late into the night, I sat on the curb feeling milk leak

through my shirt. One day I took the last breast pump bottle and filled it with found objects from my daily circling: a bottle cap, a rusted paper clip, an expired bus transfer, half a holy card with the Blessed Virgin's head ripped in two. I sent it floating away in the melting snow. Soon there was no more milk, and my breasts disappeared. Ollie and I were no longer a team.

A social worker came to see me. "I'm Miss Bennett. Could I ask you a few questions?" She was neat and pretty, like June Cleaver, the *Leave It to Beaver* mother.

What a relief to talk to someone who didn't want to poke or probe Ollie.

"We like to get a complete history whenever a family presents with birth defects. Is this your first child?" I shook my head yes. "Former miscarriages or abortions?" I shook no. "Did you ever take drugs?"

"You mean like aspirin?"

"No, I mean illegal substances."

I didn't even take Midol when I got cramps. I had tried marijuana, long before I was pregnant, but didn't like the burning in my throat so never smoked again. *They all have this thing about drugs. Does she know my father?* Miss Bennett explained that congenital malformations of the hips occur between the sixth and eighth week of fetal development. What was I doing back then? Later, I turned back the pages in my daybook to March, April, the beginning of spring. Shakespeare paper due. Boss on vacation. Matthew sold his blood to buy beer. What else? Malathion, scribbled in the margin of the calendar next to the Daylight Savings Time reminder. White fly! The begonia had white fly, and I had sprayed it with a weak mixture of Malathion. Could I have poisoned myself? The bottle did have a skull and crossbones on the warning label. Did I do anything else to cause Ollie's birth defects? Sex, masturbation, impure thoughts? Was the Church right after all? Was this punishment, retribution? Or was it something I ate. Too much red licorice? What about that time I ate the whole package of cupcakes with the pink frosting? Food dye! Could I blame the Food and Drug Administration?

During teaching rounds, doctors gathered around Ollie's crib and talked while he whimpered. If he cried too loud, the wall of white coats moved to the hall. The urologists were the worst. One doctor in particular poked and probed with analytic glee, as if my baby were a specimen for dissection. Ollie screamed long after the doctor left. I put gin in his milk to help him sleep. If it silenced my husband, it might soothe my baby. But he threw it up. I could have killed him. I wanted to kill him. He was a tiny, quivering, imperfect baby whom I was helpless to protect.

Dr. Merman, the chief urologist, said that there was something wrong with Ollie's kidneys. He wanted to explore surgically. "Only one kidney showed up on X-ray, and even that one doesn't function as it should." I got on the Halsted bus and kept riding: through Greek town, through the Cabrini Green housing project, past Ernie's Gun and Ammo. I returned to the hospital with a soft blue blanket and a fleecy white dog, small penances to tuck around my Buddha baby. Ollie's file had been left in the room. The first thing I saw when I opened it was the social worker's report: *Mother admitted to taking drugs during pregnancy.*

Surgery took place just before Christmas. The snow was heavy, and Matthew and I argued all the way to the hospital. Borrowing money from his parents had put him in a bad mood. "Couldn't they offer up ten dollars for their grandson?" We could get more mileage out of ten dollars than ten Hail Mary's. They'd reminded him that he wouldn't have these problems if he hadn't married the Polish girl.

We waited in a room for five hours with a dozen other parents on plaid couches. One woman worked a rosary, her fingertips callused, waiting out her four-year-old's sixth surgery. Another passed out donuts while her daughter, Carmen, had a shunt planted in her skull. Alone in the corner, under a painting of the Himalayas, Matthew sucked Guinness from a brown bag. Halfway through Ollie's surgery, a doctor emerged from the operating room with a progress report: "Everything's fine. We want you to know that we removed his appendix as a bonus."

In the morning, we learned about ureterostomies. During surgery, Dr. Merman had decided to cut Ollie's ureter and create an opening in his right side to take stress off his baby plumbing. The chair next to Ollie's bed was laden with dirty sheets. He was throwing up. "We came here for crooked legs." *They've butchered my son.*

"Your baby has a rare kidney condition," the doctor said. "He probably won't live to be a year old."

How will he pee? The raw pink hole in Ollie's side leaked drops of urine.

"The urine bypasses the ureter and bladder altogether now. He'll wear a bag. An elegant surgery. We've never done one of these on a baby."

"He'll pee in a bag?" *Whip out his bag when the other boys are comparing notes in the boys' bathroom?*

"This'll buy him some time." Then it hit me. There would be no life. In the spring or in the fall, we'd put Ollie in a tiny coffin and say goodbye.

I dug out the diary from my Friends of the Library tote, but words were caked in me like scum on the oatmeal pot. I was under the porch stairs again, where I went as a child to examine my bloody welts. Crouching in the musty space, my back against the third step and my head bowed under the fourth, I killed my mother, my SS officer, Scary Sophia, over and over in a spiral Raggedy Ann notebook. By eighth grade I had killed her 107 times, the Blessed Virgin thirteen times, and God twice. Now there was no one to kill.

On Christmas Eve, the five other cribs in the hospital nursery were empty, the lights dim. Ollie had a 105-degree fever. The nurse packed him in ice and hung a red Santa on his bed. I leaned over his crib, lips close to his face, tasting his baby breath. *Feel my warmth and take me in.* I had nothing to give him. Not my milk, not my arms. I was like my cat, licking her stillborn kitten back to life. But I didn't know how to protect him. "Let me stay." The voice came over the loudspeaker for the end of visiting hours.

"You can't. Against policy," the nurse said. "We don't have room for parents. If you stay, all the other parents will want to stay."

I looked around the empty room. "What other parents? Please, please, I won't take up any space, just let me stay with my baby. You can have my leather jacket. I'll do anything. Sweep the floor, file. Please. I'll hide in the closet if security comes. Please, please, he's so little, so scared. Let me stay with him."

A few days of traction turned into a month, then two. Not long after Ollie's kidney surgery, the orthopedist came to see me. Matthew was at school trying to convince a professor not to fail him, even though he had not written his *Tale of Genji* paper and had gone to class so seldom that when he showed up, the professor thought he had come to repair the leaky radiator. Having quit work and dropped out of school, I was a permanent fixture next to the steel crib. I never showed up again anywhere after Ollie was born. Nobody knew where I was, except my parents, who offered up a mass for Ollie's soul. I had damned him by not baptizing him. "The kidney is punishment," my father said. "God don't abide no pigheadedness." "*Nerka, nerka, nerka,*" SS lamented. "The baby's damaged because his mother thinks she knows things."

"He seems to be doing better," the doctor said when Ollie was out of traction. "Healing nicely." Drops of pale urine dripped from Ollie's side, and I dabbed them with gauze. His skin was too raw for an adhesive bag to stick. Everything was clear now. We'd take him home where he belonged, home where he began and where nothing would hurt him again. He'd have a sweet time on earth, however short. I was already preparing my arms for him to die.

"I've scheduled surgery for Thursday," the orthopedist said.

"He *had* surgery." Couldn't he keep his patients straight?

"No, orthopedic surgery. The traction didn't accomplish what we had hoped, so we'll go in surgically now and repair his left hip. He'll have to wear a body cast for a few months. Then we'll do the other hip."

"Why?" Was I missing something?

"So he can walk when he grows up."

"Don't you guys talk to each other?" I pulled down the crib bars and started to dress Ollie. The doctor put his hand on my arm. As if by signal, two nurses and an aide swooped down on me like a SWAT team. "I'm taking him home. Get away!" A scrimmage for my baby.

"You can't do that." He squeezed my arm harder. "I'll get a court order."

"But he's going to die."

"Maybe. Then again, he may not. In medicine, nothing's certain. At least give him the chance to walk. Without surgery, he'll never stand up. He deserves that much. Don't make me get a court order."

Did we take Ollie home to die peacefully, defying medical advice, or leave him in the hospital for further repairs, on the off-chance that he might live? Was the glass half-empty or half-full? Was there some unifying principle holding this all together? I chewed my nails and bit the skin until it bled. I had taken to snitching Ollie's chart to see what the doctors were planning. The orthopedist had scribbled in red ink: *Mother repeatedly thwarts doctors' efforts to help baby.*

Two surgeries later, wrapped in plaster from his ankles to underarms, Ollie came home to an apartment littered with empty beer bottles and open books. I put him on a soft pillow in his crib. He lay stiff, legs splayed in the full spica cast, unable to move anything but his head and arms.

It was spring, and I opened all the windows so Ollie could hear the sounds of the neighborhood and watch the dance of the origami animals on the ceiling. Matthew folded them at night while he drank. I tried to hold Ollie, maneuvering his bulky cast to bring his face close to me, but he arched his neck and pulled away, refusing my touch. He held his own bottle, as if he needed no one. I spent my days sitting by his side, mourning for my baby. Or deep in the rabbit hole of my diary, trying to write my way out of the maze. Or wandering from room to room, eating whatever I could find, thinking of things to amuse Ollie, ashamed of not loving him enough.

I stood over him, singing "You Are My Sunshine," daydreaming about the other babies at the hospital: the tiny Mexican girl with cleft palate, the Hasidic baby with cerebral palsy, and the one with the bowling ball head and the shunt for draining it. The mother of the four-year-old gave me her rosary with aurora borealis beads when her boy died. I had used it to distract Ollie when the doctor cut a circle in the side of his cast and the nurse showed me how to put Kotex over the hole in his body to soak up the pee. He whipped the rosary across my face, nicking my cornea with the edge of the crucifix. His skin was raw now. Urine leaked into the layers of plaster, burning sores into his back and wetting his cast. I fanned him with a Chinese fan, shooing away flies that landed on his toes and buzzed around his head. One day I poked my finger into the doughy plaster and noticed tiny translucent larvae wriggling in the soft spots of his cast. Flies had laid their eggs in the crevices that were soggy with urine. I put my head out the window and screamed. I put a pillow over Ollie's head and wished he would die. He was mine to protect, and I couldn't keep the maggots away.

ONE EVENING, as we were listening to the *Midnight Special,* I asked Matthew, "What are we going to do for money?" Rent was past due, and the superintendent of our building, a no-nonsense guy from West Virginia in an undershirt, had been at the door twice with threats and a shotgun. My father tried to get Matthew a job, driving a truck or washing windows like him. But even my father knew that some men are not made for work. Matthew had hands like a Florentine Jesus. His body was gaunt and stylized, nourished on tobacco and spirits. "Money's the root of all evil," Matthew said.

"Is that why you sell your blood?" Money was driving us apart. When Debbie, my acquaintance from the Maternity Center, and her husband, Sam, came to visit, we had no food to offer them. Sam couldn't bear to be around Ollie. "Man, look at that poor little thing. It breaks me up. I can't take it. Shit, Debbie, we gotta go, honey."

"Maybe if we had some cheese or a cake to offer Debbie and Sam, they would have stayed," I told Matthew.

"Yeah, and maybe if I returned Sam's kisses when he followed me into the bathroom they would have moved in." And maybe if we had a healthy boy with plump legs and perfect kidneys, the world would be different. In the night, Matthew woke me up to describe a trip to Mars and I knew he was on acid. Purple microdot had replaced poetry.

EVERY DAY I planned how Ollie would die. The details changed— in the morning, in the night, after a spring rain, during a storm—but in my fantasies, he was nestled between Matthew and me, our three hearts beating together until Ollie's stopped and there was only the two of us. That's the part that scared me. But Ollie thrived. When he didn't die by the end of his first year, I drew a tiny grim reaper in a birthday hat in the margin of my diary. Dr. Belman said, "These things are unpredictable. Your boy surprised us." Then he said Ollie wouldn't make it to his teenage years. But I stopped listening. "He has thirty percent function of one kidney," the doctor said. "I'm sorry, but no kidney with that damage can withstand the raging hormones and systemic changes of adolescence." From then on I pretended that the glass was half-full. Together we would look for the rest of the nectar.

One day, when Ollie was almost three, I sat on the stoop in front of our flat, watching him play on the sidewalk. He fed ants lumps of bread, then put the ants, along with a damaged grasshopper, into his pocket. "My friends, Mommy." Everything seemed right with the world. Matthew had a job working in a preschool, and the rent was paid. I had completed my bachelor's degree, squeezing in courses piecemeal between Ollie's hospital stays; I wasn't even sure what my degree was in. Ollie's hips were held together with steel, and he had learned to walk. He could even pee. Dr. Merman had decided to sew up his ureter. "The truth is, we don't really know what's wrong with his kidney, but thirty percent function is enough to get by, for *now*." Ollie dumped more crumbs on the sidewalk, some for the ants, some for him, and I looked up from my book. I was reading about the life of Isadora Duncan, the part where she waves goodbye to her small children, Deirdre and Patrick, and watches their rolling car plunge into the Seine, killing them. I read her words aloud, accompanied by the Spanish dance music blaring from a window across the street: "Only twice comes that cry of the mother," Duncan wrote, "at birth and at death." One the cry of joy and the other of sorrow. And they were the same. Ollie asked what I was mumbling. When he started to run, his long stick legs pumping awkwardly beneath his checkered shorts, I decided to have another baby. I would name her Isadora, and she would dance for us, teaching Ollie to move his legs with freedom and teaching me to open my heart.

Range of Desire

K. G. SCHNEIDER

"I once read an essay about a woman who spent seventy-five hundred dollars on a sick cat," remembers K. G. Schneider. "If that had been a short story, I would have said, 'Huh—I don't think so.' But because it really happened, I believed it, and it was the factualness of this detail that hung in the air like a butterfly, amazing me." Schneider's story—which appeared online in Nerve and explores her love for women and guns—lacks in such fantastic details as seventy-five-hundred-dollar vet bills but nevertheless employs vivid details that leave no doubt about the intensity of the experiences she describes.

When I talk about my experiences with guns in the military, now memories nearly two decades old, somewhere in the conversation the listener inevitably demands that I admit I never really liked guns, that they scared me, that I was nervous, that we were all nervous, that we only did it because we were told to, that guns were alien and terrifying, and that I will never, ever use a gun again, cross my heart and hope the Democrats win in '08.

But that would be like saying I never liked women, that they scare me, that I renounce my cravings, that when it comes to being a woman with a predilection for the ladies, I am truly sorry and I humbly repent.

All these statements would be lies.

THE FIRST TIME I was with a woman was a rushed, ecstatic culmination after months of a long, slow tease and decades of ignorance and denial. That is exactly how it was for me with guns. We—two dozen basic trainees at Lackland Air Force Base, 1983—had itched to be on the rifle range, and we talked and whispered about it constantly, whenever talking was allowed, through several weeks of long droning classes, endless marching, foul food, classes on personal hygiene and military discipline, four A.M. runs in military formation, and endless pull-ups. Determinism had slowly purged our ranks of the wack jobs, bedwetters, and chunky chickens (also called, in even more direct military fashion, "fat girls") who threatened our ability to Fly, Fight, and Win. A mild collective case of Stockholm Syndrome caused us to begin agreeing heartily with anything the training instructors shouted, including the prediction, "Ladies, you're gonna love shooting!"

The M16A1 is a military classic: an eight-pound, thirty-round, air-cooled, magazine-fed rifle, black and beautiful, with a cleaning kit tucked into a cunning hidden compartment in its butt-stock. When we finally picked it up, if there was a woman in the room who had the tiniest qualm (perhaps the very young thing who had arrived at basic with her teddy bear and a box of sanitary napkins), no one owned up to it. The sissy-la-las had already been kicked out, and their gender-betraying weepy ways were not missed, not even by the very young thing, whose eyes shone as she hoisted the rifle for the very first time.

In some respects, it is easy to understand why we recruits cottoned to guns so easily; why, on the day of weapons training, we rose well before the pre-dawn bugle call; why we were washed, ready, and in formation on the cement apron in front of our barracks long before our TI showed up; why, on the long, bumpy bus ride to the range, we were silent with thrilled anticipation; and why the rifle felt so good when we finally touched it, like a promise come home to roost. We were self-selected. Without a military draft in effect—let alone a draft that selected women—the armed forces were filled with young people who wanted to be there, and "there" was not just a job or an organization, but a way of life, one that hinted, however abstractly, of a world where guns were acceptable and often necessary.

For every woman who joined up with a decade of experience hunting squirrels with Daddy, there were two who had never touched, even seen, a gun. Yet somehow, in the mysterious equation wherein we know things about ourselves, these women knew they were, shall I say, predisposed. Years of research by the Department of Defense have revealed that among recruits, more women than men are unfamiliar with guns, but after qualifying on the range—which women do with expertise equal to men, despite studies I suspect were intended to demonstrate otherwise—they feel equally comfortable with guns.

WE EACH HAVE a private path to the discovery of self and desire. The universe has a pecking order that insists that early, independent knowledge is best: the young daughter who begs to go possum-hunting and bags a deer on her first trip; the gay man who always knew he was different (and, more to the point, how); the transsexual who has known since the dawn of consciousness that he had the right brain in the wrong body; the trial lawyer who as a toddler clambered onto a tree stump and exhorted. But more of us, the less highly evolved, stumble forward blindly in life, tugged this way and that by cultural rules and imperatives. A chance occurrence—an encounter with a gun or a woman's soft lips—changes everything. Then, if we are fortunate, this encounter submits us to the mysterious imperatives of life itself. I look at the objects of my desire: women and guns, yes, but also roses, Wellfleet oysters, silver earrings, dry red wine, the color green in nearly every hue, fat new books, the gentle tweezing process of revising an essay, and the peppery fragrance of eucalyptus trees after a heavy rain; I understand that these are my desires, acquired slowly and haphazardly over nearly fifty years; but I do not understand why, nor perhaps should I. I am merely grateful that my desires and I got together in the first place.

ON THE WEAPONS range I lay prone, my rifle ready. I silently begged our weapons instructor, Sergeant Ireland, to give us the order to fire. The wet heat of a summer afternoon in Texas pressed through my uniform, flattening my back like a huge unseen hand, but a broad green awning shaded my novice eyes from the fierce August sun, and my belly and breasts and thighs were deliciously comfortable from the cool, immaculate cement floor of the firing line. My breathing rasped harsh in my head, all other sounds muffled behind huge red Air Force–issue ear defenders wrapped tight around my sweating skull.

I was supposed to be eyes-forward, focused on the concentric paper target positioned in front of me across fifty feet of scruffy tan dirt, but I slid my eyes sideways just to see if the airman to my right was as excited as I was. She caught my eye and tilted a grin in my direction. We quickly slid our eyes forward again as Sergeant Ireland walked behind us, lecturing twenty-four recruits one last time about Attention to Detail, Safety (which, he frequently reminded us, was

Paramount), and Never Pointing Your Weapon at Anything You Don't Plan to Shoot.

Guns, I am told, are dangerous. But women are dangerous, too. A woman can rip your heart from your chest and drop it like a child discarding a candy wrapper, or stand in front of you, a disdainful smile on her face, tossing your heart from one hand to another while your blood drips through her fingers. It is much worse when your heart is not left behind.

No one explains the cruelest trick of life. You are happy, and life is good, and the years roll on, until you wake up one night, terrified, because you realize that the worst thing that can ever happen to you is for something to happen to her, and there is no way to avoid that eventual tragedy other than dying first, which is almost as frightening. It is all infinitely worse because she is a woman and the logic of your heart insists there is nothing better than a woman, particularly this woman. You are caught in this conundrum; your attention to detail failed you miserably and completely, way back when it was still possible to leave. So you lie fretting in the dark while your beloved breathes in and out in the night air, and you sense the entrapment of desire, the very danger of life itself.

Compared to that, a gun is harmless.

ON THE FIRING range, we finally heard the command:

"Ready!"

I lifted the M16 and cocked my head so I could focus through the rifle's sights. Now the target looked gray and distant and a little unfocused, its dark circles less distinct, but I braced my shoulder and hoped for the best.

We were all perfectly still for two long beats. My breath rattled in my head. I concentrated: Gun. Target. Gun. Target. The world contracted into a universe populated only by my arms, my eyes, my ragged breath, the M16, and a square of paper hanging motionless in the summer heat.

At last we heard:

"Fire!"

As I had been taught, I stopped breathing. The tip of my left index finger, finally liberated from waiting, retracted the trigger of the rifle. The M16 opened up with a glorious power and raucous blattering louder than anything I had heard in my life, a sound that drowned all thought and replaced it with a pure white space. For a split second, the gun was stronger than me, shaking my shoulders and causing me to levitate very slightly from the concrete floor I was splayed on, but I trained my body against the weapon and concentrated—gun, target, gun, target—as the rifle spat bullets through the moist summer air. Across the range, dark spots instantaneously pocked twenty-four targets. Flat on the ground and burdened with our rifles, we could not see one another, but I could tell we had done well by the triumphant pitch of Sergeant Ireland's voice as he shouted:

"Hold fire!"

We immediately stopped, then took breath. For one long beat the sound of machine-gun fire continued to travel across the air, the faintest echo of an echo. As marksmen do everywhere, we promptly looked at our targets, which to our gratification we had blown to kingdom come. The air was pungent with a tangy fragrance bitter in the back of my throat—the delicious tongue-coating flavor of gunpowder I would come to anticipate and crave—and my hands were warm and damp; I wiped my fingers on my fatigues, away from the creases so my uniform wouldn't lose its spray-starch edge. I was spent, amazed and almost immediately hungry for more. My body ached, partly from the unfamiliar position on the cement, and partly from joy.

I have been advised I could stop liking guns if I tried; I could excise that dark, rotten spot that threatens to spread and taint the flesh of my soul. I imagine there are books. Study tapes. Meditative exercises. I would not be surprised to hear, particularly in these parts, that someone had established an ex-gun movement, where through daily rituals and a list of proscribed thoughts and activities taped to the refrigerator door, I could claim to purge myself of the way I feel about weapons.

But denial not only makes the heart grow fonder; it makes the heart grow desperate, makes it panic with subterranean keening. I have counseled myself, in a quavering voice in my head, that I will simply not have a gun in my life, that it is far too much risk and trouble, that no one will understand, that it will be the ruin of me, that these urges are fundamentally wrong. My desire feels disloyal, shameful, and selfish; it stands between us, this secret I cannot share.

But despite my daily promises, my straining for internal discipline, in the face of desire I feel the citadel walls buckling. I look at guns on the Internet; I hide in the stacks at the public library and pore over gun catalogs; I push open the door in my head and replay every moment I ever spent with guns, reliving the finger in the trigger, the pocked target, the tang of gunpowder, the afterglow of satiation. When I can't bear it any more, when my brain itches with desire, I drive fifteen miles up the peninsula, telling myself I am merely investigating this subject for research, as if anyone asked me to write about guns. On one of the wearier blocks of El Camino Real, where every store has roll-down metal awnings to protect it at night, I park in front of a gun shop and walk in.

I am reassured that my secret is safe, because the huge storefront windows are obscured nearly to ceiling height by the store's goods: racks of hunting vests and pants, some bright orange, some camouflage; brown cardboard cases of survival food; two walls of holsters, gun belts, and bullet magazines; displays crowded with shimmering fishing lures; and vast stacks of miscellaneous gun and hunting tchotchkes, most in ever-fashionable black. I walk up to the glass counter, which is packed with pistols neatly lined up on velvet with price tags turned out so I don't even have to ask. I look for a while as a businessman in rolled-up sleeves leans one elbow on the cash register and talks about how he's going to cook the wild duck he shot last weekend. The beefy guy restocking the holster selection half-listens, nodding, occasionally cutting his eyes my way with a friendly glance.

I feel timid, the way I felt a decade earlier, freshly out of the military and trying to come out of the closet, the first few times I went into a lesbian bookstore in the Village (unsurprisingly gone today, as most gay and lesbian bookstores are gone, victims of assimilation, acceptance, and the Web). I was living in New York, a period when I was disabusing myself of the notion that I wanted to live there again. In this small store on a hard-to-find side street, I would browse the pitiful selection of well-thumbed books on dusty shelves while thick-waisted older women with crew cuts stood around jawing about some big old contretemps that had taken place at the Gay and Lesbian Center the previous night.

I always wondered if I was supposed to join in the conversation, or just buy my book and leave. Leave is what I did every time, wimp that I was, though I would ever-so-daringly remove my purchase from its bag on my way home so everyone on the subway car would know I was reading *The Price of Salt* or the latest issue of *The Lesbian Connection*. Each time I did this, tilting the book or magazine so the title was visibly displayed, I hoped I might then lock eyes with the love of my life, sitting right across from me on the Number 7 train, or at least meet someone who could give me a clue; though these things naturally never happened—well, they did, but not on the subway.

In the gun store, I am wondering what I should say to the man restocking the holsters when from behind the business end of the gun counter materializes a plump, pretty woman in a sleeveless white top, glossy brown curls streaming past her shoulders. She is smiling at me. (Perhaps the man at the counter pressed a hidden button: CHICK

ALERT! GET THE LADY CLERK!) I tell her it's been a long time since I shot a gun, and I'm really just looking. (In a gun shop, the catechism begins: "Have you ever shot a gun?" The right answer is "Yes, and it was good." I can never tell if I gain or lose points by reciting my conquests: M16, .22, .357, and the loaded .38-special I carried in wargame exercises, lightly touching its leather holster from time to time, the way I unconsciously touch my breasts when I'm reading a particularly good book.)

"Is this for personal protection, or for recreation?" asks the shopgirl, delicately.

"I'm not sure. Maybe both," I say, mesmerized by the candy in the counter.

I see from the shopgirl's smile that she knows I've been thinking about a gun all along. Without prompting, she reaches under the counter and pulls out a piece of paper listing local rifle ranges, the letters blurred from repeated copying.

Withdrawing a pen tucked into her bodice, she circles three ranges she says I will "really like" (though I don't know her criteria, and I am afraid to ask). She then says she has just the thing for me and disappears into the back of the store, returning a moment later with a smooth black plastic case. She opens it, revealing a nine-millimeter semiautomatic Glock, its black matte contours nestled in dimpled pink foam. With one brisk motion she cracks back its slide, revealing the empty, waiting chamber, then offers the Glock to me butt-first.

My heart thumps. I slowly accept the gun with my left hand, watching through the corner of my eyes so I know the shopgirl is observing how nicely, how safely, how carefully I handle the pistol, always pointing it down and away. This delicacy, this attention to detail, this awareness that I must Never Point at Anything I Don't Plan to Shoot: in my shyness, this is the closest I can get to flirting, an activity I should not be engaged in anyway—except that as long as I am in a gun shop, an activity which I know would earn me a severe scolding from my beloved, I might as well be naughty all around.

The gun feels much too good. It feels as good as the first time I cupped a woman's breast in my hands, a moment where everything I had ever known before suddenly seemed wrong or boring or gray. The Glock fits my hand perfectly, with that same compelling sense of magical, inevitable destiny. My index finger curls in the trigger, and I gently heft the pistol, considering its weight and admiring its delicately tooled crevices, its sumptuously rounded muzzle. I run my right hand across the twin nubs of its sights while inhaling the light musk scent of gun oil; then I slowly trace my fingers along the smooth, silky curves of the barrel before toying with the dark recesses of the pistol's frame. I feel myself succumb. I am born for this gun. It is costly; it is dangerous; it is beautiful. It is, perhaps, irresistible.

The Dangerous Joy of Dr. Sex

The Story of Alex Comfort, in Seventeen Positions

PAGAN KENNEDY

"When I set out to draw a portrait of sex guru Alex Comfort," says Pagan Kennedy, "I knew I had to do more than just illuminate Comfort himself: to understand this man, readers would have to hurtle back into the 1970s. After all, the biographer's job is to show the person embedded in his era, like a fly frozen in golden amber. In this case, I would coax readers to travel with me to the moment before AIDS hit, when millions of Americans—from the orgy rooms of California to the waterbeds of New Jersey—tried to re-invent love." In this previously unpublished essay that draws on extensive research and new interviews with Comfort's friends and family, Kennedy tells the little-known story of the author of The Joy of Sex *and shows how his work changed life in the American bedroom.*

Fireworks

One day in 1934, he sequestered himself in his family's greenhouse in London to perform an experiment. Alex Comfort—then fourteen years old—had decided to invent his own fireworks. He ground together sugar, sulfur, and saltpeter, an operation so dangerous that most chemists pour water over the ingredients to prevent a blast. Alex neglected to take that precaution. The container exploded. The roof of the greenhouse blew out. A red-tinted vapor hovered in the air before him. Four fingers on his left hand had vanished, leaving a lump of meat with one thumb hanging off it. He felt no pain. Indeed, he found it thrilling to be blown apart.

Or, at least, that's how he told the story later. Alex Comfort loved explosions, even the one that mutilated him. He never would admit any regret at the loss of his four fingers. As a middle-aged physician, he bragged that his stump could be more useful than a conventional hand, particularly when it came to performing certain medical procedures—exploring a woman's birth canal, for instance.

One thing was clear after the accident: Alex should avoid laboratories, at least until he was older. So he set his sights on literary greatness instead. When he was sixteen, his father took him on a tramp steamer to Buenos Aires and then Senegal; Alex scribbled notes along the way. In 1938, his final year of high school, he published a little gem of travel book, *The Silver River,* billed as the "diary of a schoolboy."

The Glove

When Alex arrived at Cambridge University, the other students stood in awe of him—a published author! He regarded himself as brilliant but ugly. A reed-thin boy in a tweed jacket, he kept his eyes caged behind glittering round glasses and wore a glove on one hand. "I didn't like to ask him why," said Robert Greacen, who befriended Alex during his university years. One day, when they shared a train car together, Alex removed the glove, and Greacen noticed the stump, but still didn't dare mention it.

The truth was, Greacen had fallen under the spell of Alex Comfort. "Even though we were the same age, he seemed like a man ten or twelve years older than me in ideas, reading, and opinion." Greacen decided that Alex was the cleverest person he'd ever met.

Indeed. At age twenty-two, Alex began sparring with George Orwell in the pages of the *Tribune*; in rhyming verse, they debated whether Britain should have entered World War II. Alex sneered at the concept of a "good war" and denounced the group-think of the British. He was, already, an anarchist.

Snail Shell

Strangely enough, for one so devoted to free thought, Alex remained a virgin throughout most of his university days. "I was a terribly learned little man. I swotted away at my books," he said later. At Cambridge, he rarely spoke to young women—except on Sundays. Then he broke from his studies to run up the stairs of a Congregational church to join an antiwar gathering, young people in corduroys and tweeds, with bobby-pinned hair and precocious pipes. There he met Ruth Harris and her friend Jane Henderson. They seemed to be opposites: Ruth, a pale girl shrouded in a dark coat, had a submissive air about her; Jane, with an explosion of curls, liked to argue about books. Both girls pined after the boy-genius with a leather glove on his hand, but Ruth confessed her love first. Once she'd spilled out her feelings to him, Alex felt honor-bound to her.

In 1943, they married. They commenced to fumble their way through sex acts, ineptly deflowering one another, then set up house in a tree-lined neighborhood outside London.

Did Ruth realize what she was getting into? Raised by church-going Congregational parents, she aspired to be a social worker, to help the poor and then return home to tea cozies. "My mother was happier in a much more stifling, suburban atmosphere than my father," according to their son Nick.

Everyone knew Alex to be an eccentric visionary, and he behaved like one, making odd demands of his shy wife. One day he asked her to wear her bikini when she gardened; he wanted to be able to peer out the window and watch her bend over their rose beds in nearly nothing. Ruth complied. Soon he wanted more. After the milkman clip-clopped down their lane in a horse-drawn cart, Alex asked Ruth to go out with a shovel and collect the manure left behind, then use it to fertilize their flowers. Could she do this in her bikini? Ruth obediently climbed into her swimsuit and headed out onto the street with the shovel.

Ruth regarded herself as the long-suffering wife of a great man. She tried not to complain, though the pure force of his intellect wore her out. He followed her into rooms ranting about whatever subject obsessed him at the moment—ballroom dancing, electricity, cell growth, dulcimers, cooking, pacifism, anarchism, utopia. "Holding a conversation with Dr. Comfort is rather like racing after an express train that has already puffed out of the station," a journalist wrote later.

For his part, Alex tried to tamp down the impulses that upset his wife, and it cost him dearly. "I suffered from a severe form of migraine and it produced an intensive depression," he said later of that period. In order to rein himself in, he resorted to following a well-established British trope: He became an introverted polymath, pottering from one enthusiasm to the next. His son Nick, born in 1946, remembers his father building a television from spare parts and glue-soaked Weetabix. Alex also wired up innumerable burglar alarms, which only went off when they weren't supposed to, emitting inappropriate shrieks.

And he wrote with blazing speed—poetry, novels, science papers, sociology. By 1950, he'd published a dozen books. A medical doctor and biologist, he became a leading authority on snails, that creature that symbolizes the slow and cautious and flabby. It seemed that the younger Alex—the boy who blew things up—had been squashed forever and replaced by a morose intellectual.

"He seemed like a workaholic—only we didn't have that word back then. He was puritanical," said Greacen, who added that the only way to spend time with Alex was to find him in his lab or or else tag along to antiwar meetings. The two belonged to a coalition of writers denouncing Cold War hostilities. After their meetings, the writers adjourned to a pub, to huff on pipes and jaw about books. But Comfort refused to join them. Instead of socializing, "he would jump in his car and go home," according to Greacen. "He thought I was lazy. Once he said to me, 'Look Bob, you shouldn't hang around in pubs with people. You'll get no work done.' When I spent two or three hours with him, I'd go away absolutely tired—my head would be filled with all he said about literature and politics. I used to wonder when he slept." Alex Comfort obsessed about poems, political rants, novels, scientific studies—always, he hurled himself into a realm of thought.

Then, in the late 1950s, Comfort developed a new obsession, one as dangerous, in its way, as the gunpowder had been. He couldn't stop wondering about Jane, Ruth's best friend from university days, now a frequent dinner guest at their house. His wife was the kind of woman who shrunk into middle age. Jane, on the other hand, blossomed at age forty. At ease in her big-boned and athletic body, she made only a token effort to keep her lipstick on straight. To hell with propriety! Her curls blew out everywhere, like springs popping from the active gears of her mind. She was as full of ideas as Alex. Instead of marrying, she'd devoted herself to books, and now she worked as a librarian at the London School of Economics. She spent all day around professors; she understood men like him.

He had to have her.

John Thomas

By 1960, Alex had performed intercourse innumerable times with Ruth, yet he knew next to nothing about sex. So he and Jane studied it together. In the beginning, they snuck around behind Ruth's back, rendezvousing at Jane's flat, which became their laboratory.

Jane, though sexually inexperienced, was just as eager to learn as Alex. She would try anything. She twisted herself into positions and he named them. The Viennese Oyster, the Goldfish, the X. She wanted him to take notes on each contortion, to draw diagrams. They somehow managed to snap Polaroid photos of themselves (one wonders how they hit the button on the camera) to document their favorite positions for later use. They were two intellectuals screwing in every contortion possible, using the full arsenal of their erudition to explode each other to smithereens of pleasure. In bed, they went to Cambridge University all over again, figuring out everything they could about erotic bliss, which was at that time an arcane art. Back then, four-letter words still shocked people. At the drugstore, pharmacists kept condoms kept under lock and key. *Lady Chatterley's Lover,* banned for thirty years, had finally appeared in print, only to be slapped with an obscenity charge; the prosecutor in the case had asked the men in the courtroom whether this was the type of book "you would wish your wife or servants to read." Sex was not just a private matter—it was clandestine.

Before Jane, Alex had suffered alone, trying to subsist on the weak tea of matrimonial intercourse. But now sex—proper sex—brought him back to life. Indeed, it made him feel so good that he decided he needed a new name. In the privacy of his mistress's flat, he dubbed himself "John Thomas."

That was what Lady Chatterley called her gamekeeper's penis. Of course, the name only applied as long as Alex was with Jane, when, like the gamekeeper, he was an adulterer. When he washed her smell off him and went out on the street, he became his usual self again: Alex Comfort, MD, DcS, a married man and snail expert who occasionally appeared on the BBC.

And here was the funny thing: despite his experiments with Jane, he still knew little about sex. How on earth did one really make a study of it? You couldn't learn anything in the library, because all the guidebooks were hopeless. Just how hopeless? A sex guide titled *The Marriage Art* warned readers that "ineptly arranged intercourse leaves [your clothes] in a shambles, your plans for the evening shot." And what about the dangers of well-planned intercourse? The dull, ritualistic acts between husband and wife? Alex Comfort was one of the first intellectuals to worry that bad sex was a plague across Europe and America.

Right from the beginning, he and Jane began working on their own guidebook, cataloging all the positions they had tried. Jane, the librarian, had a genius for organizing information. And so they decided they would go topic by topic, alphabetically. A for Anal, B for Big Toe and so on. Using this principle of tireless cataloging, they created a little homemade book, suitable for passing around among friends. The title: *Doing Sex Properly*.

Sex, however, turned out to be too explosive and anarchistic a force to do properly. It spilled out of their guidebook and changed Alex entirely. He went to work writing books that he believed would wake people out of their matrimonial comas, and by the early 1960s he had set himself up as one of Britain's most outspoken advocates for free love. He wanted to blow up Buckingham Palace and have the pieces rain down in sparks, fireworks of joy that would set everyone to rutting. He wanted to start the sexual revolution all by himself. He had also come clean to Ruth and worked out an agreement with her: He could continue his affair with Jane, so long as he kept it hush-hush.

Only a few close friends knew that he went back and forth between two wives; to strangers, his call for open marriages seemed to be just another of his outrageous political stances. A pudgy, bespectacled professor of a certain age, he appeared to only to be dreaming of a sexual utopia—not actually struggling to build one in his own home. And Alex did what he could to foster this reputation as an armchair libertine and nothing more. His 1961 novel, *Come Out to Play*, tells the story of a doctor and his girlfriend who open a sex school; though the novel sprung out of his adventures with Jane, he dedicated the book to his wife: "For Ruth, who put ideas in my head." He appeared to be a man besotted with his wife—and only her. Jane didn't like being kept a secret, of course, but she would do anything to hold on to Alex.

Nick

One day in 1958, Alex received a letter from his son's boarding school: Parents should give their sons a talk about "personal hygiene"—that is, the facts of life—as the school would not provide such delicate information. Soon afterward, Alex called his son in for a talk, fidgeting as he explained the business between man and woman. He exuded so much embarrassment that twelve-year-old Nick did not dare ask questions. "He did very little to fill in the gaps," Nick remembered later. "I probably heard less talk about sex than the average child." Nick ended up turning to his father's medical books for information, poring over cut-away diagrams of the male and female reproductive organs.

Because he boarded at school, Nick didn't see much of his father during his teenage years. He had no idea when his father began an affair with Jane Henderson, whom the boy regarded as an honorary aunt. But clearly, something strange had happened. His father seemed to be on television and the radio all the time now.

In 1962, Alex Comfort participated in an antinuclear protest in Trafalgar Square; the police threw him in jail, along with a cabal of distinguished cellmates like Bertrand Russell. In the morning, most of the other professors sprung themselves by paying a nominal fee. Alex refused to bail himself out and stayed in prison for a month, where he had a lovely time discussing roses with his guards, who were enthusiastic gardeners.

News of Alex Comfort's arrest spread through Nick's boarding school. The other boys taunted the sixteen-year-old. "Jailbird, jailbird," they called after him. For his part, Nick fumed that his father had chosen to go to prison when he didn't have to—just to get attention. Raised by his mother to value moderation, Nick abhorred his father's outrageous style.

In 1963, his father published *Sex in Society*, a book that advocated for free love, and went on the radio to push its radical agenda. He called chastity a health problem. He argued for legal prostitution. He celebrated cultures in which children had sex with one another. He lobbed his ideas like bombs, and the British public, duly scandalized, responded with scathing attacks. "Being at boarding school when that book came out wasn't the best place to be," according to Nick. He endured taunts for the actions of his faraway father. Seventeen-year-old Nick seethed over one particular remark his father had made in the book—that fifteen-year-old boys should be given condoms. Trapped at a blazers-and-neckties school, Nick hardly ever saw girls; he blushed and grew sweaty when he tried to talk to females at a school mixer. The last thing he needed was a condom. His father was busy running around decreeing what was best for theoretical teenagers, but he didn't even know his own son.

The truth was, Alex didn't have much left over for Nick. When you reconstruct his schedule in the mid-1960s, he appears to be comically superhuman, like one of those lechers in the old *Benny Hill* television show who scooted around in fast-forward, their legs flailing as they chased after naked women. Alex would dash home for dinner with Ruth and sleep there, then in the wee hours of the morning he'd hurry to Jane's flat, nuzzle with her for a while, drive her to her job at the library, then head off to his own duties at University College London. "For quite a large part of my time, I was with two different women," Alex would comment later. "It is not an arrangement I recommend."

Being married to two women could be exhausting—the driving alone wore him out. By the late 1960s, he had divvied up his week: Mondays, Wednesdays, and Fridays belonged to Jane; the rest of the week he spent with Ruth. Neither of the women had other lovers, so he had to keep both of them satisfied. His wife would tolerate anything, so long as he played the part of her devoted husband. Nick believes that his mother agreed to the arrangement because "it gave her more time. My father could be such a handful." But one senses that Ruth had simply learned to make the best of a bad situation. If her husband decided to be a free lover, well, she would just bear up and smile. Jane, meanwhile, wanted more of him. He commuted between them in a tricked-out van with a condom taped on the dashboard.

Even many of Alex's friends knew nothing about the Monday-Wednesday-Friday side of his life. Marilyn Yalom—a feminist scholar who had befriended both Alex and Jane—was one of the friends who did know. "He was proud of the fact that he had two women and that he'd arranged his life this way," according to Yalom. "There was something ineffably childish about Alex."

Jane's Underpants

In the late 1960s, Yalom was passing through London and fell sick with a high fever. While she recovered, she stayed in an extra room in the flat that Jane and Alex shared. She found the bond between Alex and his "second wife" rather touching. But Yalom had no desire to join in. "When I got better, they proposed a threesome to me. They were like two little children saying, 'This would be fun.' I brushed it off without taking them too seriously," Yalom recounted later. "When I left, packing my things, Jane brought me a pair of her underpants. It was for her some kind of symbol of what I'd missed, or of some kind of intimacy between them."

By now, even though Jane and Alex had both grown wrinkled and so podgy they wore stretch pants, "they were like a couple of teenage kids," Yalom said. All the while, they had kept on writing their book together, adding exotic positions that they learned about on their travels (sometimes with Ruth in tow) to India and across Europe. They also began to write longingly about group sex: "Subject of a whole cult today, of which we aren't members, so we speak from hearsay. It's becoming socially more easy to arrange, and personal taste apart we see no earthly reason why pairs of friends shouldn't make love together."

By the late 1960s, Alex realized that his hobby with Jane might turn into an important book indeed; he believed they had compiled and documented more sexual practices than anyone than else in the world, with the possible exception of the fourth-century scholar who edited the *Kama Sutra*. So one day, Alex scheduled a meeting at Mitchell Beazley, the UK's top publisher of illustrated encyclopedias, to show off the manuscript. The editors recognized the book as a masterpiece, the most comprehensive book on sex ever written, and every position in it "kitchen tested." They'd take it.

The Dangers of Sticking with Snails (An Aside)

"It is an iron rule in our trade that no one gets anywhere until they give up snails," biologist Steve Jones has observed, pointing out that Edgar Allan Poe, Lewis Carroll, and Alex Comfort all achieved greatness only after they lost interest in mollusks.

By 1969, Comfort had spent two decades pottering around in labs, surrounded by piles of snail shells and plastic jugs full of guppies; he'd been searching for the mechanism that causes mollusks and fish to grow old. He'd first become interested in the tick-tock of death back when he was a young man. In his twenties, as a poet-scientist sickened by the needless destruction of Hiroshima and Dresden, he'd belonged to a literary movement called the New Apocalyptics. In his poetry and in his lab, too, he'd explored the clockwork of decay. But now he'd become a different sort of person entirely. A swinger. A sex expert. A happy man. Death no longer interested him.

Picture him in his office in London, packing shells in cotton and labeling boxes. He takes apart his chromoscope and drops the pieces into a box. Soon he and Jane will fly to Los Angeles, to the blinding sun and the dry canyons where few snails crawl. There, he will study another kind of specimen. He has heard about a utopian community out in those hills, where couples are experimenting with orgies. He will finally get a chance to participate in a laboratory of free love. Alex Comfort is about to drop snails forever and go on to bigger things.

Dedicated to No One

Meanwhile, he finished up work on his sex manual. As he did so, he began to worry about the risks of publishing what was, in effect, a diary of his sex life with Jane, written in the voice of a couple: "we" prefer playing in the bedroom, "she" likes her nipples licked, and so on. Had Alex owned up to being the male half of the couple, most readers might assume his wife, Ruth, to be his toe-riding, rope-loving, corset-wearing partner. Or the audience would suspect the truth: that his co-author was his mistress. Either way, the book would destroy his marriage. It might also lead to the suspension of his license to practice as a doctor; the British medical board had been known to punish MDs who wrote scandalous tracts.

In the end, he tried to get around such problems by listing himself as the editor of the book, rather its author. He lied in his introduction, saying that he had gathered his material from other people rather than from firsthand experience. "The book is based originally on the work of one couple. One of them is a practicing physician; their anonymity is accordingly professional," he explained. He also pretended not to have written the text, saying he had "left alone" the "authors' . . . lighthearted style." Later on, he told journalists that he'd resorted to this subterfuge in order to protect his reputation as a doctor. No doubt Alex also hoped to spare Ruth the cruelty of going public with his sex life. After all, his marriage to Ruth had endured through the wild 1960s, and though he saw less of her in 1970, he still loved her.

He had dedicated almost every one of his previous books to his wife. This time, he included no dedication page at all.

The Bearded Man

The original title for the book, *Doing Sex Properly*, sounded too stern, so an editor suggested a better one: *The Joy of Sex* would capitalize on the popularity of Erma Rombauer's bestselling cookbook.

The idea of treating sexual play as if it were French cooking delighted Alex. His mother had been the first woman ever to win a scholarship to Oxford University in French studies; when Alex was born, she dropped out of school and concentrated on sculpting him to be a perfect little wunderkind. By the age of seven, Alex could speak French fluently. The language still came easily to him, and he scattered it all through *The Joy of Sex* like so much gold dust. Foreign phrases worked magic. Ass licking became *feuille de rose*. Sniffing the partner's armpit became *cassolette;* a finger up the anus, *postillionage*. He made acts that were illegal in many countries sound like rare, sought-after perfumes. Without quite realizing what he was up to, Alex had found a way to re-brand sex. He'd taken stunts seen nowhere outside of triple-X porn and turned them into entertainments suitable for a suburban couple to try after a few glasses of merlot. Looking back, his greatest stroke of genius was to abandon the one-size-fits-all model used in nearly all the previous sex manuals. Alex—himself a bondage and group-sex fan—championed the idea of different tastes for different tongues. Today, with the Internet at our fingertips, we're used to people dividing themselves up into erotic tribes: costume wearers, horse-play enthusiasts, and dungeon mistresses have found each other and formed communities. But in 1970, few people had heard of such variations. Alex treated it all as just part of the *pot-au-feu* of human desire, and his tone suggested that the reader would too. He imagined that *Joy* would become a "coffee table" book; on display in the living room, it would make an excellent ice breaker, and might even encourage the Joneses to invite their neighbors the Smiths for a foursome.

At the same time, he recognized that many of his readers would be sexual imbeciles. The book included a sewing pattern for a g-string, so that readers could make their own stripper clothing and wear it around the bedroom. What's mind-boggling now, decades on, is that g-strings were not available in any store back then. Imagine the housewife who cut out the pattern, shopped for black silk, and painstakingly hand-sewed the adornment, all so she could surprise her husband. In 1970, when Alex prepared his sex tips, most adults were married. The birth control pill had been available for less than ten years. Many of Alex's readers had wed at twenty or twenty-one, and had slept with only one partner. They were poignantly aware that they could be better lovers.

The book reflects these aspirations. Follow instructions, its tone implied, and you could develop the kind of exceptional love-making skills previously available only to the rich. Here were the tricks you might learn if you spent a few years bumming around Europe, jetsetting to nude beaches, dabbling with lovers who spoke French. World-class sex required more than just practice—you had to learn from the experts. "Chef-grade cooking doesn't happen naturally," Alex exhorted his readers. "It starts at the point where people know how to prepare and enjoy food, are curious about it and willing to take trouble preparing it, read recipe hints, and find they are helped by one or two detailed techniques. It's hard to make mayonnaise by trial and error, for instance. Cordon Bleu sex, as we define it, is exactly the same situation."

It was a message that would resonate with millions of people—their sex could be thrilling and also classy.

But what about the illustrations? *The Joy of Sex* would describe positions that few of Comfort's readers had ever encountered before—Chinese style, Indian style, *croupade, cuissade*. Obviously, it would be necessary to include pictures that showed how to insert part A into slot B. Alex handed over the Polaroid photos that he and Jane had snapped years ago to document their adventures. Couldn't artists turn these photos into sexy drawings? The smudgy, dark Polaroids of two middle-aged intellectuals smashed together in various tableaus were far from appetizing. Both Charles Raymond and Chris Foss, the men assigned to illustrate the book, decided they must go looking for inspiration elsewhere. They leafed through porn magazines and hired models, but they couldn't seem to get the right look. Furthermore, the editors at Mitchell Beazley nixed the idea of photographs, which would likely get the book banned.

In the end, everyone agreed *The Joy of Sex* should be filled with line drawings; the softness of the pencil would add a homespun intimacy and let the book slip past the censors. The drawings would be inspired by photographs of a real-looking couple—though the models would not be as real and saggy as Alex and Jane.

Charles Raymond volunteered himself and his wife, Edeltraud. Charlie had a hippie beard and the long, tangled hair of a wino, but he turned out to be well-suited for his new role as sex model. Chris Foss, who snapped the photos, could only marvel at the ease with which Charlie and his wife bent themselves into the two hundred positions they documented for the book. "Edeltraud was very Germanic, and so she would say 'Right, Charles, we start now. Position number one!'" remembers Foss. "She'd tap her leg and say 'Come on, Charles!' and off they would go and do that and she would tick it off and say 'Right Charles, now we do this one!' Poor old Charlie was only human, so every now and then he—how do I say it—blew it a bit. I'd say 'Charlie, you can't do it now. We've got fifteen more positions and just an hour left. Charlie, can you get back into business as quick as you can?'"

Afterwards, Foss produced minimalist line drawings based on the photos, gorgeous in their simplicity. His illustrations capture the many moods of two people who adore each other. In some, the lovers droop across one another, satisfied; in others, they rear back, trying to find just the right spot. But, lovely and erotic as the illustrations are, the first thing you notice about them is Charles Raymond's hair, that wild mop on his head and the obscene beard. When the book came out, much of the buzz would center around the "bearded man," who seems to be the narrator and hero of the story. His caveman coif and perpetually hard penis would do as much to sell the book as Alex's elegant prose.

Of course, as Alex worked on his manuscript in 1970, he had no idea just how popular the book would become two years later. The publisher planned an initial print run of only ten thousand copies. For Alex, *Joy* was a manifesto, a byproduct of his own revolutionary sexual life. He had begun commuting back and forth to the United States to spend weeks at a time living in a community called Sandstone. He had just discovered an erotic playground that could only have existed in his wildest fantasies—or in California.

Sandstone

"The moment [my father] went to the States, the party began," according to Nick Comfort. "He had a suffocating upbringing. When he discovered what life could be like in California there was no stopping him." *Joy* had yet to be released, but already Alex had embraced his new role as the run-amok British intellectual. In 1970, he and Jane flew to Los Angeles to get their first taste of Sandstone.

Most of the couples that made the trip to the Topeka Canyon community went in search of utopia. Like Alex and Jane, they believed Sandstone offered the first glimpse of what society would look like in the future, when Americans built their lives around pleasure rather than duty. Founders Barbara and John Williamson handpicked the members, seeking out professors, journalists, and scientists who might show up at one of the naked dinners, stay for the orgy, become a convert to the philosophy, and then spread the word in newspapers and academic studies. Their schmoozing paid off. George Plimpton, Dean Martin, Tim Leary, and Daniel Ellsberg were just some of the pop luminaries and intellectuals who rubbed up against each other, perhaps literally, during weekends. Sammy Davis Jr. materialized one night in full Vegas drag—diamonds on his cuffs and cigarette lighter—escorting both his wife and porn star Marilyn Chambers. As he stripped, a cufflink bounced to the floor and Chambers dove for it.

But this was no mere sex club. Only couples could join the Sandstone community, and everyone had to abide by a set of rules. The Williamsons saw Sandstone as a revolution in lifestyle: They wanted no less than to redesign commitment between men and women, to teach husbands and wives to put aside "hang ups" and give each other complete freedom. It was a have-your-wedding-cake-and-eat-it-too philosophy of love: men and women were supposed to be able to screw anyone they fancied, and do it on a mattress in front of their spouses; this would (in theory) deepen their trust in one another. Alex himself couldn't have designed a better test tube for his ideas.

One evening in 1970, he maneuvered a car up the Pacific Coast

Highway, heading to his first orgy. The road to Sandstone was marked only by discreet stone pillars, and the visitor had to bump along a private drive until he reached the main house.

That evening, Alex parked next to a fleet of Jaguars and Porsches and climbed out into the smell of eucalyptus, pot smoke, and suntan lotion. At the door, Barbara Williamson, a slim woman in her thirties wearing nothing but spectacles, checked his name against a list. The house was a 1970s California suburban spread—redwood deck, low-slung furniture, wagon-wheel chandelier. The wallpaper, in various shades of brown and mushroom, appeared to be paisley until you got up close to it, then you saw the naked bodies worked into the design. A sign hung above the garlands of incense, informing all visitors about the rules inside these redwood walls:

> Privacy means you see the environment as hostile. . . . Here, there are no doors on the bathrooms, the environment is gentling. Lovemaking is . . . tribalized. You are in the community. You do your thing; it is yours. Others may want to watch, learn, comment, even laugh. But they are of your tribe; the laughter is not hostile.

Once inside, Alex was free to lounge by the fire in the living room and chat with other naked professionals. Or he could descend the stairs into the "ballroom," a wall-to-wall carpet of seething flesh: breasts, butts, astonished faces, hair, writhing legs, errant arms, coos, sighs, slurps, giggles. Later, he would write about those Sandstone parties as mind-expanding experiences akin to LSD trips. Usually, the woman ended up being the more enthusiastic half of the couple, he remarked, and led the way downstairs into the orgy room; because of her superior anatomy, she could keep going all night, long after her husband was sidelined. In the morning, the first-timers tended to go on talking jags as they tried to hold on to revelations from the night before. They would linger over their coffee, "trying to work out what had happened to them," Alex wrote. "Breakfast often ended as an impromptu seminar on something" as the Sandstone-ites rapped about how to take their insights to the wider world. "Some of these morning-after experiences were even more rewarding than the specifically sexual part of Sandstone," he wrote.

Alex fell in love with the community. From 1970 through 1972 he lived there for weeks at a time. Occasionally Jane accompanied him— for they were still very much in love—but often he pilgrimaged to Sandstone solo or with a male buddy. It seemed that Alex could break the rules. Gay Talese described Alex as a fixture at the place, its *eminence grise*. "The nude biologist Dr. Alex Comfort, brandishing a cigar, traipsed through the room between the prone bodies with the professional air of a lepidopterist strolling through the fields waving a butterfly net," Talese wrote in *Thy Neighbor's Wife*. "With the least amount of encouragement—after he had deposited his cigar in a safe place—he would join a friendly clutch of bodies and contribute to the merriment."

It was at Sandstone, and often in mid-orgy, that Alex met many of the other minds behind the sexual revolution. For instance, Betty Dodson—the feminist writer who championed masturbation in her own best-selling book—first noticed Alex across a crowded room at Sandstone. At the time, Dodson happened to be stretched out on the floor with a man and a woman licking her. Looking up from the proceedings, she noticed a gent with gray curls who studied her intently. She waved him over, and he tottered toward her obligingly. When he was near enough, she reached for his left hand, as if to shake it, and found nothing there but a stump and a thumb. Unperturbed, she slapped his hand down on her crotch. "Oh, he was so happy," Dodson remembered years later.

But it all came at a cost. Alex felt he had to cut himself off from his family and old friends, even his son. "He was always strongly resistant to the idea that I or any of the family should visit him in California—largely because he didn't want us privy to the Sandstone community and all the rest," according to Nick. For all Alex's talk of freedom from shame, he was too mortified to let Nick witness the goings-on in California. Father and son had no contact for years.

Dr. Goggins

When *The Joy of Sex* came out in 1972 it hit the best-seller lists in most English-speaking countries. However, its success was most blazingly spectacular in the United States, where it climbed to the top of the charts, stayed at number one for more than a year, and remained a best seller for six. "Nothing makes a recreation more respectable for Americans than the rumor that it takes know-how," the critic Hugh Kenner would later quip about the book. Alex's writings fit perfectly with the American zeitgeist: He'd presented sex as wholesome sport, sanctified by Puritanical labor and an effortful sheen of sweat.

Even as the book became a superstar, Alex himself remained in the shadows. He might have exploded into fame as Timothy Leary had, might have become a walking advertisement for his own brand of utopia. Except, of course, Leary possessed the movie-star jaw, the Pepsodent teeth, and the boyish physicality that allowed him to transition from professor into pop-culture icon, and Alex . . . didn't. Had you met him in 1973, you might well have mistaken him for a car mechanic. He made the rounds of newspaper interviews in a blue jumpsuit—no need to wash shirts, he liked to brag, if you only wore zip-up suits. He slumped in his chair with a hunched-over posture that made him look older than his fifty-three years, kept his breast pocket stuffed with a line of cigars, and kept another stogie clamped in his mouth. Photographs of him during this period suggest that he washed his gray hair as infrequently as his costume.

And anyway, Alex did not crave fame of the Leary variety. Rather, he saw himself as the man who lobbed the bomb, caused the big explosion that changed society, and then ran away. An avowed anarchist, he lived for the moment when the old system fell apart and the new order was born.

Ever since the early 1960s, he'd imagined himself in the role of world-class trickster. In his 1961 novel, *Come Out to Play,* he had created a character, Dr. Goggins, who represented his ideal. A genius in bed, the doctor opens a school in Paris where he and his girlfriend teach their students advanced love-making skills. "Bill Masters thought I was writing about his clinic, but I was able to tell him I wrote that book back before Masters and Johnson were heard of," Alex bragged in 1974. And now it appeared that what Alex had imagined a decade earlier might come true.

In the novel, Dr. Goggins meets "a French chemist who's happened on a drug and can turn people on. Not raise the libido, but thaw the superego, the part of the mind that says 'mustn't.' I call [the drug] 3-blindmycin," Alex explained in one interview. Dr. Goggins—believing that enough orgasms could bring an end to war—constructs a Molotov cocktail, fills it with a huge dose of the drug, and sets it off in front of Buckingham Palace. The queen, parliamentarians, barristers, peers, and bureaucrats all huff in the substance and become flower children. The military brass retire to the country. The rocket scientists lose interest in building phallic weaponry and run naked through their neighborhoods. War ends forever.

In the early 1970s, Alex could believe that he had himself become the Goggins character; *Joy* was his drug, his 3-blindmycin. With the right words, he had transformed the mores and habits of the entire English-speaking world. He'd turned what used to be called perversions into "pickles and sauces"; he'd written the manifesto that people were using to refashion their lives, putting the orgasm at the top of their agendas.

For most of his life, Alex had been out of step with the main-

stream; in the 1940s, George Orwell denounced him as soft on the
Nazis; in the 1960s, moralists had crusaded against the radical agenda
he put forward in *Sex and Society*. Now, for the first time, he led the
crowd.

That Book

The runaway success of *Joy* presented one problem for Alex: He'd
made Ruth's life hell. Every one of her acquaintances, from grocer to
next-door neighbor, had likely heard about her husband's exploits
with Jane. And though Alex had gone through gyrations to pretend
he was only the editor, that subterfuge evaporated after the book
came out. The press called him "Dr. Sex." Ruth coped with this disaster by pretending it wasn't happening. According to Nick, "my
mother never discussed [*Joy*] at all." When she absolutely had to
allude to her husband's best seller, she called it "that book." The marriage, which had survived so many betrayals, now crumbled.

In early 1973, Alex negotiated a divorce from Ruth. A few months
later, he and Jane married in a quiet ceremony in London. Nick—and
many old friends—were not invited. Then the couple jetted off to
their new home in California. The Center for the Study of Democra-
tic Institutions, a liberal think tank in Santa Barbara, had offered Alex
a sun-drenched office near the beach. He'd take it.

Good Housekeeping

"Here we have a new genre: the coffee-table book that should be kept
out of the reach of the children. Higher coffee tables would seem to
be the answer," John Updike joked in the 1970s about *The Joy of Sex*.
But the coffee tables stayed low, and the book splayed its pages sug-
gestively in living rooms across the nation. It matched the Danish
Modern furniture; the understated cover was all white space, the epit-

ome of space-age minimalism. The book became a fashion accessory, a symbol of the New Good Life. Along with a waterbed, a hot tub, and a high-end stereo, this was a toy for adults at play.

And suddenly, so many were at play: in 1970, California adopted the first no-fault divorce law, and by the end of the decade splitting had become easy. Now, entire consumer empires catered to the single and middle-aged: these swingers needed fern bars, sports cars outfitted with quadrophonic 8-track tape machines, amusing drinks (Harvey Wallbanger, Harvey's Bristol Cream), aftershaves, designer jeans, beachside condos, shag rugs, silver coke spoons.

Alex Comfort had never meant to create a faddish product or storm the consumer market. Just the opposite: He dreamed of a utopia where tribes of people shared their bodies, where greed dissolved. In such a world, talking about money would be the ultimate gauchery. Examine the illustrations in *Joy,* and you catch a glimpse of what heaven might have looked like in Comfort's mind. The lovers float in the freedom of white space; seemingly they own few possessions beyond pillows and a mattress. They need nothing but their erogenous zones. In the sequel, *More Joy,* their friends come over, and now the foursome copulates on some hazy surface (the floor? a bed?). The reader of *Joy* steps into an demimonde something like Sandstone in the early years—just men, women, and mattresses. Pleasure belonged to everyone. Didn't it?

The last thing Alex Comfort had expected was for his guidebook to become a status symbol. The book made a fortune for its publisher (though not for its author) and became a must-have furnishing for the vacation house or bachelor pad. It both promoted Alex Comfort's utopia and undercut its essential message: In *Joy,* he exhorted readers to get beyond all the prepackaged ideas about sex and to fully inhabit their own minds and bodies. "Play it your own way," he lectured readers. Once "you have tried all your own creative sexual fantasies, you won't need books." Ah, but his readers did need the book; they bought it by the millions; they wanted the cool white cover; they longed for an artifact.

Likewise, his beloved Sandstone became an upscale consumer product in the late 1970s. Its original owners, bankrupted by a lawsuit, had no choice but to sell the place. The new proprieter, an ex-Marine, instituted a $740 initiation fee for members, which made the club as expensive as a Hawaiian vacation or a share in a yacht. Once Sandstone turned into a money mill, Alex divorced himself from the place. By all accounts, he gave up on group sex entirely around that time.

Monogamy

But wait! Let's not go there yet. Let's jump back to 1972, to the happy times. In those first golden years in California, Alex and Jane fucked and recited limericks and threw dinner parties. They had set up house outside Santa Barbara, in Montecito, and seemed destined to slither into old age bathed in massage oil. They padded around naked and floated in swimming pools as blue as Viagra—though, of course, Viagra hadn't been invented yet. The sex pill of choice was still 3-blindmycin, Alex's imaginary aphrodisiac.

At first, Jane "was willing, maybe even eager, to participate in the sexual play," according to Marilyn Yalom. Alex boasted about her prowess in bed, and even created a stage on which both of them could perform; in the back of their house, he installed an "Indian room" filled with batiks and pillows where he could throw orgies. "He assumed that the two of them would be the sexual gurus of Montecito," according to Yalom. "But Jane balked."

Stranded in an alien country, Jane began to regret indulging Alex's every sexual whim. In the late 1970s, she told her husband she wanted a conventional marriage—no group scenes, no experiments, no second or third wives. "I can still see the look of disappointment on

[Alex's] face," Yalom remembers. "He had more or less contracted for a sexual playmate where the doors would be open. She changed her mind."

Alex had believed that open marriage and group sex would become the model around which most people organized their lives—and he'd been wrong, on both a personal and a cultural level. According to Yalom, "He didn't realize the strength of monogamy."

In 1985 he and Jane decided to move back to Britain. Jane would feel at home there, and Alex might be able to resume serious academic work. Besides, they were now well into their sixties. "[My father] came back to the UK to enjoy his old age," according to Nick. "But that didn't happen."

Age-ism

In the late 1970s, around the time that Jane demanded his fidelity, Alex's magpie mind led him to return to a question that had fascinated him as a young man: How and why do people grow old?

Since the 1940s, he'd been reading and publishing papers on gerontology; now he hoped to do for the aged what he had once done for the sexually innocent. In 1976 he published a manifesto against the warehousing and dehumanizing of old people, titled *A Good Age*. He intended his new book to be a best seller that would radicalize the wrinkled. However, as it turned out, readers were not as eager to join this revolution. The book sold respectably but couldn't begin to match the influence of *Joy*. Still, Alex kept on with his crusade. He flew to conferences on gerontology, trying to wrangle his way to the top of the field. When the proceedings bored him, he jumped up on stage and summarized the disagreements with a limerick, written on the spot. He couldn't resist proving how much smarter he was than any of them. The scientists and doctors out there in the audience, those men with their sober expressions and sharp name tags, thought of him as a pop-culture idiot. *Joy* had ruined his reputation among serious people. He wanted it back.

He shed his jumpsuits for tweed blazers; he anticipated the breakthroughs he'd make in the field. He published a shower of books and articles. But wherever he turned, he was dismissed as the guy who had written that sex book.

"There was the publicity roller-coaster which he quite enjoyed," according to Nick Comfort. "But he wanted to be treated seriously. He was an academic of considerable gravity." Still, it wasn't just his pop-culture past that tainted his reputation as a biologist. Alex had little interest in making a scientific argument; instead, he published polemics. His crusade had been—and would be—to convince people to see their bodies as ideas. This may be one reason that he did not anticipate AIDS, even in the midst of the orgies, with fluids splattered everywhere. Alex could not seem to accept that viruses and cells and bodies themselves might have antirevolutionary agendas.

Likewise, he insisted that most of the problems of the old came from discrimination—rather than decay or illness. And now he began to imagine a new kind of utopia, a place where the gray-haired could be cherished as sexual and intellectual beings. In such a society, he believed, health problems would nearly vanish for the old.

Three Strokes

It was 1991. The house in Kent, England, smelled of curry and pipe smoke. Prints from India—which he and Jane had collected during their many trips—hung above the sofa. Alex had embraced his role as the globe-trotting gadfly; he jetted around, speaking out against age-ism.

Today he was pottering around in his study, working up notes for a nursing conference in Australia. Except he couldn't seem to concentrate. His thoughts had gone foggy. He picked up a pencil to make a correction on his manuscript. Australia. He'd never been before. He was just entering his seventies, and by his calculations, he had twenty good years ahead of him at least. The rest of his life stretched ahead, enormous as Australia, undiscovered and sunny.

And then he collapsed.

It was Jane who found him. She punched numbers into the phone. Soon paramedics crowded around, snapping their latex gloves, prodding him all over. He rode in an ambulance and then a helicopter. The next day, he woke up in a new country; it was not Australia. The monitors beeped beside him. The nurses—whom he would never again lecture in conference halls—whisked in and out. His jaw had frozen up. He shook all over. The doctor came by and explained—slowly, as if Alex were an idiot—that he'd suffered a massive brain hemorrhage. He'd obviously taken a hit to his motor cortex. Years before, writing *A Good Age,* he'd been so confident: "The human brain does not shrink, wilt, perish or deteriorate with age. It normally continues to function well through as many as nine decades," he'd asserted. But now his own brain begged to differ.

He drifted in and out of consciousness for weeks. Someone held his hand and told him Jane had died. She'd suffered a massive heart attack.

Seven months later, they put him in a wheelchair and his son Nick wheeled him out into the world of taxicabs and crowded crosswalks, where everyone had somewhere to rush. Everyone but him. Nick— the son he'd hardly known—would handle most things for him now, from bills to fan letters to updating the next edition of *Joy of Sex.* He would be installed in a little flat around the corner from where Nick, his wife, and the grandchildren lived. And do what? "Leisure is a con," he'd written, but now he had nothing but idleness ahead of him. He would enter that condition he feared most, and which he'd tried to eliminate with his theories: He'd become an unperson.

When the next stroke hit him, paralyzing his right side, he moved into a nursing home. On Sundays, he rode in an ambulance to Nick's house and sat immobilized while his grandchildren ran around him. When he spoke, people leaned in, wrinkled their foreheads, and asked him to repeat himself.

Albatross

In his midseventies, Alex Comfort had shrunk into a codger with Einstein hair and furious eyes, immobile in his wheelchair. With his right hand paralyzed, his left thumb had become his only lever on the world. He typed poetry with it, one painful letter at a time. He gestured by wiggling that thumb, so that his whole will seemed to live in that snail-like appendage.

Today a young reporter—a girl, really—would be visiting him; she'd told him she was doing a story about the twenty-fifth anniversary of *Joy*. Before the girl came, his nurse, Linda, set him up in a spotless suit and arranged him in the chair.

The reporters always asked the same question. How did he come to write *The Joy of Sex*? And behind their question lay another question that he heard in the snigger of their voices. They cared nothing about the other fifty books he'd written, now arrayed on shelves behind him. Always *Joy, Joy, Joy*. "*Joy* is frankly an albatross," he said to one journalist in 1997, pumping his thumb for emphasis. Had they not read his poetry? His scientific papers?

The reporter—a beautiful girl, just as he'd hoped—entered and reached out for his hand. But he had nothing to shake, so she smiled awkwardly. She asked where to put her tape recorder. "Stick it wherever you like," he tried to quip, but his mouth wouldn't cooperate.

The girl questioned him for hours, and because she was kind enough to flirt a little, to make him feel human for a moment, he did his best to answer.

She wanted to know whether he'd marry again.

He laughed. Who would want a cripple stuck in a wheelchair?

But your brain works, the girl said.

Yes, that's true, he replied. But no one wants to marry a brain.

He wanted to tell her it wasn't supposed to go like this. He thought he'd known his enemies: the Tories, Thatcher, the sword rattlers, the physicists who designed bombs, the prudes, the teetotalers. But now he'd been defeated in the way he least expected. The true enemy had turned out to be so small, and not the least bit political: bits of brain tissue in the motor cortex and possibly the parietal lobe. And *Joy* had become an enemy too, an albatross straight out of Coleridge.

Remember how the poem goes? A ship gets lost in a storm, and bangs around among ice floes; the sailors believe they'll die at sea. Then salvation comes in the shape of a bird, an albatross that leads them to open water. The sailors venerate the bird as an emissary from God—or most of them do. One free-thinking anarchist on board refuses to acknowledge the bird as holy. This anarchist, who loves shocks and explosions of all kinds, shoots the albatross dead.

And then the winds cease, the sails drop, and the ship founders in the terrible silence of the sea. The other men hang the dead bird around the anarchist's neck as a sign of his sin. Years pass. The anarchist recants. And yet, still he wears the ghost of that dead bird around his neck. It weighs him down. It humbles him. And eventually he and his greatest mistake merge into one.

Alex Comfort died in 2000.

Sources

Allyn, David. *Make Love, Not War: An Unfettered History.* New York: Routledge, 2000.

Banks-Smith, Nancy. "Privates on parade." *The Guardian* (London), Jan. 5, 2001.

Comfort, Alex. *Come Out to Play.* New York: Crown Publishers, 1975.

———. *A Good Age.* New York: Crown Publishers, 1976.

————, ed. *The Joy of Sex: A Cordon Bleu Guide to Lovemaking*. New York: Crown Publishers, 1972.

————, ed. *More Joy*. New York: Crown Publishers, 1974.

————. *The Silver River: Being the Diary of a Schoolboy in the South Atlantic*. London: Chapeman & Hall, 1936.

————. *Writings Against Power & Death*. London: Freedom Press, 1994.

De Bertodano, Helena. "25 Years of Joy." *Chicago Sun-Times*, Jan. 5 1997.

————. "Labour of Love." *Courier Mail* (Queensland, Australia), Nov. 23, 1996.

Dery, Mark. "Paradise Lust." *Vogue Hommes*, Spring/Summer 2005, pp. 244–47.

Gray, Paul. "Less Joy." *Time*, May 19, 1975.

Hammel, Lisa. "Will the Real Alex Comfort Please Stand Up?" *The New York Times*, June 2, 1974.

Heller, Zoe. "Where's the Beard?" *The Daily Telegraph* (London), Sept. 17, 2002.

Hunt, Liz. "Alex Comfort's Joy of . . . Poetry." *The Independent* (London), Nov. 12, 1996.

Illman, John. "Has *The Joy of Sex* Stood the Test of Time?" *The Guardian* (London), Nov. 12, 1996.

Jones, Patti. "Better than Sex." *The Seattle Times*, Jan. 27, 2003.

Jones, Steve. "Adventures in Thought: Experiment in Literature and Science." Transcript of a talk given at the University of East Anglia on June 16, 2006.

————. "My Greatest Mistake." *The Independent* (London), Sept. 3, 2003.

The Joy of Sex, a documentary produced by Twenty Twenty, first aired on BBC Channel 4 in 2001.

Kenner, Hugh. "The Comfort behind *The Joy of Sex*." *The New York Times Magazine*, Oct. 27, 1974.

Martin, Douglas. "Alex Comfort, 80, Dies . . ." *The New York Times*, March 29, 2000.

Obituary of Alex Comfort. *The Guardian* (London), March 28, 2000.

Salmon, Arthur E. *Alex Comfort*. Boston: Twayne Publishers, 1978.

Savage, Dan. "The Doctor of Love." *The New York Times*, Jan. 7, 2001.

Sayre, Nora. "Ahh!" *The New York Times*, Feb. 11, 1973.

Stuever, Hank. "*Joy of Sex* Back on Top?: Author's Son Updates a 30-Year-Old Classic." *The Washington Post*, Feb. 25, 2003.

Talese, Gay. *Thy Neighbor's Wife*. Garden City, NY: Doubleday & Co., 1980.

Updike, John. "Coffee-table books for higher coffee tables." *The New York Times,* Oct. 28, 1973.

Walsh, John. "Everything We Wanted to Know about Sex." *The Independent* (London), July 16, 2002.

Interviews

Nick Comfort, interviewed by Pagan Kennedy, 2007.

Robert Greacen, interviewed by Pagan Kennedy, 2007.

Marilyn Yalom, interviewed by Pagan Kennedy, 2007.

. . . By Any Other Name

David Bradley

On July 9, 2007, the NAACP held a funeral in Detroit for the "N" word, with an empty pine casket in a horse-drawn carriage. This essay, which David Bradley wrote for Obit, *a magazine that features stories about various aspects of death and dying, took the form of, in the author's words, "a statement cast as an omitted portion of the burial ritual."*

"Of every literary expression we can inquire: How factual is it?" Bradley says, "Which is not the same as How true is it? but is still an important question, because there are some people who simply will not recognize truth unless it is grounded in verifiable fact—and sometimes not then."

Sometimes I'm a little . . . out of the loop. I didn't hear the verdict until the 'hood was burning. I didn't hear we'd invaded Afghanistan until we'd invaded Iraq. And I didn't know Nigger was even sick.

There'd been no alteration in the vital signs. Median black family income was still 61 percent of white. Black unemployment was still twice as high as white. Unarmed black men were still being shot by cops. Thousands of black refugees still no longer lived in New Orleans.

But there had been indications. The last time I got fired, the Human Relations Commission said "race was not a factor," and the last time I didn't get hired the Equal Opportunity Employer said it was my "style" that "didn't quite fit." But the guy they hired was white, so I assumed it was just another euphemism, like "last hired, first fired." When the officer who stopped me for Jogging While Black called me "Sir," I never dreamed it was because Nigger had Blue Flu.

I did hear that Paris Hilton was freedom riding in Dixie with Nicole Richie, who, according to one tabloid, "self-identifies as African American." I did hear that Nicole Richie likes her men pale and homeless-looking—in other words, white trash. But I didn't hook it all up with Nigger until I heard about the funeral.

I know the National Association for the Advancement of Colored People has money trouble. They can't even afford to let Colored retire. But this so-called funeral was not only cheap, but wrong. A funeral is a solemn rite; you do not cheer, even if the departed was your landlord. And a pine coffin? A horse-drawn wagon? Not even a used El Dorado? In Detroit?

My daddy was a preacher. I'm not saying he would lie, but he'd eulogize the devil out of drunks, loose women, even politicians so their own mothers wanted to recognize them, because Last Words should be not only true, but kind. The preacher at Nigger's funeral told lies worse than truth. Nigger, he said, was "the greatest child racism ever birthed." Like he never heard of lynching.

Mostly the Colored People just dissed the deceased, denying Nigger's entitles, saying Nigger needed killing. The mayor said the "N" word would be buried with "all the nonsense that went with it." Like it was Nigger that invented "all deliberate speed," "separate-but-equal" and the One-Drop Rule.

I don't know why the governor attended; she's native Canadian, of Scandihoovian extraction, blonde as Paris Hilton—I doubt she's got a drop of black blood, let alone personal experience. But she was kickin' trash right along with the Colored People. At least she didn't claim Nigger interfered with her, you know? Or maybe she did. Maybe that's why the preacher didn't mention lynching, and nobody ever said how Nigger died.

I know some folks weren't fond of Nigger, but this was no decent burial. So let me say Last Words, and try to be true and kind.

Yes, Nigger did the bigots' business. As did the Constitution. Racism is the nation's baggage; Nigger just toted the load. And the trunks were packed by Thomas Jefferson. If you want definition, not just a derivation, see *Notes on the State of Virginia,* Query XIV. Yes, Nigger worked for the Man. But also against him. The Man believed Jefferson's definition; Nigger never set him straight. As a result the Man was often embarrassed. Nigger was no revolutionary, but Nigger was subversive.

And when it was just us . . . chickens, Nigger was a whole other thing. Yes, Nigger would insult you, and your Mama, too; Nigger playin' dozens was hilarious. Nobody could have a better time with less money. And Nigger could make wine from anything.

Nigger knew the trouble we'd seen better than Jesus. Yes, Nigger was part of it. Also the inspiration for "Lift Ev'ry Voice and Sing." Without Nigger there would have been no spirituals, no blues.

You find that contradictory? Nigger always was. A man owns 187 slaves. That man writes, "All men are created equal." Later, that man writes that blacks cannot be free because their hair is kinky, they're oversexed and don't use perfume. That man then takes one of his own stinking, nappy-headed ho's as his mistress and mother of his children. That's contradictory.

So yes, Nigger was cruel. Absent physical abuse, nothing can be more cruel when you're black and six years old. I do have personal experience; Nigger destroyed my faith in mankind and in Jesus, made me want to kill somebody, or myself, or both. But my uncle told me, "Don't worry what they call you, so long as it ain't late to dinner," and he taught me to counterpunch. Ever since Nigger and I went toe-to-toe, I haven't cared what anybody called me. I have cared what somebody might do to me, but who listens if there's a nightstick up your anus?

Besides, those who've done me most harm would never use the "N" word. It's too naked a reminder of what they want to bury. They prefer terms like "underclass" or "tangle of pathology." They will call you on time to dinner, provided you're "articulate," but expect you to be silent while their heirs are served first. Later, they'll ask you to do the dishes.

Despite that day job for the Man, Nigger worked for me. Nigger protected me from self-delusion, harmonized my cognitive dissonance, immunized me to the contradictions of American history. Jefferson's definition was the thesis. The Colored People wasted time with antithesis. But Nigger is synthesis. That's why I loved Nigger.

And that's why the Colored People should not have buried Nigger like a sharecropper. Nigger deserved to lie in state. Congress, the Supreme Court, the executive branch—also the vice president— should have had to pass and pay respects. For it is they who must declare Nigger persona non grata.

The Colored People didn't even have a viewing. I therefore suspect that reports of Nigger's death have been greatly exaggerated. They've been premature before; they buried Jim Crow in 1944, but still had to put Nigger in a colored cemetery.

And I hear Michigan voters amended their constitution to ban affirmative action. I hear the IRS taxed the Colored People for criticizing the president. I hear three of New York's Finest were indicted for killing an unarmed black man again. I hear Nicole Richie just got fired.

Ceremony

ANDER MONSON

"When I write essays I feel naked," says Ander Monson. "There's a bit of rush in it, that of heights or exhibitionism, or other sorts of dares. I have always hated roller coasters: they're no fun for me at all: too much real terror there, the body's response not pleasing. But nonfiction (particularly when pried open with the awkward terms 'creative' or 'literary') is an open space, seen from far above, and somehow the height and speed doesn't put me off from it." This vertiginous tour of President Gerald R. Ford's funeral events first appeared in The Believer.

Procession

3:06 P.M., Tuesday afternoon, January 2, 2007. Former president Gerald R. Ford's remains have landed in Grand Rapids, at the airport bearing his name, and I am in position on a bridge overlooking I-196, which feeds into I-96, one of two major expressways cutting east-west across the bottom half of Michigan. There are already sixty people lined up on this or the next overpass east of here. We are waiting for the motorcade, which the police officer tells me is running late.

It is light outside. Bright and clear. A good day for ceremony.

According to one of the many press releases, "the remains will depart the museum with ceremony and proceed to Grace Episcopal Church for a private funeral service." The remains will arrive at the church with ceremony, and will depart the church with ceremony.

Two University of Michigan songs will be played as part of the arrival ceremony: "The Victors" and "The Yellow and Blue." Most people know the first one from television, though probably not the second. Ford played football for the University of Michigan; his number was ceremonially retired. This music is meaningful and specific, and was selected in advance by Ford himself for the various ceremonies. The funeral and interment services, arrivals, and departures will be soundtracked by a preponderance of Bach and a number of traditional hymns, most of which I recognize.

I return to my car for warmth and music. I sit here on this strange-weathered, unseasonable day contemplating Gerald R. Ford, who is referred to almost exclusively with the full name and the R. I listen to pop music on the factory-installed stereo in my Subaru, specifically "Ceremony," by the British band New Order. I am here along with these other thousands gathering to "line the streets," as the television stations' Web sites exhort us to do, in honor of Ford's remains' return to their childhood home. Can remains be said to have a childhood home? Our culture certainly thinks so. Place of burial is important. It accrues meaning. Ford had asked to be interred here, in the crypt on the Ford museum grounds that has been waiting for him ever since I moved back to Michigan four years ago.

Ford is one of two important Fords in Michigan.

Now the crowd has doubled. They are waiting. I am waiting. I am waiting for them and for the motorcade, for the ceremony of it, the pomp and circumstance. Many people are dressed up for this. Black is appropriate, goth appropriate, funeral appropriate, though I'm not wearing it.

"Ceremony" is almost certainly one of New Order's best songs. I say *almost* because it's an iffy choice since it was recorded as their first single, "Ceremony" (1981), their first as New Order after they ceased being Joy Division after their former lead singer Ian Curtis's suicide. It was actually penned by the band as Joy Division, but never recorded past the demo stage. Bernard Sumner, who assumed singing duties in New Order, sounds a lot like he's channeling Ian Curtis on this track. The band reportedly had agreed to split if one of them left the band, so they re-formed as another band, the sort-of-martially-named electronic pop outfit New Order.

I don't know what Curtis's funeral was like, if he had one, or what.

What I wish is that I had brought my vintage Ford election campaign sign so I could hold it over my head like John Cusack does the boom box in the film *Say Anything,* an act that has become a kind of ceremony, a recognizable gesture, repeated I'm sure by tens of thousands of wooing boys. It is even iterated on an episode of *South Park.* See the boys queue outside your bedroom window, boom boxes directed up like satellite dishes to your cold, cold heart.

"Temptation," another New Order song, and the song that I'd argue is the best pop song of the last twenty-five years, and probably the best pop song ever written, plays on the car stereo.

A Ford pulls up to the curb in front of me.

The police officer conducting crowd control for this event has informed me we are not allowed to be on the side of the interstate approaching us; we are not allowed to be above Ford's body as it comes. We cannot darken the path with our shadows, if there was sun to be had here at all. The light is bleakening now, white and weak and obscured by clouds, filtering through only intermittently. It feels appropriate, as if the weather is complying with the collective mood. If there won't be snow, it will look like there could be snow. Dead puffs of leaves line trees, a little, and the cloud cover looks threatening behind it.

Here's a douchebag in a Chevy pulling in. Those sunglasses are hard to take seriously. Come on, man.

World in Motion

According to local news channel Wood-TV8's Web site, "During the interment service, a twenty-one-aircraft flyover in a 'missing man' formation will fly south to north up the Grand River." This is a sentence taken exactly from a press release (a kind of ceremonial offering to the public that describes the various rites that will be performed as part of the national, state, and private ceremonies), "Public Participation in Michigan for State Funeral Ceremonies for President Gerald R. Ford" by JTF-NCR Public Affairs. This document describes our role.

Missing Man formations, which had their roots in the British Royal Air Force in World War I, demonstrated upon return how many planes returned from a mission.

Charles Schulz, the creator of the comic strip *Peanuts*, got a flyby at his funeral, possibly in tribute to his use of Snoopy and the Red Baron. By British World War II–era fighter planes, no less. Daniel Ford (no relation to any of the obvious Fords), author of *Flying Tigers: Claire Chennault and His American Volunteers, 1941–1942*, has an interesting article on the Missing Man formation in which he traces the history of official flybys at various funerals and important events.

The last time I saw any kind of formation of jets live was at a University of Alabama Crimson Tide football game in 2002 or 2001. The game of football, and the Alabama brand of it in particular, generates a lot of ceremony. There are fight songs ("We're gonna beat the hell outta you. . . . Rammer jammer yellow hammer, Give 'em hell, Alabama"). The various processions of the home team with their bands and phalanxes of cheerleaders, dancers, and backers proceed to the stadium. There are the mascots, the drum corps. The *College GameDay* show on ESPN with the donning of the mascot's heads. The gathering of thousands upon thousands to line the streets for the progression of the glorious teams. The marching bands, remainders of a martial culture. Various military people were present at this game in a tribute to I don't remember what. Probably the war in Iraq, iteration one or two. The fighter jets flew over during "The Star-Spangled Banner." It was a totally exhilarating surprise. That's what it's for.

Ford prearranged all of this. He reportedly "kept it simple" compared to other presidential funerals. He knew of course that he would die, and made arrangements for everything, chose the songs to be played, the pallbearers, and even asked President Jimmy Carter to speak at his funeral if Ford died first (and promised that he would return the favor if Carter died first). All (or most, anyway) of this aggregated ceremony is designed for us, not for him, by him. It is a last offering to the public.

In a Lonely Place

Today is a national day of mourning, an official day off for many. What can this man, this name, this president, or possibly the presidency, mean to the public, so that we should spend a day considering his life and legacy? What does it mean to Grand Rapids that the president is *from here*? He is a hero, a local. They would like to claim him as their own. I am not one of them, one of the West Michiganders (or Michiganians, if you prefer—there is some discussion about which nomenclature is preferred), but I am *from* this state where Ford's body will soon be laid to rest. Meaning I was born here, have lived the majority of my life within its perimeters, within its Great Lake embrace.

The interstate traffic will be entirely stopped from three to four thirty P.M. going west toward downtown Grand Rapids. There are cars still coming through as we wait; two pull over to try to get a good view of the proceedings and are immediately shooed away by the police, lights and all. The flow starts to dwindle. I could call it a trickle and recognize this for the cliché that it is. Clichés are a kind of ceremony, I think, well-worn ruts, smooth stones, sayings that we like to say because they reassure us, communicate a popular idea over and over, so much so that its meaning begins to fade. Pop music is filled with clichés: It is not about lyrical invention inasmuch as it is about the hook, the bit that plays on the radio, that can be repurposed now to play on cell phones as ringtones, announcing your musical taste to the world. Some pop songs in the new millennium (think the Black Eyed Peas, for instance, their music repurposed to fit commercials for the NBA finals in 2002) sound a lot like jingles, themes, ringtones with some added breaks, though I don't mean this as a critique. It is evolution: music is now being written for this new technology, and of course it is structured differently.

We could hear jets a couple hours ago. Clearly a squadron of something. A bunch of jets flying pretty low. They sounded like fighters, maybe preparing for the Missing Man.

A guy wanders onto his porch with gut, sandwich, and drink. He is here to tailgate Ford's motorcade, a collision of two different ceremonial occasions. Both are broadcast on television; both are a public spectacle. He is getting it partly right. He is maybe here to observe or be part of the crowd gathering outside his house.

I don't want to appear irreverent in this crowd, though I mostly am. I don't have any personal feelings about Ford. He is a president, and that deserves something, capitalization and the permanent present tense until death, for instance, and the state funeral, and media coverage, and so forth. I don't want to appear irreverent toward Ford in what he considers his hometown, however, for the sake of the family, for the sake of the public here slowly gathering to line the streets.

Only an asshole shows up to mock or be ironic about the dead in a moment like this.

The Christmas trees are coming down, that opportunity for ceremony over. They're still set out with the trash, reminders of the recent holiday.

My brother and his wife had their first child last April. In preparation, they have been actively developing traditions that they can pass on: It's more obvious this year than last, and I respect this, this forward thinking. They are adapting their parents' ceremonies and adding things of their own. This is the way ceremony is passed down when not writ in Bible or law, or helpfully on the Internet. My wife and I didn't do much to officially celebrate this Christmas. We had a tree and lights and presents. We drank absinthe (her present), listened to *A Life Less Lived: The Gothic Box* (also a present for her), newly released by Rhino, played Boggle. Watched a Christmas (horror) movie (*Black Christmas,* the original version, not the shitty 2006 remake). Ate a huge dinner. Ate leftovers. Regretted it a little. I suppose if we had a child we might need to make more of an effort to create an experience for said child to remember and dread or look forward to each year seemingly forever.

Fine Time

Gerald Ford dead today at the age of 83.

Gerald Ford dead today at age 84.

Gerald Ford shot dead today at age 83.

Gerald Ford shot dead today at the senseless age of 83.

Gerald Ford senselessly shot dead at the age of 83.

Gerald Ford dead today after jumping out of an office building senselessly.

Gerald Ford dead today from an overdose of crack cocaine.

Stunning news from Michigan as former president Gerald
Ford was chopped into little bits by the propeller of a com-
muter plane.
Tragedy today as former president Gerald Ford was eaten by
wolves.
He was delicious.
Stunning news from Yorba Linda as Richard Nixon's corpse
climbed out of its grave and strangled Gerald Ford today.
Gerald Ford was mauled senselessly by a circus lion in a con-
venience store.
Gerald Ford is dead today and I'm gay.
—*from a* Saturday Night Live *broadcast in 1996,*
with Dana Carvey playing Tom Brokaw

I remember watching this sketch and finding it very odd. Why Ford, I
wondered? Who cared about Ford? Why foretell his death in particular? Mostly the bit is a send-up of Brokaw, projected onto Ford, a
somewhat blank and serious Midwestern face. It's hard to say why it
continues to resonate, why the idea of a former president's then-
future death was entertaining, or why anything stays with us in the
incomprehensible matrix of memory, but somehow this remains, and
remains entertaining, and is now pertinent once more. You can watch
it on YouTube if it has not been removed by the time this essay is published. Watch it in collision with the Ford funeral footage, which is
probably not exciting enough to have been reposted to YouTube,
though you can buy a four-DVD set of the news coverage.

And now Ford is actually dead. His crypt had been waiting for the
last several years on the grounds of the Gerald R. Ford Presidential
Museum in Grand Rapids, yawning (or so I imagine, projecting the
human onto the world), awaiting the body. After the death of Reagan
and the surprising amount of emotion and ceremony surrounding

that, I have been waiting for Ford to go (it is weird to say, but true) until this week, when it occurred. Potential energy, now kinetic.

And now Dana Carvey, like Gerald Ford, has passed into a kind of oblivion, if not yet physical cessation. At the time of this writing, Carvey's most popular fan Web site, danacarvey.net, had not been updated since 2005. According to this Web site, he no longer has an official fan club, if he ever did. Maybe he will return at death, have a well-attended, broadcast funeral procession. Really, I feel closer to him, have more memories of him stored in my brain, than I do to former president Gerald R. Ford. He entertained, even haunted me. He is best associated with his impression of the first Bush president, probably, or the Church Lady bit. And as those characters have ceased to matter, so has he.

> Dana Carvey, dead at 84, forgotten by the public until this very
> moment. He will be remembered for his bit on Gerald Ford; at
> least one of them is dead from an overdose of crack cocaine.
> Dana Carvey passed away today, passé no more at last.
> Dana Carvey, dead at 83, devoured by wolves.

Vanishing Point

There are far more people now in the street ahead. It will be a serious crowd.

I will join them and brave the cold, a statement in itself of my support for them, for the city, for the state, for its lowercase *s* and flags. There will be many of us citizens out here. The media will be out in force. Hundreds of thousands are coming into the city to pay their respects. It is more than a little strange, a kind of tourism, maybe.

This anticipation is somehow festive. A crowd of about one hundred fifty is on the south side of Eastern Street NE waiting for the president's body. Probably twenty kids are in attendance, and they yell periodically: "Is he coming?" "Is that him?" "He's coming!" and so on. They could be talking about Santa, Jesus, Justin Timberlake. A man is there with a large flag that he unfurls and waves. It is surprisingly emotional, at least a little bit. Like the others in attendance, I am not sure how to respond. A woman next to me asks if we should cheer or applaud. Yet when the motorcade comes—thirty to forty cars—there is only silence, the sound of wind, of thinking, of memory.

My crowd, the growing *us* of this experience, is diverse. A lot of parents with their kids, eager for some kind of celebration. Our bodies are adjacent to each other; we share pheromones. It could be a parade, almost, if not for the cops and the photographers and television cameras. I'm sure there is a specified order as to who comes first in these things—it always has the appearance of order, which is what ritual, ceremony is all about. Ford's casket comes fourth. Maybe fifth. Probably the number is symbolic. He, or what remains of him, is followed by a phalanx of American-made cars: Lincolns, Chevys, and—yes—Fords.

The public is invited via press release to queue to see the body. Ford is now seven days dead but still on display.

This Time of Night

Eight P.M. I am finished baking bread and two friends and I go down to queue for the viewing of the body in repose. We park and go down only to find out that the wait time is seven hours. Thousands are lined up down here, curlicuing around corners and blocks. Neil Diamond is in the air since the queue starts next to Rosa Parks Circle, where teenagers are skating on artificial ice. It hasn't been below freezing for a week or so, though it's cold enough to make this more of an ordeal than it probably needs to be.

Seven hours? For *this* president?

We turn around. My backup plan is to come back at 2 A.M., when the line must surely be more reasonable.

One fifteen A.M. My friend Charlie and I go back in his large Japanese-made SUV and join the line. We get to sit inside. There are still at least three thousand people here surrounding us. The old are here. The very young are here. A lot of high-school-age kids. There are tents. Sixty-plus lines snaking back and forth in the huge convention center. At least it's warm enough inside. The collective energy of our thousands of bodies, all that breath and body heat collected, is something to feel. It is a little bit electric, exciting. No one has an official time on the wait, but we wait for close to two hours, and make it about a third of the way. I feel it is decision time. Charlie's willing to go for it, but it will be an all-night experience, and he proposes an early breakfast if we can find a place that's open. I see a handful of my students, people I have passed on the street. Some of them were probably in the crowd along the interstate with me before.

It turns out that I do not care enough to hold the line all night, lacking the proper reverence or motivation. At the halfway point, at my behest, we check out. I wonder what it would mean for me to stand in line for six hours to make it through to stand in the same room as the flag-draped closed coffin. My left foot has been aching badly for the last several days and standing for this time has not improved it. Who stands all night to be in the same room with the body of the former president just for a moment before being ushered through?

No active cell phones were officially allowed. Nor were cameras, though many had their cell phones anyhow. The idea was to preserve a kind of silence, probably, or to make it impossible for people to snap pictures?

In the next days I talk with a couple dozen people who stayed in line, who got into the inner sanctum, had their minute or two with the flag-draped coffin, signed the official guest book, got their name inscribed in history. Of course the coffin isn't open, so there is a barrier between the world and the body, not to mention the whole thing is roped off, and security is everywhere so as to enforce order, decorum. So they waited to pay their respects.

State of the Nation

Back to the procession. A set of kids are snacking on a bag of Doritos as we watch the motorcade. They treat this like a parade, sans music and candy. The television news commentators tell us that we are all becoming a part of history. Is that our motivation, to be one with history? Or is it an outpouring of support for the hometown boy turned president? Or a show of confidence in what Ford represents to the culture, meaning (with air quotes) "Midwestern values" like hard work and honesty and unpretentiousness? Are the crowds gathering to make a statement to the contrary of the current red-state/blue-state culture? Is the caption for this photograph "We Are in Fact One"?

It's strange to be part of a crowd here in reverence for a dead president. It is unsettling to be standing in a crowd at all, physically part of an obvious *us,* in proximity, and probably in solidarity by default. In my lifetime I have disapproved of most of our presidents and have not had much reverence for them. I don't listen to country, kick ass for the Lord, or support the war. My family has few connections to the military, though we spent several years in Saudi Arabia, where my dad worked for the government, and we spent significant time on a military compound. He did not go to war. Went to grad school, quite probably with the intention of avoiding the draft. He and my mother went to Africa soon after. We are a crowd of recent academics. While I have a friend in the service, I don't think about the idea of serving one's country in this way much, if at all, except to think about how strange it is, and to be thankful for others' observation of this duty, at least in the abstract. I know something about that culture, and the world beyond this country. I watch the coverage of the wars on television.

Regret

A week after Ford's remains have been finally and permanently interred, and several days after the media coverage has subsided in favor of something more exciting and less reverent, I am at the bar where I sing karaoke some Friday nights. A woman dedicates the Bette Midler song "Wind Beneath My Wings" to her son, who's coming home in a couple weeks from Iraq, and whom everyone in the bar seems to know well. There are cheers. My instinct is to laugh, but I cannot. I feel embarrassed not to have anyone close to me who is serving in this way. It's easy to distance myself from these ideas, this part of our culture, of our culture's martial interactions with other cultures, all the procedures designed to corral the edge of the inhabited world into the impression of solidity. I can laugh it off. I can be irreverent. This irreverence implies a kind of recognition, though, that the subject at hand does have some potential gravity that I have no access to. I can have my ironic moment listening to this performance: I can hold myself above the crowd here at the Point, on Grand Rapids' more blue-collar west side—and the crowd is totally into it, not examining but enjoying it, as it should be, as we should be, since karaoke is a participation in a culture, both the culture that produced the song being sung and the culture that is listening to the (often not very good) performances of the song. If I am a good citizen of karaoke, I need to get behind her. Part of you can sit back and remark how everybody (but you, but us, as this implies) sucks, or how good they are, but part of you—again, if you are a good citizen of karaoke country, if you live by its bill of rights, its constitution, its random set of bylaws (no jumping the rotation, no booing the singers, no matter how bad, though maybe if they're unenthusiastic it's acceptable: If they're not buying into the culture, the culture does not need to buy into them)—must endorse it. Your presence endorses it. By virtue of your ass being in the chair, and your hand probably lifting a drink to your open mouth, you're there, and that counts for something. So I applaud. And she is good, and her son will, I think, be proud, as she is proud of him.

I think you should sing periodically too, though I don't think this is the rule. If you are an enthusiastic member of the audience, you are doing your part here as a citizen, but still It Is Good to participate more actively. It's like you're running for public office, not just voting, though you're likely to lose, and that losing is part of the experience, a civic lesson, a contribution. Losing, you fall backward into a network of other arms—if this isn't making too much of this—and are conveyed back to the stage for your encore.

I do sing, though my instinct is to do Erasure, or Cher, or something celebratory and provocative in straight bars like this. My first song flops totally, though for the life of me (a weird cliché, again, that familiar stone in the hand, designed to increase the gravity of the statement, suggesting that if it were worth my life even then I could not possibly remember) I can't remember what I sang now when trying to revisit this experience. This is even weirder that I can't remember, can't recover the memory of not being rewarded or appreciated.

The second one is a more considered choice: you can't go wrong with "Every Rose Has Its Thorn" (which I have gloriously performed at an open mic in college, culminating with me smashing my guitar on the stage and storming off—the closest I got to my rock moment, my preaching from the pulpit, my place on the ballot, really), and it goes well, though the guy in the rotation just in front of me does another Poison song, "Something to Believe In," which is more ponderous, is later, post-awesome Poison, but to his credit, it is a much less obvious choice, and I am suddenly self-conscious about my own decision. Is it too easy, I wonder? Too open for camp? As the intro starts up the crowd is suddenly entirely with me: We are, no doubt, an us, and it is fabulous. I am part of something. I tell CC to take it to the bridge, and at least I think the crowd cheers. Last week I did Billy

Idol's "Dancing with Myself" (song number two, chronologically, on my best-pop-songs compilation) and that went over well, as it should, a song about our essential (maybe even existential) aloneness and working through it. When we sing these songs we are one with Billy Idol, with the soul of pop, with the populace. Regardless of our inability to perform them adequately, our participation is important. Buying the records and making mix tapes in high school for girls we totally loved was important, and remains important. Ranking songs and making exhaustively researched lists is important, both to my participation in the culture (teenage geek boy) and to my demonstration of knowledge of and in this culture, my acknowledgment of the importance of pop.

This is my civic participation, and as I do it, my little shell of irony recedes. It will go back up later, certainly, but for now I am subsumed in something new for me.

Even the guy who insists on doing the same songs every Friday night (The Beastie Boys' "Fight for Your Right to Party" with added swears; Puddle of Mudd's "She Hates Me" receiving the same treatment), and not all that well, but with great enthusiasm: He pats me on the back later, introduces himself. He is a genial guy. We are men here. Possibly we will play some pool.

All of this is unexpectedly moving.

Round & Round

Ceremony is order, arbitrary, evolving, but not too quickly, stilled by the call to history, to stricture, to authority. I have applied an artificial order to this essay, parceling this story into unrelated moments, titling each section after songs by New Order (an Easter egg for music geeks, and now you get your invitation into the club), creating a kind of new order, a momentary rigidity, an exoskeleton through which fact or thought can move and become a citizenry, a sudden we.

Dreams Never End

"The Gerald Ford Funeral Video Compilation features the arrival ceremony at St. Margaret's Episcopal Church in Palm Desert, California, official ceremonies in Washington, DC, services in Grand Rapids, Michigan, and final interment at the Gerald Ford Presidential Museum. Official events in Washington include the arrival at Andrews Air Force Base, the funeral motorcade to the Capitol, official funeral services in the Capitol Rotunda and the National Cathedral. This video set is available on four DVDs or five VHS tapes."

Everyone
Everywhere

According to press releases and the FAQ page at the Gerald R. Ford Library and Museum Web site, "nearly 50,000 people signed the Condolence Books on the grounds of the Gerald R. Ford Presidential Museum in Grand Rapids and Library in Ann Arbor beginning at 1:30 A.M. on Wednesday, December 27, 2006, through 5:00 P.M. Thursday, January 4, 2007.

"An estimated 36,000 visited the U.S. Capitol Rotunda as President Ford lay in State.

"As President Ford lay in repose at the museum, Tuesday afternoon through Wednesday morning, some 62,000 people paid their respects, including the estimated 57,000 people who entered the queue through DeVos Place and waited patiently in line.

"In addition, an estimated 75,000 people lined the streets of Grand Rapids to welcome President Ford home on January 2, 2007, and during the funeral services on January 3, 2007.

"Pallbearers for the services in Grand Rapids, Michigan: Martin J. Allen Jr., Mary Sue Coleman, Richard M. DeVos, Richard A. Ford, David G. Frey, Pepi Gramshammer, Robert L. Hooker, Frederick H.

G. Meijer, Jack Nicklaus, Leon W. Parma, Glenn 'Bo' Schembechler (In Memoriam), Peter F. Secchia, L. William Seidman, and Steve Van Andel."

Some of these people—most, even—are honorary pallbearers (at least one was dead at the time). They did not physically bear the pall, the cloth spread over the coffin, hearse, or tomb. It is a ceremonial designation.

Anti-Aliasing

BRIAN OLIU

"The excitement and true joy in nonfiction is taking something that is universal and finding something absurd or even impossible while still remaining inside the confines of truth," says Brian Oliu. As it turns out, this is an apt metaphor for his story, which appeared in Swink *and takes the form of instructions for manipulating not only digital photographs but, perhaps, memories themselves.*

Step One: Open up source image barcelona010.jpg (1488 x 1984 pixels) taken 06/15/2005 in a third-floor hotel room on Passeig de Mallorca, adjacent to Passeig de Gràcia, using an Olympus D550Z digital camera.

She is posed in the center of the frame, left leg kicked up behind her body, fingertips pressing against the wall for balance. If you zoom in on the photo and focus on her fingers, you'll notice that her nails have been painted a dull pink, the color of a pastel Easter egg pulled out of the dye too soon. Her dress is white with red flowers, though the lighting turns them a grapefruit red-orange. She always reminded you of citrus. The first time you visited her apartment she offered you a clementine, and her hair often smelled like lemon drop candies. Now what comes to mind is grapefruit juice, the tart taste, how it reduces the potency of certain medications.

In the photograph she pulls at the strap of her shoe—one of the gold high heels she'd worn to dinner that evening. You shared stale bread drenched with olive oil and tomato pulp.

You didn't expect her to come to Barcelona, not with you living at home in New Jersey and her at school in London, your relationship sinking, submerged in the Atlantic Ocean around latitude thirty. But you were going to Barcelona to visit family, and she'd hinted at your making a stop at Heathrow, presumably to eat Cadbury Crème Eggs and lock arms by the Thames. You told her if she wanted to see you, she could come to Spain, something you knew she'd never do. But she did—met you in Terminal A of the Aeroport de Barcelona, gave double kisses to your great-aunts, held your hand while walking down subway steps.

This picture is a reenactment. She wasn't posing to begin with; it was a practical act, the removing of footwear, its beauty utilitarian. But by the time you'd extracted the camera from your left pocket, the shoe was off. You asked, then, that she put the shoe back on and assume the same pose, so you could capture it. She obliged, but the moment was lost. Before, her head had been down, light brown hair hanging over her face; this time she looked into the camera and smiled. Inspecting the photo later, this upset you, not only the artificiality of the pose and smile, but because now there is no mistaking that it is she, her. Before, you could pretend she was just a girl, face masked, concentrating on a simple action. No hidden meanings, no rite of discalceation at temples, just the taking off of heels after an evening walk past street performers who stand on pedestals emulating statues of Greek goddesses.

Step Two: With the Selection tool, draw a box around the body to isolate her from the rest of the image. Choose Edit>>Crop to eliminate the background.

The only thing you cut out is the top right edge of a blue couch. You are not in this photo. There is not a single picture of the two of you together taken during this five-day European jaunt. Tieta Rosa-Maria did not take a photo of you two together at your grandfather's childhood home in Cantoni. None of your uncles ever took a photograph of you and her in front of the La Rambla street performers during your evening walk. You didn't throw a euro into a hat or a guitar case to thank the mime for his ideal stillness. There are no photographs of the two of you cheek to cheek, the paleness of a forearm reflecting the flash from the camera as you hold it in the air, pointed down at your faces smashed together into a pillow and propped up on the headrest. She insisted on sleeping on the blue couch alone. You'd already been cropped out of the picture.

There's a story you recall from your childhood about a camera that would take pictures of things that had not yet happened. Most often these pictures were disturbing: A portrait taken of a person is developed without the person in the frame, indicating that he or she would not survive the coming weeks. It is almost as if this photograph were one of those, a moment of prophesy captured long before the trip to Barcelona, in some other room the year before, or perhaps the year before that. Instead of her hand holding the wall for support, it could be your shoulder. You could be looking to your left, watching her flex her calf muscle as she reaches back to remove her shoe. This picture, if taken a year before, might have been a warning. The frame of things to come. Even if you had ignored all the other signs, you'd have had this photograph to let you know that she didn't need you by her side; she would hold herself up.

The image will shrink in size from 1488 x 1984 pixels to 972 x 1432.

Step Three: Using the Extract tool, draw a line around her face, taking the time to carefully outline every hair wisp. In doing this, you may remember another picture, gala016.jpg (1488 x 1984, taken 05/12/2004), in which you are featured prominently, your hand on the waist of her dress made of glittered fabric the color of antifreeze. At the evening's end, you moved that hand from her waist to her hair, traversing it, removing hairpins as you went, each toss of her head releasing the scent of hair spray and pomegranate.

Using the Fill Bucket, click on the area you wish to retain. Pressing the "OK" button will remove her body in that dress, the shoe, the walls of the hotel room, Barcelona, the month of June. The background will cease to exist. You will be left with the floating image of her head parted from her body, hair cascading like serpents. At this moment, you are Perseus. At this moment, she is the one turned to stone, she is the one caught looking back and turned to salt, a sleek white column outside the falling cities. Before, she was a hazel-eyed girl from the suburbs of Philadelphia with a name and a phone number; now she is mythological.

This is not what you had planned.

Step Four: Open up every item in the folder labeled Every Woman You Have Seen Since She Left You, created 01/28/2005. In this folder, you will find a photo of every woman you have come in contact with since late January.

Some of these pictures are crisp and clear: high dpi, large resolution, thirty-two bits per channel. The pharmacist in scrubs the color of mint-chip ice cream, delivering antipsychotics to the mental health unit you worked in. The Audrey Hepburn in pigtails who bought you a rose and a white chocolate Reese's peanut butter cup on Valentine's Day. The Long Island princess who sleeps next to firefighters. The majority of the photos stored here are blurry (girlbehindretail counter001.jpg, girlbehindretailcounter002.jpg, girlbehindretail counter003.jpg). Furthermore, there are photographs concentrated with blurs of colors accented by lens flares and water droplets. They are pictures of patterns, beautiful and colorful, but without any form. These fractals represent an endless ideal, the purples and reds of sensuality and heat swirling to create a perfect vortex. Staring through the center of the centrifuge, you might see a rendering of a romanticized Joan of Arc with a pixie cut, Venus on a half shell, a twenty-first-century Myrna Loy.

Step Five: Using the Lasso tool, draw a rope around her skull, then choose Edit>>Copy to place her head on the Clipboard. You can paste her face on anything. There is an infinite supply of her now. At one time she existed only in a photograph in a Catalan apartment with an ironing board in the kitchen, and before that, she existed as a 118-pound container of apples, ancient Egyptian curses, and orchestra swells that would toast you an Eggo waffle some evenings after ten. Now she exists in duplicate, triplicate, quadruplicate, infinity. Her face will remain on your Clipboard until some other girl, whose lips and eyes you can't even imagine or begin to vector-draw at this moment, takes her place.

Step Six: Paste her head into every photograph in every image in your Every Woman You Have Seen Since She Left You folder. Select her head and move it into position, overlapping and masking the face of the original woman. Rotate. Rotate. Her forehead is too large. Shrink. Her jawline is too slight. Stretch. Manipulate until her head on this new body could almost be perceived as normal, although the schematics of head-to-body ratio as well as facial structure can never permit this to be absolutely perfect. Her head will never fit on a shield. She will turn your hand to coral.

Step Seven: Click Layer>>Flatten Image. This will fuse the layer of her face to the background of the photo. Once this is done, she will become synonymous with whatever image she was pasted into, her face the face of every woman you've seen since she left you.

She has become a part of everything you see, and therefore everything has been either ruined or remedied.

Step Eight: Click File>>Save. Make sure to save over the original document. You have no need for it anymore. barcelona010.jpg does not exist. Barcelona does not exist. You have new memories of her now, ones that require neither her participation nor her consent.

Now the rats of Philadelphia are scattering and diving into the Schuylkill as Broad Street burns. The seal tanks in the National Aquarium at the Inner Harbor swell and crack from the heat. Casa Batlló becomes Casa dels Ossos, the House of Bones. You are the one looking back, and she is the one frozen in place, her skin and hair made of pixels, shining granules of light.

Everything That's Wrong with Facebook

PHILSPROOF.COM

Today, I did the unthinkable.

I did something I said I'd never do.

I joined Facebook.

Yeah. I did. I can't go back and undo it now.

THE PROBLEM WITH Facebook is that it's sort of like having a relationship with a cheap hooker. Or at least, how I always imagined it to be. It's cheap, quick, and I suppose, the overwhelming sense of satisfaction afterward is enough to override any residual feelings of guilt you may have had going into the whole mess.

On the other hand, there's nothing particularly special about it. In the long run, it's just not that satisfying.

There's an uncomfortable disconnect when you use Facebook. For one thing, the site is designed to shed light on people's personal lives. It's supposed to reveal everything you'd want to know about your friend, your friend's friend, or (more likely) that girl you met the other night. It's supposed to connect people.

But because the information is so effortless and so unkempt, it fights against the very purpose it was designed for!

It becomes impersonal.

Suddenly, when all your friends have been reduced to teensy avatars, canned quotations, and endless "favorites" lists, they don't seem quite as special as you may have once remembered them.

So I'm updating my profile and I see several options about Current Relationships.

I frown very slightly, check Single (because I am), and check all the boxes under Looking for . . . , which includes Friends, Relationship, Dating, Random Play (play what?), and Whatever I Can Get (what does that mean?).

Hey, I'm not picky.

Immediately, a cutesy heart shows up on my profile along with, "Phil is listed as single."

What the hell?

It's not that I'm not single (I am), nor is it that I'd be terribly disappointed if I were to catch the eye of, say, a gorgeous, leggy girl that Mommy would wildly approve of. It's rather the fact I want to be able to say, "Phil is listed as single but . . ."

I need that "but."

That "but" is the story of my life. That "but" is so I can tell riveting stories about my tragic singleness and my unyielding search for Ms. Right.

The "single" part—pssh—that's just the title. The "but" part, that my friend, that's the journey.

The bottom line is, we all have our own wants and needs. We all have intriguing stories to tell and life-defining experiences to relive. But what's important is that we should all aspire to tell it our way.

Facebook is like that girl who comes to the party dressed in the low-cut blouse, skirt showing off everything and, well, wearing nothing much else. You know who I'm talking about.

She walks in. We all gape. Eyebrows hit the ceiling. Jaws hit the ground. And that's about it.

Because, really, it's just a turnoff. When someone goes to such lengths to bare all, there's nothing left of interest. There has to be an air of mystery. There has to be room for imagination.

Facebook, with its cheap, fast, easy, and naked virtues, is that kind of girl.

So why—why in the world—would I do it?

Why would I join Facebook?

Because I'm a fucking hypocrite, okay?

Oh, don't look at me like that. I've totally searched all of y'all.

So I know that you know that I know that you're on Facebook, too.

Now go ahead and add me so you can entertain my pet polar bear, Sprinkles.

It Was Nothing

CAROL RICHARDS

In a montage essay, an author can approach a narrative in fragments, adding to a story a bit at a time. In this piece from Alaska Quarterly Review, *Carol Richards documents the progression of her vitiligo in snapshots that capture her growing awareness of and changing thoughts about the condition that is slowly causing parts of her skin to lose pigment.*

Look at me. Turning white. An albino. A ghost. I'll blend in with the snow. I'll lie perfectly still on my white sheets. See me? See where the sheets end? And I begin?

I WASN'T ALWAYS this way. It happened bit by bit. First I found one perfectly round circle. White. Dime-sized. On the inside of my left wrist. Hidden under the clasp of my metal watchband. I thought I was allergic to something. To time, maybe. To my watch, probably. So I cleaned my watchband with alcohol and swabbed my wrist and didn't think of it again.

I didn't think of it again until a boyfriend found the circle when he was stroking my bare wrists. What's that? Nothing, I said. You should have it looked at. It's nothing, I repeated.

I WAS RIGHT. It was nothing. The absence of something. The start of the absence. The beginning of nothing.

MY KNEES. I skinned my knees. Late for a plane, I sprinted toward the shuttle bus and tripped over my own feet. Falling in slow motion, arms outstretched like I was flying, then landing hard on my knees, bouncing on my belly. People on the bus mouthed, Oh. Looking, pointing. Waiting for me to get up, to half-limp, half-run to the bus. I thanked the driver for waiting, thanked the passengers, too. Yes, I'm okay. My knees, bleeding through my torn jeans. I made the flight. The flight attendant examined me, pulled out her medical kit. I washed and patched up my wounds. When they healed there was no scar. Just one spot, on each knee: one the shape of England, the other, Australia. English-speaking spots.

STILL I THOUGHT it was nothing.

MY FACE. The corners of my mouth. That's where I saw them next. Little white spots. One on each side. Symmetrical. Small. Friendly. They made me look like I was always smiling. Slightly. It was nothing. A highlight, sort of. I liked them, sort of.

WHEN MY SKIN first started losing color I was living in Portland. By the time I moved to Minneapolis, I knew the name for it. In New York I saw a dermatologist. Vitiligo. Loss of color to the skin. Loss of melanin. My immune system stuck in high gear. My immune cells attack the pigment-producing cells. My skin, a battlefield. Like the game of Risk, white overtaking the brown.

I'd lived Outside, far from Alaska, for years. Back home, my Aunt Bea claimed my vitiligo was the Eskimo and the White Man fighting. White was winning. Bea says, they usually do. I always said I was half-Eskimo. Both my parents were half-Eskimo. Now, it seems, bit-by-bit, White was claiming me.

THE LITTLE CIRCLE on my wrist was soon besieged by dots on the back of my hand. First left, then right. On my knees England and Australia morphed to include Scotland and New Zealand and other neighboring countries. My skin became a collection of reverse freckles, light spots instead of brown. A constellation. In the bath, or naked in bed when I couldn't sleep, I'd study my changing skin. I could make out countries, or, more sleepily, shapes, like clouds of elephants and horses and dragons. One spot on my right forearm resembled a sperm, or a snail. I couldn't decide which. My legs, nearly colorless. My nipples faded to pink.

THE EMERGENT WHITE patches are especially susceptible to sunburns and to skin cancer. Sunscreen becomes vital. I never was much for sunbathing. Now I can't tan, only burn. I started sporting wide-brimmed hats. Post-vitiligo, in Hawaii with friends, I slathered on 45-SPF sunscreen. When I took surf lessons I wore a long-sleeved, high-necked wetsuit top with built-in UV 50 sunscreen. Thick sunscreen, no makeup. At the beach I saw a boy, a good-looking surfer dude. In a wheelchair. We looked each other in the eye. With curiosity. What happened to you?

I USED TO be jealous of girls with perfect complexions, their lovely, smooth skin. Now I say to them, to me, enjoy it while you can.

WHEN I WAS still more brown than White I didn't wear much makeup. Post-vitiligo I splurged. I bought Chanel bronzer. I coughed up big dough at a day spa and got exfoliated and bronze leafed, "to create the illusion of a sun-kissed body." Now I shake my head. Silly me. It's not like I was fooling anyone. Besides, who was seeing my "sun-kissed body"? Nobody. Nobody noticed. No before, no after. I only tried it once. The exfoliation felt kind of good. But the results were short-lived. They washed off.

The dermatologist prescribed Tri-Luma, a bleaching agent that reduces dark circles. The idea is, if I can't get back to brown, to even out the spots, to go lighter. The spot-reducing cream is smelly. It didn't yield immediate results. I was impatient. Expecting instant transformation.

THE VITILIGO WEB sites allude to the psychological consequences, the self-consciousness. Yet most everyone I know is selfconscious. The older I get, the more I realize this. I was probably always afraid to be intimate. I didn't want to get naked. Before vitiligo I never was a nudist. Now that the disease has progressed further, I've somehow relaxed more. Maybe it's just a matter of being older.

VITILIGO DOESN'T HURT. Vitiligo is not a birthmark. Vitiligo is not a burn. Vitiligo is not contagious. It can be hereditary. It usually appears by the time you're thirty. And only one percent of the population gets it. So I am different.

I'M NOT ALONE. My brother has vitiligo. He's older. He had it first. Once my vitiligo showed up, my mother wondered if she was responsible. She worried, was it something she did? She was Catholic. She already had enough burdens.

VITILIGO. Michael Jackson claims to have it. His revelation on *Oprah* made him the poster child for vitiligo. He may well have it, but usually one does not lose pigment so evenly all over. So, maybe he has it, but he's used makeup or bleaching agents to mask any remaining pigment. Or, he doesn't have it, and he used chemical bleaching agents to lighten his skin color. One doctor says, "Patches on hands may explain his early use of the one glove." I don't care whether he has it or not. It just makes it easier to say, when people ask about my skin, "Oh, it's what Michael Jackson says he has." They nod, ah, like they know.

I CATCH MY reflection in a window, in the mirror. I see someone with very white skin and very dark hair, dark brows, dark eyes. I look. It takes me a minute to recognize myself. Every day. Every night before I go to sleep. Every morning. In the mirror, that's me brushing my teeth. I'm still there. It's still me.

THERE'S THIS ESKIMO legend, probably a true account, of a hunter who licked his finger after nicking it while butchering a polar bear. The bear's liver was poisonous. He lost all skin color. Turned white. White as the bear.

Shrinks Get It Wrong Sometimes

SHRINKTALK.NET

I work in a nursing home for a few hours each week in the South Bronx. It's near Yankee Stadium, a particularly daunting area of the city for unarmed, skinny guys wearing a tie and carrying a *How Do You Feel Today?* workbook. I started working there when I first got my license to practice, a common strategy among new psychologists. Before you get to graduate school, you think that you'll one day just throw up a shingle and the phone will start ringing off the hook. Good professors disabuse you of that fact quickly and help you to identify real jobs that pay a modest salary while you network and build up a client referral base. In New York, many new graduates take jobs providing therapy to the geriatric population, ultimately decreasing their time over the years as private practice begins to unfold.

I've been at the same nursing home (also called a Skilled Nursing Facility) for more than four years now, although I have visited others. They are, for the most part, very depressing environments. The long and narrow hallways have patients lying on gurneys and sitting in wheelchairs, calling out to family members who never visit. The nurses are overworked and underpaid and are often forced to ignore screaming patients after having checked on them six times in the past hour for what they call "phantom complaints." Bedpans are everywhere, and I've even had a patient throw one at me after I told her I couldn't write her a prescription for painkillers.

Most of the patients are depressed about spending their remaining years outside of the home. At some point they become too sickly to be cared for by their families, and most people in this part of the city can hardly afford home care. My job is to try to help many of the people here find meaning with their lives, to help them "see the bright side" of having twenty-four-hour care at their disposal, and to face the fact that they are, in all likelihood, in the final stage of life.

Erik Erikson, a famous developmental psychologist and psychoanalyst, describes the life cycle as a series of psychological crises that are to be resolved. The first, "Trust vs. Mistrust," begins within the first year of life. The infant ideally learns through a nurturing mother figure that others can, within reason, be trusted. This establishes the foundation for positive and healthy interpersonal relationships in later life. The last stage is known as "Integrity vs. Despair," which is the stage for the patients at the nursing home. Essentially, a person looks back on his life at this stage and says either "I did the best I could with what I had; I lived as best as I knew how, and my life was fairly well-lived," or "I am full of regret. I did not do what I wanted; my life was wasted." In reality, most of us hold elements of both mindsets, but if we can get close to the former, we experience significantly less psychological distress and greater overall life satisfaction.

After four years, only five patients remain on my caseload. I started with more than forty. Some I have treated with success, others have resisted treatment or have intractable conditions (such as a blazing psychosis that won't allow them to open up to me), some begin to suffer from dementia and are unable to effectively communicate, while others have passed away. Unless you are specializing in geriatrics, they don't teach you much in graduate school about coping with the death of a patient, unless he or she commits suicide. It's assumed that your patients will all be alive when they are done seeing you, even if they're not psychologically healthy.

A few weeks back, my last patient of the day was Andy (name changed for purposes of confidentiality). Andy is in his late eighties, with a history of psychosis, although he has been stable for many years. While his memory isn't what it used to be, he is still cognitively sharp and is quite a chatterbox when his mood is at least somewhat upbeat. He'll talk endlessly about family, sports, and his girlfriend on the third floor with whom he has lunch every afternoon. Today, however, he was somewhat reticent, with a tinge of anxiety in his voice.

"Andy, how are you today? It's nice to see you."

"Doc."

"Right, I'm Doc. Catch me up on your week, man."

"Doc. Doc, there's something wrong."

"Tell me."

"I feel it, it feels like I'm dying. I know."

Because all the residents at the nursing home are older and physically compromised, I do a weekly check-in with one of the nurses to see if there are any major changes in the patients' health. As far as the nurse knew, Andy was fine.

"Andy, I checked in with the staff, and they say that nothing is wrong with you. If you keep taking your medications and follow doctor's orders, there's no reason you can't live many more years."

"Doc, you're not listening."

"No Andy, you're not listening. Trust me, your nurses told me so."

I'm right, of course. I'm a Ph.D. I checked with the staff, he's fine. He's got a history of psychosis; he's being paranoid. This place is disgusting, and I want to go home.

I leave Andy after about twenty minutes of what feels like unproductive arguing. One week later I'm back in the Bronx. "Dr. Dobrenski," the nurse says, "Andy expired."

Expired. The politically correct term for dying in a medical setting. I hate it. It's like he's a jar of fucking mayonnaise or something.

"When did this happen?" I ask.

"Last night. We don't understand it. He was fine. He died in his sleep."

I didn't understand it either. I called my mom from the nursing home. She is a retired nurse who spent most of her career working with the aged. I told her what happened and asked for some help in understanding it. My mom generally will take any and every opportunity to make fun of me and enjoy a laugh at my expense (when I was eighteen she called me and pretended to be the hottest girl in my high school and asked me on a date, and then she and my stepfather laughed their asses off when I came down dressed in my favorite Duran Duran–type outfit). However, like most moms, she can hear her kid's distress, and immediately goes into helpful mode.

"Mom, how does this happen?"

"I don't think it's something you explain; it's something you experience. People know their bodies better than any doctor does. They can sense something is wrong, like an aura. Whether or not it comes up in a blood test or an MRI or CAT scan is irrelevant; some people just know, like your patient did. I know you were good to him during your last session together."

No Mom, I was a preoccupied, self-possessed prick who ignored Andy's last words to me and dismissed him like the fuckface I am.

"Mom, I gotta go."

I spent the next two nights drinking wine and pondering how much of an asshole I am. I proceeded to do the same for two more nights, adding thoughts about my own mortality and how I hope I don't end up with someone like me as their shrink if and when I'm Andy's age. I hate the nursing home because I'm scared of it, I'm afraid I'll end up there. Alone. I talked about it with colleagues and friends, and of course my therapist, who told me that I have a few responsibilities at this point. The first is to forgive myself for being human and fucking up, like all professionals do at one point or another. I also have to start to understand and embrace my own mortality, to recognize that I won't be under forty forever, that I will be old and need to be taken care of, and to be prepared to deal with Erikson's final stage of life.

"All of us need to be prepared," she said.

I have a lot of work to do.

George

STANLEY JENKINS

First-person narrative is sometimes criticized for being self-indulgent, a way for a writer to plumb the depths of his or her own experiences. But memoirists can also tell the stories of others, as Stanley Jenkins does in this essay that never loses focus from its primary subject, bearing witness to the writer's father-in-law's final illness. It first appeared online in Eclectica.

1.

George is a crotchety old man. George is my father-in-law. George is the father of Ms. Mary and her sister. And George is terminal. They can't deal with the cancer because of the heart, and they can't deal with the heart because of the cancer. So he's going to die. Or better, because George is a good Catholic, he's going to go home. He's eighty. "I'm doomed," he says, "Aw, what the hell . . ."

The family sent me on a mission here to Chicagoland—I'm back on the prairie of my origins—to take care of George because Ms.

Mary's sister is dealing with the chemo for her third recurrence of breast cancer (it's in the spine now) and can't travel, and because Ms. Mary was here for a month and today they started demolitioning our kitchen for the eight-week remodel (apparently they found an old fireplace where the stove used to be), and besides she was going a little crazy out here in the land of ranch houses, parking lots, blond brick, and flatlands—and because I'm a minister and today the oncologist was going to try and make it clear again to George that he is terminal. Stage four cancer. Four to six months to live.

So today, the long and short of it is that George got it that he was going to die. You could see it happen. He's a proud man. World War II vet. So it wasn't like you were going to see an opera. George just got it. We went home. I made hamburgers. He drank a big glass of wine. Had a beer. (Why not?) Fell asleep on the couch.

George owns a ranch house in the south suburbs of Chicago. Just outside of Kankakee. Not too far from Joliet. When he bought the place twenty-five or thirty years ago, there were thirty-five hundred people in town. Now there're over nine thousand. A bunch of them drive BMWs, and they live in the lonesomest mansions—each on a hill that exists only metaphorically. Traffic is a nightmare. He doesn't go to any of the new restaurants. He likes Klaus's, where you can get a pint and a schnitzel.

Anyway, when George bought the place, there was just a crawl space beneath the house. Well, damned if he didn't dig out a basement beneath the foundation, bucketful by bucketful—had a neighbor kid to help him—and built a finished basement. I'm sitting in it now. And in his basement he installed a workshop where he built his own violins. I shit you not. Glued them together, varnished them, did it all—and he built a model railroad on a huge platform with switches and bridges and big ole cigar ashes on the floor.

George grew up in Cleveland, and he still thinks of it as home although he told me today that he thought that was odd considering how he only lived there eighteen years. After that he got drafted. He was on his way to Japan when they dropped the bomb on Hiroshima. On Nagasaki. Didn't see a day of fighting. He seems pleased as punch about that. Tickles him pink. Like he got one over on the sons-abitches. His younger brother signed up for Korea and was worried that their Dad, who worked in the coal mines of Pennsylvania and still received Socialist and Commie literature in the mail, might be a problem for him . . . Goddamn bohunk!

Anyway, George is kind of grateful that I'm here, he says, because I don't tell him what to do, like the women. The women are Ms. Mary and her sister, who can both be kind of bossy. Reminds him of their mother, Ms. Alice. (Who I love also with a gratitude that I don't quite understand, though I can attest to her bossiness.) And George still loves her, too. And that's kind of sad—because she divorced him more than twenty years ago and has since found a couple of sugar daddies to take her beyond her—Boy howdy! She was a bit younger and innocent as a babe—origins. I gather they fought a bit. She wanted strange things. Bright Lights, Big City. And never did like to drink beer with the cousins in basements all night until morning came too soon and the boss was gonna be an asshole about it—although she did seem to love his violin playing. Wasn't George the concertmaster for the Kankakee Symphony for years? And didn't he own his own goddamn tux? I mean, he owned it, dammit.

George thinks it's okay that I'm a Protestant, although he seems to be a little nervous that my dad is Republican. Still—on the whole—he figures I'm a good guy. He lets me tell him when it's time to take his medicine, and he wanted me to be there when the doctor told him the bad news. He already knew the news, by the way. He's known it for a while. He just lets news be true—bad or good—on his own terms. He wanted me to be there, though, and I gotta say, I am grateful beyond words to be able to be a son in a way that my father would never let me be.

So we watched some more Court TV. And then when he was ready to go to bed, he said, "You know, the dishwasher won't stop. It just keeps running its cycle. It's all bust."

"Uh-huh."

"And when Mary and my brother were here, the garage door broke and the windshield on the car got cracked . . ."

"It's like your house is breaking down with you, George. Sympathy pains."

"Yeah." He liked that, too. Made him chuckle.

"Good night, George."

"Good night, Stanley."

I gotta go. Plane is going to leave tomorrow, and they need me back home. Family is coming Saturday, and then after they leave, Ms. Mary and her sister are coming in for a couple of days. He's got neighbors that love him, that are gonna check up on him.

He's fading fast though. I don't know that I'm going to see him alive again. He doesn't need me anymore. Others are coming.

But here's the thing. I've been real good. Charon ferrying him across. You do your duty. You get out of the way and let the fellow feeling flow through. Yeah. And then you want to break things. And smash things and just fucking keen. Like the coyotes out here. You know, there really are coyotes out here. I heard them. On the prairie at night. Didn't believe it at first. But yeah. Coyotes.

And you know what? Jesus really is just calling him home. And he really will see all the home-folks again. And there won't be any pain or sorrow, and every tear shall be dried. Amen.

And he is turning away from us and turning toward something else, and I don't want him to go. And I miss my dad. I miss my mom.

And I'm just all tied up in knots about it. Like water that's gotta go downhill and don't have a say in it. Not a mumbling word.

It is what it is. You just got to get out of the way. Why do you have to learn the same lessons over and over again? When does it stick?

3.

Well, I'm back on the prairie, just a few miles south of where I used to live, where way back in 1934 they gunned down Dillinger in that alley beside the Biograph theater in Chicago—on that night when he was looking good in his "gray slacks, black socks, red Paris garters, and white buckskin Nunn Bush shoes"—but this time, today, George, my father-in-law, is in a hospital bed in his den with diapers and an old T-shirt, stuck between two worlds, all hopped up on morphine— Man they aren't ever going to take me alive! Take that, copper!—and he's all gaped mouth because he lost his partial somewhere in the bedclothes—Got one foot on the platform, one foot on the train— and he's making wild, defiant gestures. He's having conversations with dead people. He's neither here nor there. I mean, he's nowheresville, man.

"George, are you in pain?"

"George, do you need your morphine?"

He's clutching at the bedclothes. He's grimacing.

He's reaching for things I can't see.

"George . . ."

Last night with his broken femur he tried to crawl out of bed, clawing at the bed railings, because there was a train accident, he said, and he had to get to the trolley so he could help—Cleveland in the '40s—but they never gave him a chance, all those laws and g-men and cycles of life. We had to hold him down, me and the hospice nurse. He reached for his pistol—he was struggling to get out—but the fix was in. Blown away in a filthy alley. And all the pretty ladies—Mary Aubaschon called today to say she loved him—dipped handkerchiefs in his blood that just pooled there in the alley beside the Biograph and dreamed of good-time johnnies. But Dillinger is always already gone, boys. Out of range. You ain't getting out of this world alive, George. No sir.

Yeah, you can watch little Georgie making his mad dash. Little Georgie who played the violin in Cleveland when they beat up kids for hearing something they didn't. You can watch it happen in real time. And tonight, I swear I'd carry a cross, harbor a fugitive, and smuggle one more wooden gun into the Crown Point Jail if only George could just make it this time. One more escape. One more last breath. Just gone.

There is evidence of a terrible struggle. Jacob and the angel. You can watch peace being born. George is going out in style. He's going out on his own time. Like a man. Like a musician. Or a killer. It's enough to bring you to your knees. It's enough to make you believe. Hallelujah.

What is there to do but to bow at the passing of a living man? And to fear God? Mountains must tremble at such a moment. And surely there is great rejoicing in heaven. Little Georgie is coming home, boys.

Yeah. And all we get is this body. This body that lies twitching and drooling. This body that shits on itself and babbles stupidly. This thing that will be consumed and turned to ashes. This boat. This raft. This thing that we will find burnt and abandoned on the shore—like a salt and pepper shaker you find on the lawn after a tornado and the house is just gone. Just like the obscene corpse of John Dillinger lying in an alley beside the Biograph theater in 1934.

Yeah. Even so. They can shoot us in the back, George. They can pretend like we weren't ever here. And erase our names and write other names over ours, pretty as you please, as if the writing weren't indelible. All those laws and g-men and cycles of life. They can make out like a man never lived. Well they can just kiss my ass, George. Because I was here. And I'm going to remember. It just can't end this way. There ought to be fireworks.

At 6:10 this morning, as the sun came up over the prairie, George passed. It was very quick. Three short breaths and he was gone. The birds were making a commotion.

Errands in the Forest

William deBuys

"There is mystery in even the smallest events," says William deBuys, "and making sentences and telling stories about them almost always produces surprise. . . . When the writing goes well, a sense of discovery comes with it, and the discoveries change how the world looks." In this story, which first appeared in Orion, *deBuys delves into the mystery of a strange totem that appeared in the woods near his mountain ranch. "Writing intensifies the sensed animation of the world by directing and heightening awareness," deBuys concludes. "[It] is like taking the mind and heart for a walk. It is basic to getting around."*

The forest did not keep the body of the dead mare long. After two weeks, close to Christmas, when I returned to the knoll where I shot her, the skeleton was already picked clean. I had not imagined the hunger of the forest to be so swift. Coyotes must have done most of the work, vultures having migrated south, or perhaps a bear gorged on the carcass before heading to winter sleep.

A week later, I noticed that the tips of the short ribs had been gnawed away, and rabbit tracks dimpled the glaze of snow beside them. I had never thought of cottontails as scavengers, but here was proof. It seemed that every creature participated in the slow reduction and disassembly of the old mare's parts.

We called her Geranium. She'd been my kids' horse for six or seven years, after a well-earned retirement from service as a cowpony in the rugged New Mexico high country of the Pecos Wilderness. The woman who named her—she was two owners removed from me—said one morning she went out to buy a pot of geraniums to brighten her kitchen, but when she came home she brought with her not flowers, but a compact, even-tempered mare about fourteen hands high.

A working horse takes a lot of pounding in its forelegs. Too many sharp turns cutting cattle. Too many long days up and down mountain steeps, sometimes with a rider, sometimes with a pack. Geranium's knees began to give out a few years after we got her. A few years more and the arthritis pained her so much she could barely hobble around to graze. I consulted a vet as well as my retired sheep-herder neighbor, a lifelong horseman. They agreed that it would be cruel to put her through another winter on our little mountain ranch.

The vet offered to provide me the barbiturates to put her down, but I declined. That would have involved a backhoe and a giant grave, lest the drugs poison the creatures that came to feed on her. Instead, I waited as long into December as I dared and then led her one morning to a pretty knoll in the forest where I put a soft cloth over her eyes and unholstered the pistol.

On a horse, if you draw imaginary lines from the root of each ear to the opposite eye, the lines cross in the center of the flat plane of the skull. That is where you shoot a horse to kill it. And that is where I shot Geranium, who buckled and dove into the ground even before the gunshot's roar reached its peak.

Killing her was a wrenching duty, made of large parts of obligation and regret, and for months afterward I kept going back to the knoll where I left her.

All this happened a decade ago, and, in fact, I still go back.

One day, in those first months, I visited the knoll, approaching through a thicket, not by the path I used when I took her there. The head and spine were now yards from where she'd fallen, and a gristled leg had been dragged into oak brush. The winter was dry, and no snow lay on the ground to record the tracks of visitors. I left by the usual path, which was an alley through the scrub of young pines that guarded the site. Where the scrub opened out, something lay in the trail. Something white like a bone. Some piece of Geranium, I thought. But no, it was the skull of a cow. There was no mistaking that it had been placed to lie at the entrance to Geranium's death site. The cow skull was a funerary marker, and it had not been there long.

Any creature bringing the skull would have crossed a patch of bare ground, devoid of duff, where the only tracks were those I had left on earlier visits and the lighter, less distinct prints of coyotes and my own dog. In my years of wandering this patch of forest I had rarely encountered sign of another person this far back from both the river and the road, and never had I found such sign in winter. I was sure no person had brought the skull to the entrance of the knoll. But I believed I knew the skull's origin.

Some years earlier a cow had died—or a dead cow had been discarded—at the head of a gully beside a logging road a quarter mile away. The carcass appeared in summer, when food was abundant, and the forest community dawdled in consuming it. For months the gully reeked. In those days I rode the logging track frequently, and I would kick my horse and hold my breath as I passed by. Back then I also collected skulls, and I kept my eye on the cow's, but it vanished before it was clean enough to take home. Now, perhaps, this was that very skull, reappeared.

Tales that cast coyote as a trickster abound in native lore. No other creature seems so instinctively inclined to mischief. The fox may be sly, but he is not bold enough for joking. The wolf is bold, but not lighthearted. Bear is both bold and strong, but too hazy-witted to deal in irony or symbolism. Cougar and bobcat, like all felines, are too self-absorbed. Among our cast of forest characters only raven also possesses the requisite curiosity and knack for mockery, but raven, being a bird, is too small for muscular pranks.

The business of the cow skull, however, was more than mischief. It was a declaration. I have encountered only one other statement of similar heft and seriousness, and coyote unmistakably was its author. I stumbled upon this message years ago in deep forest at the foot of a mountain. Scrub oak blanketed the upper slopes and made the area rich in acorns. And thick with bears. Within the forest I followed a well-worn game trail. Where this trail met another there lay a bear skull, upside down, exactly in the center of the crossing. No other bones were close by; the skull had been brought there and conspicuously placed. It was old and whitened, and the base of the cranium had been opened and the brains eaten or rotted out. But the cranium was not empty. Bears no doubt think often, if fuzzily, about coyotes and coyotes surely reflect even more upon the bears whose territories they share. In this instance a coyote that held strong views about its neighbors had deftly filled the cranium of the defunct bear with a compact mound of turds. The message was hardly subtle. It might have been a general statement about all bears or a more specific declaration about this particular bear, but in either case the author's point of view was unmistakable.

The shat-in bear skull having enlarged my idea of what a coyote might do, it did not seem a stretch to believe that a coyote might place the skull of a cow to mark the death place of a horse. I believe that a coyote did this in the same way that I believe in small miracles and in the frequent intendedness of coincidence. Odd, dreamlike things happen in the forest that beggar belief, and we learn only of a few, while explaining fewer still. When D. H. Lawrence wanted to invoke the mystery of the soul, he summoned the image of the forest. The image works because the reverse is also true: To invoke the mystery of the forest, only something as grand and inexplicable as the soul will do. Here is what he said:

> This is what I believe: That I am I. That my soul is a dark forest. That my known self will never be more than a little clearing in the forest. That gods, strange gods, come forth from the forest into the clearing of my known self, and then go back. That I must have the courage to let them come and go.

Lawrence's image of the soul is like the forest I think I know. It is a place more often dark than light, where the half-light of dawn and dusk lasts longer than in other places. It is a place where creatures on strange errands trot through the gloom bearing odd burdens and odder messages that are rarely deciphered. It is a place where bones and other strange things vanish and later reappear only to vanish again. But in the forest, as in the soul, nothing is lost. Or so I believe.

So it must be with the skull of the cow, which disappeared from Geranium's knoll three weeks after it was placed there. I have searched for it repeatedly, but I have not seen it again. It simply vanished, and when I noticed it was gone, the tracks in the mud and crusty snow revealed no more or less than they had before.

about the contributors

Emily Bernard is an associate professor of English and ALANA US Ethnic Studies at the University of Vermont. She has edited two books, *Remember Me to Harlem: The Letters of Langston Hughes and Carl Van Vechten* and *Some of My Best Friends: Writers on Interracial Friendship*. Her essay, "Teaching the 'N' Word," appeared in *Best American Essays 2006*.

Patricia Brieschke has worked in a variety of settings, from a fertilizer factory, a five-and-dime, and a hospital to universities. As a professor of leadership and policy studies in Ohio and New York, she used literature in lieu of textbooks to help students explore life in organizations. She writes full time now. Her work has appeared in *Rainbow Curve, Appalachee Review, Sou'wester, Karamu, The MacGuffin, PMS,* and other publications.

Alice Bradley is the author of the blog finslippy.com. Hailed as "the greatest of the mommy blogs" by the National Review Online, *Finslippy* has also been featured in *Redbook, The Oakland Tribune, The Newark Star-Ledger,* and *The New York Times*. Alice writes a weekly column on current events for *AlphaMom,* and has contributed to *The Onion, Wellesley* magazine, and PBS.org. She has an MFA in writing from the New School University, and her fiction has appeared in *The Berkeley Fiction Review* and *Fence*. She lives with her family in New Jersey.

David Bradley earned a BA in creative writing at the University of Pennsylvania and an MA in United States studies at the University of London. He is the author of two novels, *South Street* and *The Chaneysville Incident,* which was awarded the 1982 PEN/Faulkner Award. His nonfiction has appeared in *Esquire, The New York Times, The Los Angeles Times, The New Yorker,* and *The Nation.* He is the recipient of fellowships from the John Simon Guggenheim Foundation and the National Endowment for the Arts. He is currently an associate professor of fiction in the creative writing program of the University of Oregon.

William deBuys is the author of six books, including *Enchantment and Exploitation: The Life and Hard Times of a New Mexico Mountain Range* and *River of Traps: A New Mexico Mountain Life,* which was a finalist for the Pulitzer Prize in 1991. His most recent book, *The Walk,* from which "Errands in the Forest" is excerpted, is set in the same remote valley as *River of Traps.*

Katie Campbell is an award-winning writer and photographer. Her work has appeared in publications throughout the country and in Costa Rica and Wales. She worked as an enterprise reporter for newspapers in Minnesota and Florida before coming to the University of Oregon, where she is now studying in the literary nonfiction graduate program. She is the multimedia editor for the online literary nonfiction magazine *Etude* and her blog, Telling Stories, contains her musings about writing, media, and life.

Hauquan Chau has been living in Japan for the past ten years. A self-proclaimed modern nomad, he has roamed from the chaos of Tokyo to the serenity of rice field villages. He has yet to unpack his bags.

Rob Dobrenski received his doctorate in clinical psychology in 2001. He lives and practices in New York City. In addition to writing his Web site, ShrinkTalk.Net, Dr. Dobrenski contributes quirky and off-beat articles to various publications about psychology and therapy. He is currently completing his first book, a humorous and educational take on the private thoughts and reactions therapists have about their patients.

Stefan Fatsis writes about sports for *The Wall Street Journal* and talks about them on National Public Radio's *All Things Considered.* He is the author of the best seller *Word Freak: Heartbreak, Triumph, Genius, and Obsession in the World of Competitive Scrabble Players,* as well as *Wild and*

Outside: How a Renegade Minor League Revived the Spirit of Baseball in America's Heartland. His latest book is *A Few Seconds of Panic: A 5-Foot-8, 170-Pound, 43-Year-Old Sportswriter Plays in the NFL.*

Donovan Hohn's work has appeared in *Harper's, Civilization, Agni, The Bedford Reader,* and the Italian magazine *Internazionale,* which published a translation of "Moby-Duck." He is the recipient of the Academy of American Poets Prize and Hopwood Awards in essay and poetry, and with Adrienne Rich he shared the Laurence Goldstein Prize for the best poem published in *The Michigan Quarterly Review* in 2004. A former magazine editor and high school English teacher, he is now working on his first book.

Stanley Jenkins's writing has been published widely in electronic and print magazines, including *Amelia, 32 Pages, The Blue Moon Review, Cross-Connect, Living Forge, The Oyster Boy Review,* and *Eclectica Magazine.* An ordained pastor of twenty years, he lives with his wife and stepson in New York City.

Heidi Julavits is the author of three novels, most recently *The Uses of Enchantment.* She is a founding co-editor of *The Believer.*

Pagan Kennedy has published nine books. Her biography *Black Livingstone* was named a New York Times Notable. Her novel *Spinsters* was shortlisted for the Orange Prize and was the winner of the Barnes & Noble Discover Award. She has written for the *New York Times Magazine, The Boston Globe Magazine,* the *Village Voice, Dwell, Details* and dozens of other publications.

Gwendolyn Knapp is a native of New Port Richey, Florida. She lives in New Orleans, where she works as a cheese monger. Her favorite cheese is Comte. She is working on an essay collection called *Lightning Capital of the World.*

Patrick Madden teaches creative writing at Brigham Young University and edits *Quotidiana,* an online anthology of classical essays. His essays have appeared in *The Iowa Review, Hotel Amerika, Fourth Genre,* and other journals, as well as in the *Best American Spiritual Writing 2007.*

Desirae Matherly is a Harper Fellow at the University of Chicago, where she teaches in the Humanities. Her most recent essays appear in *Eureka Literary Magazine* and *Columbia: A Journal of Literature and Art,* and she takes great delight in a crossword puzzle book review she wrote for *Brevity*. Currently she is a contributing editor for *Quotidiana*, an online anthology of classical essays, and in 2004 she finished her doctorate in creative nonfiction at Ohio University.

Laura Sewell Matter is an MFA candidate at the University of New Mexico and a high school teacher at Albuquerque Academy. She is currently at work on an essay collection.

Sarah Miller-Davenport's work has appeared in the *St. Petersburg Times*, the *Montreal Gazette*, and on *Mr. Beller's Neighborhood*, among other publications. A native New Yorker, she is currently in graduate school at the University of Chicago.

Ander Monson is the author of three books: *Neck Deep and Other Predicaments* (essays), *Vacationland* (poems), and *Other Electricities* (fiction). He lives in Michigan, where he edits the magazine *DIAGRAM* (thediagram.com) and the New Michigan Press.

Brian Oliu is originally from Readington Township, New Jersey, and is receiving his MFA in creative writing at the University of Alabama. His work has been published in *The New Ohio Review* and *The Southeast Review*.

Rolf Potts is the author of *Vagabonding: An Uncommon Guide to the Art of Long-Term World Travel*. He has reported from more than fifty countries worldwide, and his adventures include piloting a fishing boat nine hundred miles down the Laotian Mekong, hitchhiking across Eastern Europe, traversing Israel on foot, bicycling across Burma, and driving a Land Rover from Sunnyvale, California, to Ushuaia, Argentina. His nonfiction work has appeared in *The New York Times Magazine*, *National Geographic Traveler*, *The Believer*, *The Nation*, *Outside*, *Slate*, *The Best American Travel Writing*, and other publications. Each summer he can be found in France, where he is the summer writer-in-residence at the Paris American Academy.

James Renner is a staff writer for the *Cleveland Free Times*. His articles have earned awards from the Society of Professional Journalists and the Press Club of Cleveland. He is also an aspiring film director, and was granted the rights to film an adaptation of a Stephen King short story, by the author, in 2004. The completed movie, *All That You Love Will Be Carried Away*, premiered at the Montreal World Film Festival in 2005. He has been named one of Cleveland's "30 Most Interesting People" by *Cleveland Magazine*. In 2006, Renner published his first book, *Amy: My Search for Her Killer,* a nonfiction "novel" about a famous Cleveland cold case.

Carol Richards was born and raised in Alaska. She worked as a designer and art director Outside (which, to Alaskans, means anywhere outside the state), before returning to live in Anchorage. While in San Francisco, she took courses at the Writer's Studio through Stanford's Continuing Studies program. Her writing has appeared in the *Alaska Quarterly Review* and in Alaska Airlines' in-flight magazine.

K. G. Schneider is a writer and librarian who recently relocated to Tallahassee, Florida, from northern California. When she is not writing, reading, or rendering unto Caesar, she can be found procrastinating in real-time at freerangelibrarian.com.

Susan Schultz is the author of four books of poetry, including *Memory Cards & Adoption Papers* and *And Then Something Happened,* as well as a book of essays, *A Poetics of Impasse in Modern and Contemporary American Poetry.* She edits Tinfish Press out of her home in Kane'ohe and is professor of English at the University of Hawai'i at Mānoa. Her blog, at madridws .blogspot.com, covered several months in the decline of both the author's mother and the republic.

Vijay Seshadri is the author of *Wild Kingdom* and *The Long Meadow,* both from Graywolf Press. His poems, essays, and reviews have been widely published and anthologized. He has received grants from the New York Foundation for the Arts, the National Endowment for the Arts, and the John Simon Guggenheim Memorial Foundation, and he has been awarded *The Paris Review*'s Bernard F. Conners Long Poem Prize, the MacDowell Colony's Fellowship for Distinguished Poetic Achievement, and the Academy of American Poets James Laughlin Prize. He lives in Brooklyn and teaches at Sarah Lawrence College.

Phil Trinh is a doctoral student at the Mathematical Institute of the University of Oxford. A graduate from Hillcrest High School in Ottawa, Ontario, he received B.Math and M.Sc. degrees at Carleton University. Day by day, he struggles to balance his professional love for math with his clumsy zeal for creative writing—two opposing passions forming the inspiration for his blog, Phil's Proof.

Anne Trumbore teaches writing and grammar at EPGY at Stanford, and has written ad copy for about four hundred movies and television shows. She has an MA in creative writing from SFSU and lives with her family in Oakland.

where we found
the best creative nonfiction

Alaska Quarterly Review, published by the University of Alaska Anchorage, celebrated its twenty-fifth anniversary in 2007. Featuring new and emerging writers, and open to a wide range of styles and content, *Alaska Quarterly Review* has been recognized by *The Washington Post Book World* as "one of the nation's best literary magazines" and as a "fresh treasure" by *The New York Times Book Review.* Professor Ronald Spatz, the editor, says, "If the creative nonfiction we publish has certain characteristics, they are freshness, honesty and a compelling subject. . . . We look for the experiential and revelatory qualities that engage and surprise. The joy in reading such a work is in discovering something true."

The Believer, published ten times a year by McSweeney's, features articles about authors, artists, and literary issues of the past and present. Its editors state, "We will focus on writers and books we like. We will give people and books the benefit of the doubt."

The Big Ugly Review showcases emerging and established writers, photographers, musicians, and filmmakers. Each issue contains fiction, nonfiction, poetry, photo essays, original music, and short films of five minutes or less, all based on the same theme. The magazine is published twice a year online at biguglyreview.com.

Cleveland Free Times is a writer-driven alternative newsweekly committed to innovative and provocative storytelling as well as accuracy and relevance. Its writers and editors strive to offer both style and substance, in whatever measures each topic warrants.

Creative Nonfiction was the first and is the largest journal devoted to the genre from which it takes its name. Since its first issue, in 1994, *Creative Nonfiction* has featured the work of established writers, including Diane Ackerman, John McPhee, and John Edgar Wideman, and has published early work by Lauren Slater, Mark Bowden, and many others. Essays from *Creative Nonfiction* have been reprinted in the Best American Essays series, the Best American Nonrequired Reading series, *Utne,* and elsewhere.

Eclectica Magazine, founded in 1996, is an electronic, literary variety publication featuring some of the best and most diverse writing on the Web, including fiction, nonfiction, poetry, travel, reviews, opinion, artwork, and miscellany by authors from all over the world. One of the longest running and best-known literary sites, eclectica.org receives in excess of forty thousand visitors a month and nearly four million hits per year. Editor Tom Dooley says, "I approach a submission the same way a fickle reader, who can easily turn the page or click the mouse, approaches a piece of writing in a newspaper or online. . . . If I read all the way to the end, ideally the sum total will have an impact: knock the air out of me, make me laugh, something. Often it's the 'something' that I really appreciate—an impact I wasn't expecting and maybe haven't encountered before."

Etude, an online quarterly since 2002, showcases narrative nonfiction and immersion reportage by new and emerging writers. The magazine celebrates evocative storytelling, fresh perspectives, and intelligent voices backed by extensive, thoughtful journalistic and anthropological fieldwork. Each issue features four major pieces of narrative journalism and one essay. *Etude* also publishes multimedia pieces, book reviews, and author Q&As. The magazine is published at the University of Oregon School of Journalism and Communication. Editor Lauren Kessler describes the work that appears in *Etude* as "timely stories that tap into the moment. But they are also timeless tales that transcend it."

Fourth Genre encourages a writer-to-reader conversation, one that explores the markers and boundaries of literary/creative nonfiction. It publishes works that cut across the genre's full spectrum, ranging from personal essays and memoirs to literary journalism and personal criticism. In addition, it includes interviews with prominent nonfiction writers, individual commentary, and roundtable discussions of craft and topical genre issues, and both full-length and capsule book reviews. Given the genre's elasticity and scope, it invites submissions that are traditional, hybrid, and experimental in form, content, and style. Editor Michael Steinberg says, "When I founded *Fourth Genre* in 1998, one of our associate editors came up with the subtitle 'Explorations in Nonfiction.' It was an apt description of the way we view the genre—as an exploratory and sometimes experimental literary form."

The Georgia Review, published quarterly at the University of Georgia since 1947, seeks to bring the best short stories, poems, reviews, interdisciplinary essays, and visual art to an audience of educated, intellectually curious readers. Winner of the National Magazine Award in Essays for 2007, *The Georgia Review* sees its contents regularly reprinted in a wide range of "best of" anthologies.

Harper's Magazine, the oldest general interest monthly in America, explores the issues that drive our national conversation through such celebrated features as *Readings, Annotation,* and *Findings,* as well as the iconic *Harper's Index.* With its emphasis on fine writing and original thought, *Harper's* provides readers with a unique perspective on politics, society, the environment, and culture. The essays, fiction, and reporting in the magazine's pages come from promising new voices as well as some of the most distinguished names in American letters, among them Tom Wolfe, Annie Dillard, Barbara Ehrenreich, T. C. Boyle, Jonathan Franzen, David Foster Wallace, and Mary Gaitskill.

Hayden's Ferry Review showcases the voices of emerging and established talents in creative writing and visual art from the national and international community. Because editorship changes annually and involves the cooperation of two editors per genre, the *Review* is not tied down to particular styles, schools of thought, aesthetics, or ideologies. The current editors say, "We look for nonfiction that explores topics we don't read about every day.... We like to laugh, riotously. We like our eyes opened. We like our nonfiction to honor and explore the imagination, to be brutally honest, and to move us with the intensity of its subject and its language."

In the Fray (inthefray.org) is an online magazine that produces independent journalism, commentary, and images that question, inform, and inspire conversations about identity and community. *In the Fray* tells the stories of today's global village with an eye toward issues concerning belief, class, gender, body, sexuality, nationality, and more. Each month's postings feature personal essays and commentary, as well as provocative visual essays, reportage, book reviews, poetry, fiction, interviews, and travel narratives. The editors write, "We look for pieces that provoke thought, discussion, an emotional reaction, and which offer unique points of view and the writers' definition of the world around them."

Mr. Beller's Neighborhood (mrbellersneighborhood.com) combines a magazine with a map. It uses the external, familiar landscape of New York City as a way of organizing the wildly internal, often unfamiliar emotional landscapes of the city dweller. It is about a specific place—New York—and it is about the many different consciousnesses that thrive and wilt and rage and reminisce there. The site publishes reportage, personal essays, urban sketches—any piece of writing that might illuminate a corner of life in the city. The site began publishing in spring 2000. In 2002 it was nominated for a Webby Award in the Print and Zine category. That same year, a collection of pieces from the site appeared in book form, *Before and After: Stories from New York.*

Nerve is an online magazine (nerve.com) that publishes essays, reportage, and fiction about dating, relationships, sex, politics, and pop culture—exclusively and in combination. "What we look for in good creative nonfiction is a voice that is honest and strongly personal but has enough perspective to be contextual; a sense of humor; a general disdain of clichés and shtick; and a topic that isn't addressed anywhere else (or a fresh view of topics that aren't addressed honestly elsewhere)," say the editors.

Obit Magazine features articles that range from memorializing the figures who have shaped our culture over the past decades to departments and columns that profile new attitudes about aging and death. By offering new perspectives on death, legacy, and memory, *Obit* takes on a taboo subject with the aim of challenging assumptions about death and dying through life stories and innovative thinking. "The subject of our magazine is often dark and heavy," the editors comment. "Writing that finds the humor and grace that complement life's gloomier moments captures our attention."

Open City Magazine has been publishing since 1991; its books division launched in 1998. The magazine publishes short stories, poems, essays, and art projects. Its opening credo, announced in a classified ad in the *Village Voice* calling for submissions, was "Primary sources, nervous voices." The magazine has been the venue for many debuts and has also published work by established writers, including Mary Gaitskill, David Foster Wallace, Dennis Johnson, and Michael Cunningham. The editorial taste is eclectic, though a common thread that runs through the issues and the books is an attempt at exposing, elucidating, and getting as close as possible to the human predicament in all its facets, with whatever intimacy, candor, irony, and wit is required for that particular piece.

Orion publishes writing that artfully examines the collision of nature and culture, the comingling of people and place. Although the articles in any given issue of the magazine range widely over a vast terrain, the notion of ecology is the glue that holds it all together. *Orion* distinguishes itself from the din of common culture through its depth of inquiry, commitment to interdisciplinary thought, and focus on the soulful qualities that inform our daily lives. Insight and imagination are qualities the editors encourage, alongside a big-picture approach to problem solving. While paying due respect to the past and present, *Orion* is typically forward looking, anticipating the challenges and opportunities that lie ahead for people and nature.

PMS poemmemoirstory is a women's literary journal published annually by the University of Alabama at Birmingham since 2001. While *PMS* publishes the best work written by women today, each issue also features a memoir from a woman who has experienced something of historic, national, or global import. Selections from *PMS* have been reprinted in *Best American Poetry* (2003 and 2004), *Best American Essays* (2005 and 2007), *New Stories from the South* (2005), and *Best Creative Nonfiction* (2007 and 2008). Editor

Linda Frost says, "Creative nonfiction harbors hidden dangers, the most central being, for me, mediocrity. But when it's good, when the words in the sentences reach without apology into what we the readers feel to be the very heartstuff of life and love and pain; when those letters grab and get hold of and squeeze our eager little readerly heads—it's just wonderful."

Portland Magazine, published by the University of Portland, in Oregon, is "the finest spiritual magazine in America," according to Annie Dillard. It has five times been named the best small university magazine in the country, and an anthology of the best essays from its pages was published in 2003 as *God Is Love.* The magazine is edited by Brian Doyle, who says, "We look for bone, salt, prayer, zest, naked hearts, wit, humor, a direct taut spirit. Sort of. Generally we are interested in pieces about spiritual matters and education of all sorts. Generally we like shorter than longer. Generally we are less interested in lovely writing and more interested in ragged honesty."

Swink is a bicoastal, biannual magazine dedicated to identifying and promoting literary talent in both established and emerging writers, from debuts to works by such luminaries as Geoff Dyer, Janet Fitch, Daniel Alarcón, Elissa Schappel, Neil Labute, Amy Bloom, and Thomas Lux. *Swink* publishes fiction, nonfiction, poetry, and interviews. The online edition features several departments intended specifically to encourage and promote creative nonfiction, and the online editors actively seek out and develop nontraditional writing, from microfiction to impressionistic memoirs like Brian Oliu's elegant, elegaic "Anti-Aliasing."

World Hum (worldhum.com) is an online travel magazine. Its editors see travel as much more than means of spending a couple weeks' vacation every year. They write, "For us, travel is a way to see the world when we're abroad, but also a way to see the world when we're at home. Travel is a state of mind. *World Hum*'s stories, essays, interviews, and blog are dedicated to exploring travel in all its facets: how it changes us, how it changes the way we see the world, and finally, how travel itself is changing the world."

credits